28

How to Do *Everything* with

PHP &
MySQL

D0509411

Vikram Vaswani

McGraw-Hill/Osborne

New York Chicago San Francisco Lisbon
London Madrid Mexico City Milan New Delhi
San Juan Seoul Singapore Sydney Toronto

The McGraw·Hill Companies

McGraw-Hill/Osborne
2100 Powell Street, 10th Floor
Emeryville, California 94608
U.S.A.

To arrange bulk purchase discounts for sales promotions, premiums, or fund-raisers, please
contact **McGraw-Hill**/Osborne at the above address. For information on translations or book
distributors outside the U.S.A., please see the International Contact Information page
immediately following the index of this book.

How to Do Everything with PHP & MySQL™

234567890 FGR FGR 019876

ISBN 0-07-225795-4

Editorial Director	Wendy Rinaldi
Acquisitions Editor	Nancy Maragioglio
Executive Project Editor	Mark Karmendy
Technical Editor	Sara Goleman
Copy Editor	Marcia Baker
Proofreader	Susie Elkind
Indexer	Valerie Perry
Composition	International Typesetting & Composition (ITC)
Illustrator	International Typesetting & Composition (ITC)
Series Design	Mickey Galicia
Cover Series Design	Dodie Shoemaker
Cover Illustration	Jacey

This book was composed with Adobe® InDesign®.

Dedication

For the baby:
an e'er-fixed mark
that looks on tempests and is ne'er shaken

About the Author

Vikram Vaswani is the founder and CEO of Melonfire (**http://www.melonfire.com/**), a company specializing in software consultancy and content creation/syndication services. He is a passionate advocate of the open-source software movement and frequently contributes articles and tutorials on open-source technologies, including Perl, Python, PHP, MySQL, and Linux to the community at large through his weekly column at **http://www.melonfire .com/community/columns/trog/**. His last book was *MySQL: The Complete Reference* (**http://www.mysql-tcr.com/**).

Vikram has over eight years of experience in the IT world, and has spent six of those years working with PHP and MySQL as user, administrator, and application developer. He is the author of Zend Technologies' *PHP 101* series for PHP beginners (**http://www.zend.com/php5/abs/**), and has extensive experience deploying PHP and MySQL in a variety of different environments (including corporate intranets, high-traffic Internet web sites, and mission-critical thin client applications).

When he's not plotting to rule the world from a heavily guarded conference room at Melonfire HQ, Vikram amuses himself by reading crime fiction, watching old movies, playing squash, fiddling with his ever-growing collection of electronic gadgets, and keeping an eye out for unfriendly agents. Read more about him, download sample code, and connect with other open-source enthusiasts online at **http://www.everythingphpmysql.com/**.

Contents

Acknowledgments

I wrote this book over a period of eight months, in fits and starts, and with numerous breaks for travel, research, examinations, college applications, and other equally stimulating activities. Needless to say, this isn't the best way to work, and I'm sure I stressed out a bunch of people along the way. This section is their reward.

First and foremost, I'd like to thank my family, for providing me with a quiet place to work, and for their forbearance with my odd work hours (and even odder behavior) while this book was being written.

The editorial and marketing team at McGraw-Hill/Osborne has been fabulous to work with, as usual. This is my second book with them, and they seem to get better and better with each one. Acquisitions editor Nancy Maragioglio, acquisitions coordinators Athena Honore and Alexander McDonald, technical editor Sara Golemon, project editor Mark Karmendy, copy editor Marcia Baker, and editorial director Wendy Rinaldi all guided this book through the development process. I'd like to thank them for their expertise, dedication, and efforts on my behalf.

PHP and MySQL have grown up over the last couple of years, to the point where they're barely recognizable from the toddlers they once were. The only thing that hasn't changed is how much fun I have playing with them. Special mention, then, of Zend Technologies and MySQL AB, both of whom have built two incredibly cool pieces of software. Keep rockin', guys!

Finally, for making the entire book-writing process less tedious than it usually is, thanks to: Lawrence Block, Bryan Adams, the Stones, *MAD* magazine, Scott Adams, Gary Larson, MTV, Jamelia, Kylie Minogue, *Buffy,* Farah Malegam, Stephen King, John le Carre, Subway, Harish Kamath, Barry White, Steph Fox, Apple, Robert Crais, Robert B. Parker, Baz Luhrmann, Jonathan Stroud, FHM, Canon, Anna Kournikova, Swatch, Zak Greant, Ling's Pavilion, Tonka, HBO, Mark Twain, the cast of *The Woman In Black,* Tim Burton, Pablo Picasso, Randy Cosby, the cast of *Friends,* John Sandford, the London Tube, Jeroo Dayal, Pixar, Dido, Google.com, Nicole Kidman, *The Matrix,* Alfred Hitchcock, Bruno D'Costa, Woody Allen, PalmOne, Susanna Clarke, Saïd Business School,

London Business School, Anahita Marker, Michael Schumacher, Mark Haddon, Mambo's and Tito's, Kalindi Mehta, John Kerry, Humphrey Bogart, the Library Bar, Bombay Travels, Amazon.com, U2, The Three Stooges, Oscar Wilde, Punch, Harry Potter, Scott Turow, Slackware Linux, Calvin and Hobbes, Vincent van Gogh, Fiona D'Silva, Kelley Armstrong, Blizzard Entertainment, Dhara Dusija, Stanford University, Popeye and Olive, Dennis Lehane, Trattoria, Xerxes Antia, Dire Straits, Bruce Springsteen, David Mitchell, and all my friends, at home and elsewhere.

Introduction

If you're reading this book, you probably already know what PHP is—one of the world's most popular programming languages for web development. Flexible, scalable, easy to program in, and supported by an international community of developers and users, PHP is today in use on over *fifteen million* web sites, an impressive achievement, especially considering that the language was originally developed by volunteers who made its source code freely available to anyone who cared to ask for it!

One of the most important factors driving PHP's popularity over the last couple of years has been its support for a variety of databases, including MySQL, mSQL, Oracle, and Microsoft Access. By simplifying and streamlining database access, PHP enables developers to build complex data-driven web applications, while enjoying short development cycles because of the simplicity and flexibility of the language.

One of the most powerful combinations in the open source arena today is the PHP/ MySQL combination. Like PHP, MySQL has open-source roots: it is a fast and reliable database management system that is rapidly acquiring a worldwide user base. By using PHP and MySQL together, users can benefit from the cost savings that accompany community-driven software, and also leverage off the immense number of freely available PHP/MySQL applications to reduce development and deployment time.

That's where *How to Do Everything with PHP & MySQL* comes in. If you're a business professional looking to reduce your software costs by using open-source tools, a developer interested in creating database-backed applications for the Web, or simply a hobbyist curious about what the Linux, Apache, PHP, and MySQL (LAMP) combination can do, the book you're holding in your hands is all you'll need to get started on your journey into the world of PHP and MySQL.

Overview

How to Do Everything with PHP & MySQL has been designed as a comprehensive tutorial that will teach developers everything they need to know to begin creating database-backed web applications. It contains information on both the PHP programming toolkit and the MySQL RDBMS (including coverage of relevant features in both PHP 5.*x* and MySQL 4.1.*x*), and provides one-stop coverage of software installation, language syntax and data structures, flow control routines, built-in functions, and best practices.

Every chapter in *How to Do Everything with PHP & MySQL* contains code snippets and examples that you can try out yourself. The concepts taught in each of the main sections are further illustrated with a sample application at the end of each section; this sample application is a practical tool, such as a web-based shopping cart or a news publishing system, which you can immediately use and modify for your web site.

Audience

How to Do Everything with PHP & MySQL is targeted at novice web developers interested in server-side scripting and database usage. Such developers are typically already familiar with HTML, CSS, and client-side scripting, and they are keen to add server-side programming skills to their repertoire. The PHP-MySQL combination is one of the most popular for server-side application development, and this book provides an easy introduction to using it.

A number of other reader segments will also find this book useful: students looking for a free RDBMS on which to practice their SQL, developers experienced with other programming languages who now want to translate their skills to the PHP platform, individuals interested in inexpensively adding bells and whistles (online polls, discussion forums, and content management tools) to their personal web sites, and administrators concerned with migrating their data to an open-source platform. This book contains the theory and practical examples needed to get all these users up and running with the powerful PHP-MySQL combination.

Unlike many other books, *How to Do Everything with PHP & MySQL* doesn't assume prior knowledge of programming or database fundamentals. Rather, it teaches by example, using tutorials and real-world examples to explain basic concepts and, thus, increase your familiarity with both PHP programming and MySQL usage. Throughout the chapters that follow, you're encouraged to try out the various examples on your own LAMP installation. You won't break anything, and you're sure to gain a great deal from the hands-on experience.

Organization

How to Do Everything with PHP & MySQL is structured primarily as a tutorial, so it's probably best if you read the chapters sequentially (this is especially true for users new to both technologies). That said, if you're already familiar with either one of the two technologies, feel free to skip ahead to the bits that are new to you.

How to Do Everything with PHP & MySQL is broadly divided into four sections. Here's what each section contains:

Part I provides an introduction to PHP and MySQL, and guides you through the process of installing and configuring a PHP-MySQL development environment on both UNIX and Windows. **Chapter 1, Introducing PHP and MySQL** discusses the history and evolution of PHP and MySQL, looks at their individual feature sets, and explains why the combination of the two is such a compelling value proposition. **Chapter 2, Setting Up a PHP-MySQL Development Environment** discusses how to obtain, install, configure, and test a PHP-MySQL development environment, for both Windows and UNIX users.

Part II focuses on the basics of PHP programming, introducing you to PHP syntax and language structures and demonstrating practical PHP applications in the web context. **Chapter 3, Using Variables, Statements, and Operators** gets you started with PHP, by showing you how to embed PHP code inside HTML documents and use statements, comments, variables and operators. **Chapter 4, Using Conditional Statements and Loops** teaches you to use PHP's comparison and logical in conditional statements and loops to make your PHP scripts respond intelligently to different events. **Chapter 5, Using Arrays and Custom Functions** shows you how to group related data into PHP arrays and define your own functions for greater reusability of your PHP code. **Chapter 6, Using Files, Sessions, Cookies, and External Programs** contains a grab-bag of common techniques and tools you will find yourself using frequently in your PHP development. **Chapter 7, Session-Based Shopping Cart** builds on everything taught thus far to create a session-based shopping cart you can plug in to your web site.

Part III introduces the MySQL RDBMS, teaching you the basic commands and concepts you need to use it efficiently. **Chapter 8, Understanding an RDBMS** gives you a crash course in basic RDBMS concepts and introduces you to the MySQL command-line client. **Chapter 9, Working with Databases and Tables** looks at the database and table structures used by MySQL to store its data, and explains the SQL commands to create, alter, and delete databases, tables, and indexes. **Chapter 10, Editing Records and Performing Queries** continues where the previous chapter left off, explaining how to insert records into a MySQL database and use the `SELECT` statement to create filtered subsets of the records in a database; sort, group, and count records; use session variables; and import and export data in a variety of different formats. **Chapter 11, Using the MySQL Security System** discusses the MySQL security and privilege system, and the management of user accounts and passwords (including what to do if you forget the MySQL superuser password). **Chapter 12, Order Tracking System** takes you through the process of designing a larger, more challenging database for a small business's order tracking system, and also teaches practical database normalization.

Part IV brings PHP and MySQL together, teaching you the tools and techniques you will need to retrieve and use the results of MySQL queries in a dynamic web application. **Chapter 13, Querying a MySQL Database with PHP** examines the built-in MySQL support in PHP, and explains how it can be used to perform and process MySQL queries. **Chapter 14, Validating User Input** teaches you to maintain the integrity and passwords of your database by sanitizing and validating user input before it is saved to the system. Among the items covered: ensuring required fields are never left empty, validating the length and data type of user input, and using regular expressions to validate e-mail addresses. **Chapter 15, Formatting Query Output** discusses common techniques used by PHP developers to make the results of MySQL queries more readable and useful. Both PHP and MySQL come with numerous functions for output manipulation and display, and this chapter explains how to use them on strings, numbers, and timestamps. **Chapter 16, Sample Application: News Publishing System** concludes the tutorial, using everything you've learned to build a real-world application that retrieves data from a MySQL database with PHP to create a news publishing system for a public web site.

Conventions Used in This Book

This book uses different types of formatting to highlight special advice. Here's a list:

- **Note**   Additional insight or information on the topic.

- **Tip**   A technique or trick to help you do things better.

- **Caution**   Something to watch out for.

- **How to…**   Instructions or advice for performing a specific task.

- **Did you know?**   Information that is tangential to the topic at hand, but that you should know about.

In the code listings in this book, text highlighted in bold is a command to be entered at the prompt. For example, in the following listing:

```
mysql> INSERT INTO movies (mtitle, myear) VALUES ('Rear Window', 1954);
Query OK, 1 row affected (0.06 sec)
```

the line in bold is a query that you would type in at the command prompt. You can use this as a guide to try out the commands in the book.

Companion Web Site

The best way to learn PHP and MySQL is through hands-on interaction with . . . yup, PHP-MySQL applications. To this end, you can find the SQL commands used to create many of the example databases in this book on the companion web site at **http://www.everythingphpmysql.com/**, together with the source code for the various applications and scripts demonstrated throughout. And, while you're there, take a look at the online case studies, connect with other PHP users, and share your thoughts on PHP and MySQL development with the rest of the community.

Part I

Learning the Basics

Chapter 1

Introducing PHP and MySQL

If you think back a little, you'll remember how the Web first began, with static HTML pages on which image maps and animated GIFs were considered cutting-edge. And you'll remember how web users clamored for more interactivity on those static pages, interactivity that became simpler once dynamic HTML and JavaScript became standard accessories for your Internet browser.

Well, it isn't your grandmother's Web any more. . . .

The current generation of web designers thinks nothing of animated GIFs and pop-up boxes, preferring instead to use brightly colored Flash animation and live video feeds. And that's just what they're doing in your browser. A similar revolution has been taking place in the backroom, with the current crop of server-side languages giving web developers a brand new sandbox to play in.

That's where this introductory chapter comes in. The next few pages give you a quick overview of how server-side scripting can be combined with a database system to create some useful and powerful applications. This chapter also introduces you to the stars of this book—PHP and MySQL—explaining what they are, how they came into being, and why they make such a good couple.

Server-Side Applications...

Server-side scripting is not new. It's been around for quite a while, and almost every major web site uses some amount of server-side scripting. Amazon.com uses it to find the book you're looking for, Yahoo! uses it to store your personal preferences, and eBay uses it to process your credit card number for that gigantic eight-headed stone eagle you just bought. What *has* changed, however, is that it's no longer the domain of the big guns—as programming languages have matured and the barriers to entry have lowered, independent web publishers are increasingly using server-side technologies to deliver a better experience to their users.

If your primary experience with web development has been with JavaScript, the popularity of server-side languages like Perl and PHP might be hard to understand; after all, you've already seen what a few JavaScripts can do. However, JavaScript runs within a client application—the browser—and as such can only access resources, such as the current date and time, on the client machine. JavaScript also has limited storage capabilities for user data—for example, while a web site can certainly store user preferences in a *cookie* on the user's hard drive with JavaScript, those preferences can only be retrieved if the user returns to that site from the same computer (because the cookie will not exist on any computer other than the one that was originally used).

A Fine Balance

Just because you can do a lot more with server-side scripts doesn't mean that you get to bin your copy of the JavaScript manual. Often, client-side scripting is the most efficient way to perform tasks localized to the user interface. It's hard to imagine, for example, how a server-side script could help with an image rollover or a page transition effect. Similarly, when dealing with user input in web forms, client-side checks are a necessary first step to verifying the validity of entered data; performing basic checks on the client alerts the user to errors faster and reduces the number of round-trips to the server. A judicious mix of the two is thus essential to creating web applications that are fast and easy to use, yet robust and error-free.

Server-side scripts run on the web server, usually a powerful UNIX or Microsoft Windows system with oodles of RAM and CPU cycles; they can, therefore, be used to access server resources, such as databases or external files, and perform more sophisticated tasks than regular client-side scripting. For example, a server-side script could store a user's shopping cart in a database, and retrieve it on the user's next visit to save him some time reselecting items for purchase; this translates into an improved customer experience (and it doesn't matter which computer the user logs in from, because the settings are all on the server and, thus, are always available).

... And the Databases That Love Them

The large majority of server-side scripts are related to either getting information from the user and saving it somewhere, or retrieving information from somewhere and presenting it. This "somewhere" is usually an animal called a database, and if you're at all serious about building useful web applications, you're going to need to make friends with it.

A *database,* fundamentally, is a collection of data organized and classified according to some criteria. The traditional analogy is that of a filing cabinet containing many drawers, with each drawer holding files related to a particular subject. This organization of information into drawers and files makes it easy to retrieve specific bits of information quickly—to lay your hands on a particular piece of information, you pull open the appropriate drawer and select the file(s) you need.

An electronic database management system (DBMS) helps you organize information and provides a framework to access it quickly and efficiently. The drawers that contain the files are referred to in database parlance as *tables,* while the files themselves are called *records*. The act of pulling out information is referred to as a *query,* and it's usually expressed using Structured Query Language (SQL). The resulting data is referred to as a *result set*. These terms might seem foreign to you at the moment, but by the end of this book, you'll be tossing them around like a pro.

A *relational database management system* (RDBMS) takes things one step further by creating relationships among the tables that make up a database. These relationships can then be used to combine data from multiple tables, allowing different perspectives and more useful reports. By creating links among related pieces of information, an RDBMS not only makes it possible to store information more efficiently (by removing redundancies and repetition), but it also makes visible previously undiscovered relationships among disparate segments of data and permits efficient exploitation of those relationships.

Thus, server-side scripting languages and relational database management systems possess unique capabilities and advantages in their own right. Put them together, however, and the world really is your oyster: the combination of the two makes it possible to create innovative products and services that enhance the customer experience, simplify and speed business processes, and enable new Internet applications.

These are among the things you can do with server-side scripts and an RDBMS:

- Build a search engine that responds to user queries

- Record user input provided through web forms and save it for future reference

- Create web sites that dynamically update themselves with new content

- Manage a *blog* (or more than one)

- Process electronic payments and track customer orders

- Build customized bar graphs, pie charts, and other statistical reports from raw numeric data

- Carry out online surveys and polls, and create reports of the results

In recent years, one of the most popular combinations in this context has been the PHP scripting language and the MySQL RDBMS. The following section discusses these two products in detail, highlighting the capabilities and features of each, and illustrating just why they work so well together.

The PHP Story

According to its official web site at **http://www.php.net/**, PHP is ". . . a widely used general-purpose scripting language that is especially suited for web development and can be embedded into HTML . . . the main goal of the language is to allow web developers to write dynamically generated web pages quickly." In English, what this means is that PHP is a programming language that makes it possible to incorporate sophisticated business logic into otherwise static web sites. The language is rapidly becoming the popular choice for data-driven web applications because of its wide support for different database systems.

Typically, PHP code is "embedded" inside a regular HTML document, and is recognized and executed by the web server when the document is requested through a browser. Because PHP is a full-featured programming language, you can code all manner of complex thingummies into your web pages using this technique; the server will execute your code and return the output to the browser in the format you specify. Because PHP code is executed on the server and not on the client, developers don't have to worry about browser-specific quirks that could cause the code to break (as commonly happens with JavaScript); PHP code works independently of the user's web browser.

Now, while this is fine and dandy, you might be wondering exactly what makes PHP so popular. After all, web developers have been creating Perl/CGI scripts to dynamically generate HTML pages for a long time, and the gradual adoption of W3C standards by modern browser vendors has made JavaScript far less susceptible to the vagaries of proprietary extensions. So what makes PHP the preferred web scripting language for developers around the world?

I've always thought the reason for PHP's popularity to be fairly simple: it has the unique distinction of being the only open-source server-side scripting language that's both easy to learn and extremely powerful to use. Unlike most modern server-side languages, PHP uses clear, simple syntax and delights in nonobfuscated code; this makes it easy to read and understand, and encourages rapid application development. And then, of course, there's cost and availability—PHP is available free of charge on the Internet, for a variety of platforms and architectures, including UNIX, Microsoft Windows, and Mac OS, as well as for most web servers.

Geeks will be happy to hear PHP is an interpreted language. Why is this good? Well, one advantage of an interpreted language is that it enables you to perform incremental, iterative development and testing without going through a compile-test-debug cycle each time you change your code. This can speed the development cycle drastically. A variety of data types, a powerful object-oriented engine, an extensive library of built-in functions, and support for most current web technologies and protocols complete the picture.

A bonus, especially for developers building web applications that must interface with a database, is PHP's support for the MySQL RDBMS, as well as other commercial database systems; this support is the primary draw for web developers dealing with data-heavy web applications, like content portals or electronic-commerce applications. The close-knit relationship between PHP and MySQL, both open-source projects, makes possible some powerful synergies. See the section "Sample Applications" at the end of this chapter for examples.

NOTE *The sky's the limit . . . for a list of what you can do with PHP, see the PHP manual at **http://www.php.net/manual/en/intro-whatcando.php**.*

History

The first version of PHP, PHP/FI, was developed by Rasmus Lerdorf as a means of monitoring page views for his online resumé and slowly started making a mark in mid 1995. This version of PHP had support for some basic functions, primarily the capability to handle form data and support for the mSQL database. PHP/FI 1.0 was followed by PHP/FI 2.0 and, in turn, quickly supplanted in 1997 by PHP 3.0.

PHP 3.0, developed by Andi Gutmans and Zeev Suraski, was where things started to get interesting. PHP 3.0 was a complete rewrite of the original PHP/FI implementation and it included support for a wider range of databases, including MySQL and Oracle. PHP 3.0's extensible architecture encouraged independent developers to begin creating their own language extensions, which served to increase the language's popularity in the developer community. Before long, PHP 3.0 was installed on hundreds of thousands of web servers, and more and more people were using it to build database-backed web applications.

PHP 4.0, which was released in 2003, used a new engine to deliver better performance, greater reliability and scalability, support for web servers other than Apache, and a host of new language features, including built-in session management and better OOP support. And, as if that wasn't enough, the current version of PHP, PHP 5.0, offers a completely revamped object model that uses object handles for more consistent behavior when passing objects around, as well as abstract classes, destructors, multiple interfaces, and class type hints.

PHP 5.0 also includes better exception handling, a more consistent XML toolkit, improved MySQL support, and a better memory manager. So far, all these changes have conspired to make PHP 5.0 the best PHP release in the language's ten-year history . . . a fact amply illustrated by the April 2004 Netcraft survey, which shows PHP in use on over fifteen million web sites.

Features

As a programming language for the Web, PHP is hard to ignore. Clean syntax, object-oriented fundamentals, an extensible architecture that encourages innovation, support for both current and upcoming technologies and protocols, and excellent database integration are just some of the reasons for the popularity it currently enjoys in the developer community.

Simplicity

Because PHP uses a consistent and logical syntax, and because it comes with a clearly written manual, even novices find it easy to learn. In fact, the quickest way to learn PHP is to step through the manual's introductory tutorial, and then start looking at code samples off the Web. Within a few hours, you'll have learned the basics and will be confident enough to begin writing your own scripts. This adherence to the KISS (Keep It Simple, Stupid) principle has made PHP popular as a prototyping and rapid application development tool for web applications. PHP can even access C libraries and take advantage of program code written for this language, and the language is renowned for the tremendous flexibility it allows programmers in accomplishing specific tasks.

Portability

With programming languages, *portability*—the ease with which a program can be made to work on different platforms—is an important factor. PHP users have little to fear here, because cross-platform development has been an important design goal of PHP since PHP 3.0. Today, PHP is available for a wide variety of platforms, including UNIX, Microsoft Windows, Mac OS, and OS/2. Additionally, because PHP code is interpreted and not compiled, PHP scripts written on one platform usually work as is on any other platform for which an interpreter exists. This means that developers can code on Windows and deploy on UNIX without any major difficulties.

Speed

Out of the box, PHP scripts run faster than most other scripting languages, with numerous independent benchmarks putting the language ahead of competing alternatives like JSP, ASP.NET, and Perl. When PHP 4.0 was first released, it raised the performance bar with its completely new parsing engine. PHP 5.0 improves performance even further through the use of an optimized memory manager, and the use of object handles that reduce memory consumption and help applications run faster.

Open Source

Possibly the best thing about PHP is that it's free—its source code is freely available on the Web, and developers can install and use it without paying licensing fees or investing in expensive hardware or software. Using PHP can thus significantly reduce the development costs of a software application, without compromising on either reliability or performance. The open-source approach also ensures faster bug fixes and quicker integration of new technologies into the core language, simply due to the much larger base of involved developers.

Extensible

Keeping future growth in mind, PHP's creators built an extensible architecture that enables developers to easily add support for new technologies to the language through modular extensions. This extensibility keeps PHP fresh and always at the cutting edge of new technology. To illustrate this, consider what PHP lets you do through its add-on modules: dynamically create image, PDF, and SWF files; connect to IMAP and POP3 servers; interface with MySQL, Oracle, PostgreSQL, and SQLite databases; handle electronic payments; parse XML documents; and execute Perl, Java, and COM code through a PHP script. And as if all that wasn't enough, there's also an online repository of free PHP classes called PEAR, the PHP Extension and Application Repository, which provides a source of reusable, bug-free PHP components.

XML and Database Support

Regardless of whether your web application sources its data from an XML file or a database, PHP has you covered. PHP 5.0 comes with an improved MySQL extension that enables you to take advantage of new features in the MySQL RDBMS (including subqueries, transactions, and referential integrity), and the language also supports DB2, PostgreSQL, Oracle, mSQL, MS-SQL, Informix,

Sybase, and SQLite. Alternatively, if it's XML you're after, PHP 5.0 offers a completely redesigned XML API built around the `libxml2` toolkit; this API supports SAX, DOM, and XSLT, as well as the new SimpleXML and SOAP extensions.

The SimpleXML extension is particularly note-worthy—it takes all the pain out of parsing XML by representing an XML file as a PHP object. This object can then be processed using standard PHP constructs like loops and indexes.

And speaking of databases. . . .

The MySQL Story

If you've had even the slightest bit of experience with relational databases, you've probably heard of MySQL: It's a high-performance, multiuser relational database management system that is today the de facto standard for database-driven software applications, both on and off the Web.

Designed around three fundamental principles—speed, stability, and ease of use—and freely available under the GNU General Public License, MySQL has been dubbed "the world's most popular open-source database" by its parent company, MySQL AB. And with good reason. Official statistics reveal over five million sites are creating, using, and deploying MySQL-based applications, with more coming into the fold on a daily basis. You may even have heard of some of MySQL's customers: do the names Yahoo!, Google, Cisco, NASA, and HP sound familiar?

History

The MySQL story hasn't always been about rocketing growth rates and high user satisfaction ratings, however. MySQL has an interesting history, with roots going back to 1979, when Michael "Monty" Widenius created a database system named UNIREG for the Swedish company TcX. UNIREG didn't work for TcX on account of performance issues, and so TcX began a search for alternatives. They tried mSQL, a competing DBMS created by David Hughes, but when that attempt also failed, a new approach was called for. Thus, Widenius decided to create a new database server customized to his specific requirements, but based on the mSQL API (to simplify porting applications between the two). That system, completed and released to a small group in May 1996, became MySQL 1.0.

The Name Game

Wondering where the names MySQL and PHP came from? Well, the acronym PHP originally stood for "Personal Home Page Tools." When PHP 3.0 was released, it was changed into a recursive acronym meaning "PHP: Hypertext Preprocessor." More tidbits from PHP's history are available from the PHP web site, at **http://www.php.net/manual/en/history.php**.

MySQL's roots are not quite as clear. An entry in the MySQL manual suggests that even MySQL's developers don't know where the name came from: "The derivation of the name MySQL is not perfectly clear. Our base directory and a large number of our libraries and tools have had the prefix 'my' for well over ten years. However, Monty's daughter (some years younger) is also named My. Which of the two gave its name to MySQL is still a mystery, even for us." More MySQL history is available online at **http://www.linuxjournal.com/ article.php?sid=3609** and **http://dev.mysql.com/doc/mysql/en/History.html**.

A few months later, MySQL 3.11 saw its first public release as a binary distribution for Solaris. Linux source and binaries followed shortly; an enthusiastic developer community and a friendly, GPL-based licensing policy took care of the rest. As MySQL grew in popularity, TcX became MySQL AB, a private company that today is the sole owner of the MySQL server source code and trademark. MySQL AB is responsible for maintenance, marketing, and further development of the MySQL database server and related products. Today, MySQL is available for a wide variety of platforms, including Linux, MacOS, and Windows.

Features

MySQL's development history has always been characterized by a clear-eyed focus on the most important attributes of a good RDBMS: speed and stability. This has resulted in a system that outperforms most of its competitors without sacrificing reliability or ease of use, thereby gaining it a loyal base of developers, administrators, and users worldwide.

The following sections describe MySQL's most compelling features.

Speed

In an RDBMS, speed—the time taken to execute a query and return the results to the caller—is everything. MySQL scores high on this parameter, with better performance than almost all its competitors, including commercial systems like

What the Experts Say

In a February 2002 benchmark study published by *eWEEK* (at **http://www.eweek .com/article2/0,3959,293,00.asp**):

- MySQL was found to have the best performance and scalability, along with Oracle 9*i,* of the systems under comparison.

- MySQL was the easiest RDBMS to tune and optimize, along with SQL Server, of the systems under comparison.

- MySQL scaled efficiently at loads from 50 to 1,000 simultaneous users, with performance dropping only marginally once the 600-user limit had been crossed.

In a December 2003 study by Reasoning (at **http://www.reasoning.com/ downloads/mysql.html**):

- MySQL code quality was found to rank higher than comparable commercial software, with a defect density six times lower.

- MySQL's development team was extremely responsive to defect reports, resolving them rapidly and efficiently.

Microsoft SQL Server and IBM DB2. This blazing performance is more the result of intelligent software design than luck: MySQL uses a fully multithreaded architecture; special optimizers for complex tasks like joins and indexing; a query cache, which improves performance without any special programming needed by the user; and the capability to use different storage engines on a per-table basis, so that users can mix and match different feature sets to squeeze the maximum performance out of the system.

Reliability

When it comes to reliability, MySQL's creds are impeccable. The MySQL RDBMS has been tested and certified for use in high-volume, mission-critical applications by some of the world's largest organizations, including NASA, HP, and Yahoo! Because MySQL has deep roots in the open-source community, every new release is typically "battle-tested" by users all over the world, on different operating systems and in different operating conditions, to ensure that it is completely bug-free before being certified for use. Further, every new release of MySQL first has to pass MySQL's in-house test suite, affectionately known as *crash-me* because its primary goal is to attempt to crash the system.

Security

Security is an important concern when dealing with multiuser databases, and MySQL's developers have taken a great deal of care to ensure that MySQL is as secure as possible. MySQL comes with a sophisticated access control and privilege system to prevent unauthorized users from accessing the system. This system, implemented as a five-tiered privilege hierarchy, enables MySQL administrators to protect access to sensitive data using a combination of user- and host-based authentication schemes. Users can be restricted to performing operations only on specified databases or fields, and MySQL even makes it possible to control which types of queries a user can run, at database, table, or field level.

Scalability and Portability

MySQL can handle extremely large and complex databases without too much of a drop in performance. Tables of several gigabytes containing hundreds of thousands of records are not uncommon, and the MySQL web site itself claims to use databases containing 50 million records. And once you've got your tables filled with data, you can move them from one platform to another without any difficulty—MySQL is available for both UNIX and non-UNIX operating systems, including Linux, Solaris, FreeBSD, OS/2, MacOS, and Windows 95, 98, Me, 2000, XP, and NT. It runs on a range of architectures, including Intel *x*86, Alpha, SPARC, PowerPC, and IA64, and supports many different hardware configurations, from low-end 386s to high-end Pentium machines.

Ease of Use

Most commercial RDBMSs are intimidating, with cryptic command-line interfaces and hundreds of tunable parameters. Not this one, though—well aware that a complex interface adds to the total cost of ownership of an RDBMS, the MySQL

The Tale of Sakila

The official MySQL logo is a dolphin named Sakila. According to the MySQL manual at **http://dev.mysql.com/doc/mysql/en/The_Original_MySQL_logo.html**, the dolphin was chosen because it is ". . . a smart, fast, and lean animal, effortlessly navigating oceans of data." Whoever said programmers didn't have a sense of humor?

development team has taken pains to make MySQL easy to use, administer, and optimize. A simple SQL command-line interface (SQL commands are covered in Chapters 9 to 11) is the primary user interface to the server; users with a more visual bent can, instead, use MySQL Control Center or MySQL Administrator, two GUI clients developed by MySQL AB for MySQL usage and administration. A number of other browser-based tools are also available, and the application is well supported by a detailed manual, a knowledgeable developer community, and some excellent books and tutorials.

Compliance with Existing Standards

MySQL 4.0 supports most of the important features of the ANSI SQL-99 standard, with support for missing features slated to be added in future versions. MySQL also extends the ANSI standard with its own custom functions and data types designed to improve portability and provide users with enhanced functionality. On the internationalization front, MySQL 4.0 supports a number of important character sets (including Latin, Big5, and European character sets), with full Unicode support scheduled for future versions.

Wide Application Support

MySQL exposes APIs to many different programming languages, thereby making it possible to write database-driven applications in the language of your choice. This book focuses specifically on using PHP with MySQL, but readers working with other programming languages will be pleased to hear that MySQL AB also provides native ODBC and JDBC drivers for the Microsoft Windows and Java platforms. Additionally, hooks to MySQL are available in C, C++, Perl, Python, and Tcl, to offer developers maximum freedom in designing MySQL-backed applications.

Easy Licensing Policy

The MySQL RDBMS is licensed under the GPL, and users are free to download and modify the source code of the application to their needs, and to use it to power their applications free of cost. This licensing policy has only fuelled MySQL's popularity, creating an active and enthusiastic global community of MySQL developers and users. This community plays an active role in keeping MySQL ahead of its competition, both by crash-testing the software for reliability on millions of installations worldwide and by extending the core engine to stay abreast of the latest technologies and newest developments.

To GPL or Not to GPL . . .

While the MySQL server and associated drivers are licensed under the GPL, you need to be aware of some caveats. You are permitted to use MySQL in your own software applications, free of charge, provided that you agree to license those applications also under the GPL, or any other MySQL AB-approved open-source license. MySQL may also be used without purchasing a license in a non-GPL application *provided* that the application is neither used for commercial purposes nor released for others to use. This enables end users to use MySQL for hobby sites without releasing their script source.

However, if your MySQL-powered application is not licensed under the GPL or equivalent licensing scheme, and you do intend to redistribute it (whether internally or externally), you are required to purchase a commercial license for MySQL.

A clear explanation of this "dual-licensing" model is available on the MySQL web site, at **http://www.mysql.com/products/licensing/**.

PHP and MySQL: The Well-Matched Couple

As noted previously, one of the most important factors driving PHP's popularity over the last couple of years has been its support for a variety of databases, including MySQL, mSQL, Oracle, and Microsoft Access. By simplifying and streamlining database access, PHP enables developers to build complex data-driven web applications while enjoying short development cycles.

Support for MySQL has been available in PHP since version 3.*x*, and has gradually improved over subsequent releases. PHP 5.0 promises even better integration with the latest version of MySQL: the new MySQL extension in PHP 5.0 provides developers with both function- and object-oriented APIs to common MySQL functions, and includes support for new and upcoming MySQL features like transactions, stored procedures, and prepared statements.

NOTE *The PHP 4.x release included a bundled version of the MySQL client libraries, which made it possible to access a MySQL server out-of-the-box. With PHP 5.0, this practice has been stopped and the MySQL client libraries are no longer bundled with the PHP release archive due to incompatibilities between the licensing terms for PHP and MySQL. PHP 5.0 users, therefore, need to download the MySQL client libraries separately and manually link them into PHP before they can begin using PHP's MySQL functions. The process is far less cumbersome than it sounds; see Chapter 2 for details.*

PHP's ease of use in the web arena, together with its tight integration with MySQL, has thus made it the preferred programming language for web-based, data-driven applications. Additionally, because both tools are available under open-source licenses, developers using PHP and MySQL can provide customers with huge savings on the licensing costs of other commercially licensed software, and also benefit from the tremendous amount of thought that PHP and MySQL developers have put into making sure that the two packages work together seamlessly and smoothly.

The applications that the PHP-MySQL combination have been used for range from the small to the large: content management systems for web portals, search engines, time- and resource-tracking tools, reporting and graphing tools, web-based personal information managers . . . the list goes on. In essence, if you can think of an application that uses (1) a database for storage of user data and (2) a browser as the primary user interface, it's a good chance the PHP-MySQL combination will work for you.

Architecture

It's interesting, at this point, to see what the typical PHP and MySQL application development framework looks like. Usually, such applications are developed on the so-called "LAMP" (Linux, Apache, MySQL, and PHP) platform, wherein each component plays a specific and important role:

- Linux provides the base operating system (OS) and server environment.

- The Apache web server intercepts HTTP requests and either serves them directly or passes them on to the PHP interpreter for execution.

- The PHP interpreter parses and executes PHP code, and returns the results to the web server.

- The MySQL RDBMS serves as the data storage engine, accepting connections from the PHP layer and inserting, modifying, or retrieving data.

Figure 1-1 illustrates these components in action.

An Open Invitation

The interesting thing about the LAMP platform, in case you haven't already noticed, is this: all the components are open-source!

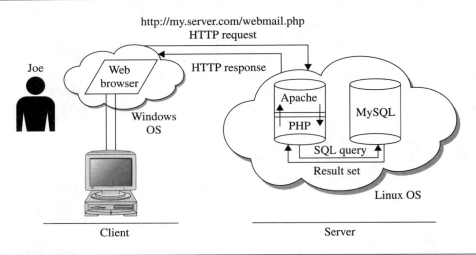

FIGURE 1-1   The LAMP development framework

NOTE

*Notice I said the development platform is "usually" LAMP. It's also possible to develop command-line PHP-MySQL applications, which run at the shell prompt and don't require a web server. Take a look at **http://www.php.net/manual/en/features.commandline.php** for more.*

Here's what's happening in Figure 1-1:

1. Joe pops open his web browser at home and types in the URL for his online Webmail client. After looking up the domain, Joe's browser (the client) sends an HTTP request to the corresponding server IP address.

2. The Apache web server handling HTTP requests for the domain receives the request and notes that the URI ends with a `.php` suffix. Because the server is programmed to automatically redirect all such requests to the PHP layer, it simply invokes the PHP interpreter and passes it the contents of the named file.

3. The PHP interpreter parses the file, executing the code in the special PHP tags. If the code includes database queries, the PHP interpreter opens a client connection to the MySQL RDBMS and executes them. Once the script interpreter has completed executing the script, it returns the result to the browser, cleans up after itself, and goes back into hibernation.

4. The results returned by the interpreter are transmitted to Joe's browser by the Apache server.

From the previous explanation, it should be clear that to get started building PHP and MySQL applications, your development environment must contain a web server (this doesn't always have to be Apache, although that's the most common) and working installations of PHP and MySQL. Chapter 2 discusses how to go about setting up this development environment, using both the Linux and Windows operating systems.

Sample Applications

Here's a small sample of the types of applications that developers have used PHP and MySQL for:

- **phpMyAdmin** (**http://www.phpmyadmin.net/**) is a browser-based GUI to administer one or more MySQL database servers. One of the most popular applications on the SourceForge (**http://www.sourceforge .net/**) network, phpMyAdmin provides users with an HTML interface to insert, edit, and delete records; execute queries; view real-time MySQL performance statistics; import and export data; and manage user privileges.

- **phpAdsNew** (**http://www.phpadsnew.com/**) is a banner rotation and tracking system for web sites that enables site administrators to manage advertisers, display banners in rotation, and generate reports on views and clickthroughs.

- **Horde** (**http://www.horde.org/**) is a PHP-based application development framework that provides the foundation for a suite of web-based applications, including a Webmail client, a contact manager, a file manager, and a news client.

- **Midgard** (**http://www.midgard-project.org/**) is a template-based content management system (CMS) that provides a WYSIWYG interface for building web sites. It includes a web-based administrative interface to easily add and delete content, as well as support for content in multiple languages.

- **phpBB** (**http://www.phpbb.com/**) is a PHP/MySQL-based bulletin board package that enables web site administrators to quickly add unlimited discussion forums to their web site. phpBB includes a multitier privilege system, a powerful search engine support for multiple languages, private messaging, and public and private discussion rooms.

- **phpNuke** (**http://www.phpnuke.org/**) is an open-source portal-in-a-box solution that uses MySQL for data storage. phpNuke provides all the features most commonly found in a web portal, including user personalization, polls, bulletin boards, downloads, banner management, FAQs, a search engine, and more.

- **Drupal** (**http://www.drupal.org/**) is a content management system that enables users to publish and manage many different types of content. It supports news articles and content, polls, discussion forums, weblogs and download archives, and comes in handy if you need to jump-start a community-based web site or personal weblog.

- **phpGroupware** (**http://www.phpgroupware.org/**) is a PHP-based multiuser, multilanguage application suite. Usable through a web browser, it provides a calendar, to-do list, e-mail client, file manager, and address book.

- **Gallery** (**http://gallery.menalto.org**) uses PHP and MySQL to create a highly configurable digital photo archive, complete with automatic thumbnail creation, image captioning and editing, keyword search, and gallery-level authentication.

Summary

This chapter provided a gentle introduction to the world of data-driven web applications, setting the stage with a description of how server-side scripting and databases work, and then proceeding to an overview of PHP and MySQL. It offered insight into the history and evolution of both tools, identified the core

1

features that have made them so popular with developers all over the world, and discussed some of their most common applications. Finally, it wrapped things up by identifying the essential components needed to build a PHP-MySQL development environment, together with an explanation of how the various components interact with each other.

The next chapter expands on this last section, guiding you through the process of obtaining, installing, and configuring the components of this application development environment—a necessary first step before you can begin building your own PHP and MySQL applications.

Chapter 2

Setting Up a PHP-MySQL Development Environment

In the previous chapter, you learned about the components of a typical PHP-MySQL development platform and how they work together to provide a framework for database-backed application development. As a necessary first step to exploiting this framework, you must install these components on your workstation, and then create a development environment that can be used to run the code examples in subsequent chapters.

That's where this chapter comes in. Over the next few pages, I will guide you through the process of obtaining, installing, configuring, and testing a PHP-MySQL development environment on your Windows or UNIX workstation.

How to...

- Obtain MySQL, PHP, and Apache software from the Internet
- Install these components, compiling them from source code, where necessary
- Perform basic testing to ensure that your development platform is working as it should
- Automatically activate all required components on system startup
- Take basic steps to safeguard the security of your MySQL installation

 *This chapter is designed merely to provide an overview and a general guide to the process of installing and configuring MySQL, PHP, and Apache on UNIX and Windows. It is* not *intended as a replacement for the installation documentation that ships with each software package. If you encounter difficulties installing or configuring the various programs described here, visit the respective program's web site or search the Web for detailed troubleshooting information and advice (some links are provided at the end of this chapter).*

Obtaining the Software

The first step is to make sure that you have all the software you need. Here's your shopping list:

- **MySQL**   The MySQL database server provides robust and scalable data storage/retrieval. It is available in both source and binary versions from **http://www.mysql.com/**. Binary distributions are available for Linux, Solaris, FreeBSD, Mac OS X, Windows 95/98/Me/2000/XP/NT, HP-UX, IBM AIX, SCO OpenUNIX, and SGI Irix, and source distributions are available for both Windows and UNIX platforms. The binary version is recommended for two reasons: it is easier to install, and it is optimized for use on different platforms by the MySQL development team. At press time, the most current version of the MySQL database server is MySQL 4.0.21.

- **PHP**   PHP provides an application-development framework for both web and console applications. It can be downloaded from **http://www.php.net/**. Here, too, both source and binary versions are available for Windows, UNIX, and Mac OS X platforms. UNIX users should download the latest source archive, while Windows users should download the latest binary release. At press time, the most current version of PHP is PHP 5.0.1.

- **Apache**   Apache is a feature-rich web server that works well with PHP. It can be downloaded free of charge from **http://httpd.apache.org/** in both source and binary form for a variety of platforms. UNIX users should download the latest source archive, while Windows users should download a binary installer appropriate for their version of Windows. At press time, the most current version of the Apache server is Apache 1.3.31.

   *PHP and Apache 2.0.x are not completely stable when used together. It is, therefore, recommended that you use Apache 1.3.x to avoid compatibility issues.*

In addition to these three basic components, UNIX users may also require some supporting libraries. Choose from:

- The libxml2 library, available from **http://www.xmlsoft.org/**
- The zlib library, available from **http://www.gzip.org/zlib/**

Finally, users on both platforms need a decompression tool capable of dealing with TAR (Tape Archive) and GZ (GNU Zip) files. On UNIX, the tar and gzip utilities are appropriate, and are usually included with the operating system. On Windows, a good decompression tool is WinZip, available from **http://www .winzip.com/**.

Behind the Scenes

The examples in this book have been developed and tested on MySQL 4.0.21 and MySQL 4.1.3, with Apache 1.3.31 and PHP 5.0.1.

Installing and Configuring the Software

Once the required software has been obtained, the next step is to install the various pieces and get them talking to each other. The following sections outline the steps for both Windows and UNIX platforms.

 *If you use an Apple workstation, you can find instructions for installing PHP on Mac OS X in the PHP manual, at **http://www.php.net/manual/en/ install.macosx.php**.*

Installing on UNIX

The installation process for UNIX involves a number of distinct steps: installing MySQL from a binary distribution, using the supplied MySQL client libraries to compile PHP from a source distribution, and compiling and configuring Apache to properly handle requests for PHP web pages. These steps are described in greater detail in the following subsections.

Installing Supporting Libraries

If you're using PHP 5.x, you might need to install some supporting libraries first: libxml2 2.6.0 (or better), which is used by the new XML API in PHP 5.x, and zlib 1.0.9 (or better), which provides compression services to many PHP 5.x extensions. If you already have these libraries installed, skip to the next section. If not, use the following steps to install them.

1. Log in as the system's root user.

    ```
    [user@host]# su - root
    ```

2. Extract the contents of the libxml2 archive to the system's temporary directory.

Did you know?

Bundle of Joy

The UNIX version of PHP 4.*x* included a set of MySQL client libraries, which were used by default to communicate with the MySQL server. Because of licensing issues involved with bundling these libraries, and because these included libraries often conflicted with previously installed MySQL client libraries and led to unexpected run-time behavior, the PHP Group decided not to bundle MySQL libraries with the UNIX version of PHP 5.*x*.

The result of this apparently minor shift in policy has significant implications for you, the end user. If you're using PHP 5.*x* in your UNIX-based development environment, it is now mandatory for you to first obtain the MySQL client libraries on your own (usually by installing MySQL from a binary distribution or RPM, or by compiling it from the source code), and then point the PHP installer to these libraries to activate MySQL support in PHP. The procedure to accomplish this is explained in detail in this chapter.

```
[root@host]# cd /tmp
[root@host]# tar -xzvf /tmp/libxml2-2.6.11.tar.gz
```

3. Next, change into the newly created directory and set variables for the compile process via the included *configure* script (note my use of the `--prefix` argument to `configure`, which sets the default installation path for the compiled libraries).

```
[root@host]# cd /tmp/libxml2-2.6.11
[root@host]# ./configure --prefix=/usr/local/
```

You should see a few screens of output as *configure* configures and sets up the variables needed for the compilation process.

4. Now, compile the library using `make`, and install it to the system using `make install`.

```
[root@host]# make
[root@host]# make install
```

At the end of this process, the `libxml2` library should be installed to */usr/local/*.

In a similar manner, compile and install the `zlib` library as well.

Installing MySQL

Once the libraries are installed, proceed to install MySQL from a binary distribution, using the following steps:

1. Ensure that you are logged in as the system's `root` user.

   ```
   [user@host]# su - root
   ```

2. Extract the content of the MySQL binary archive to an appropriate directory on your system, for example, */usr/local/*.

   ```
   [root@host]# cd /usr/local
   [root@host]# tar -xzvf ↵
   /tmp/mysql-standard-4.0.21-pc-linux-i686.tar.gz
   ```

   The MySQL files should get extracted into a directory named according to the format *mysql-version-os-architecture,* for example, *mysql-standard-4.0.21-pc-linux-i686.*

3. For ease of use, set a shorter name for the directory created in the previous step by creating a soft link named *mysql* pointing to this directory in the same location.

   ```
   [root@host]# ln -s mysql-standard-4.0.21-pc-linux-i686 mysql
   ```

   Change into this directory and look at how the files are arranged. You should see something like Figure 2-1.

4. For security reasons, the MySQL database server process should never run as the system superuser. Therefore, it is necessary to create a special `mysql` user and group for this purpose. Do this with the `groupadd` and `useradd` commands.

   ```
   [root@host]# groupadd mysql
   [root@host]# useradd -g mysql mysql
   ```

5. Initialize the MySQL tables with the *mysql_install_db* initialization script, included in the distribution.

   ```
   [root@host]# /usr/local/mysql/scripts/mysql_install_db
   ```

   Figure 2-2 demonstrates what you should see when you do this.

   As the previous output suggests, this initialization script prepares and installs the various MySQL base tables, and it also sets up default access permissions for MySQL.

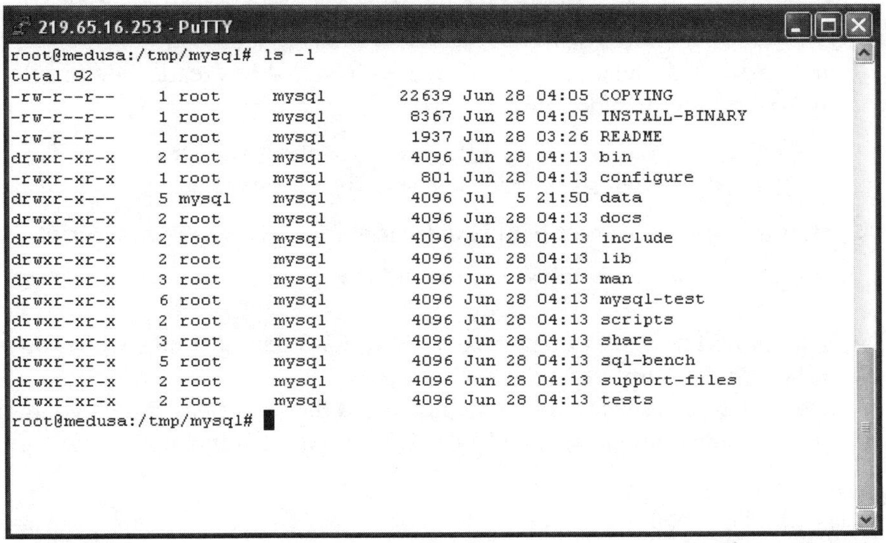

```
219.65.16.253 - PuTTY
root@medusa:/tmp/mysql# ls -l
total 92
-rw-r--r--    1 root      mysql        22639 Jun 28 04:05 COPYING
-rw-r--r--    1 root      mysql         8367 Jun 28 04:05 INSTALL-BINARY
-rw-r--r--    1 root      mysql         1937 Jun 28 03:26 README
drwxr-xr-x    2 root      mysql         4096 Jun 28 04:13 bin
-rwxr-xr-x    1 root      mysql          801 Jun 28 04:13 configure
drwxr-x---    5 mysql     mysql         4096 Jul  5 21:50 data
drwxr-xr-x    2 root      mysql         4096 Jun 28 04:13 docs
drwxr-xr-x    2 root      mysql         4096 Jun 28 04:13 include
drwxr-xr-x    2 root      mysql         4096 Jun 28 04:13 lib
drwxr-xr-x    3 root      mysql         4096 Jun 28 04:13 man
drwxr-xr-x    6 root      mysql         4096 Jun 28 04:13 mysql-test
drwxr-xr-x    2 root      mysql         4096 Jun 28 04:13 scripts
drwxr-xr-x    3 root      mysql         4096 Jun 28 04:13 share
drwxr-xr-x    5 root      mysql         4096 Jun 28 04:13 sql-bench
drwxr-xr-x    2 root      mysql         4096 Jun 28 04:13 support-files
drwxr-xr-x    2 root      mysql         4096 Jun 28 04:13 tests
root@medusa:/tmp/mysql#
```

FIGURE 2-1   The directory structure created after unpacking a MySQL binary tarball

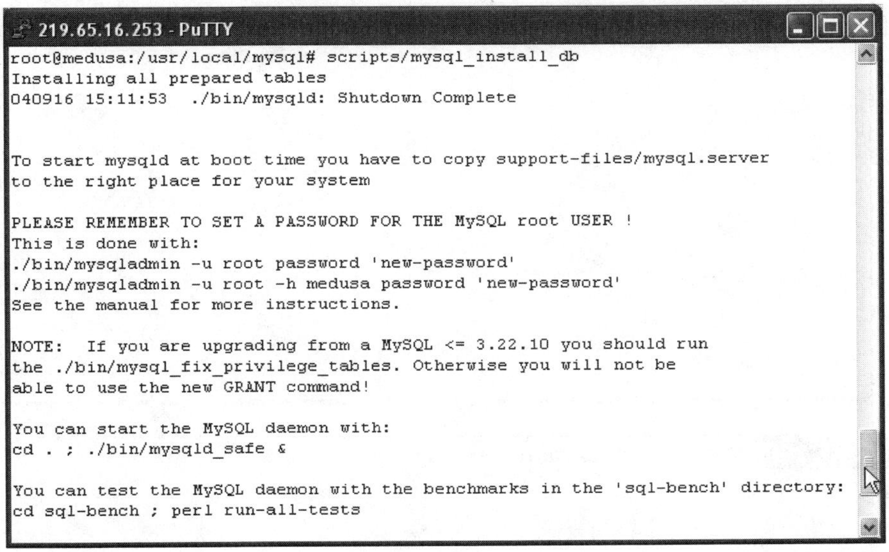

```
219.65.16.253 - PuTTY
root@medusa:/usr/local/mysql# scripts/mysql_install_db
Installing all prepared tables
040916 15:11:53  ./bin/mysqld: Shutdown Complete


To start mysqld at boot time you have to copy support-files/mysql.server
to the right place for your system

PLEASE REMEMBER TO SET A PASSWORD FOR THE MySQL root USER !
This is done with:
./bin/mysqladmin -u root password 'new-password'
./bin/mysqladmin -u root -h medusa password 'new-password'
See the manual for more instructions.

NOTE:  If you are upgrading from a MySQL <= 3.22.10 you should run
the ./bin/mysql_fix_privilege_tables. Otherwise you will not be
able to use the new GRANT command!

You can start the MySQL daemon with:
cd . ; ./bin/mysqld_safe &

You can test the MySQL daemon with the benchmarks in the 'sql-bench' directory:
cd sql-bench ; perl run-all-tests
```

FIGURE 2-2   The output of the `mysql_install_db` script

6. Alter the ownership of the MySQL binaries so they are owned by `root`

```
[root@host]# chown -R root /usr/local/mysql
```

and ensure that the `mysql` user created in step 4 has read/write privileges to the MySQL data directory.

```
[root@host]# chown -R mysql /usr/local/mysql/data
[root@host]# chgrp -R mysql /usr/local/mysql
```

7. Start the MySQL server by manually running the *mysqld_safe* script.

```
[root@host]# /usr/local/mysql/bin/mysqld_safe --user=mysql &
```

MySQL should now start up normally. Figure 2-3 demonstrates what you will see as the server starts up.

Once installation is successfully completed and the server has started up, move down to the section entitled "Testing MySQL" to verify it is functioning as it should.

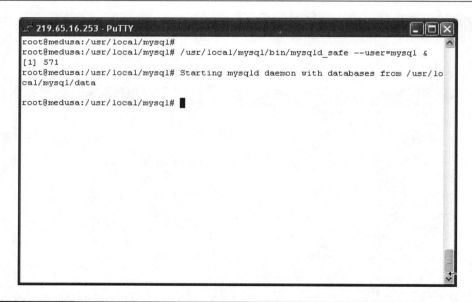

FIGURE 2-3   MySQL server startup messages

Installing Apache and PHP

PHP can be integrated with the Apache Web server in one of two ways: as a dynamic module loaded into the web server at run time, or as a static module integrated into the Apache source tree at build time. Each alternative has advantages and disadvantages:

- Installing PHP as a dynamic module makes it easier to upgrade your PHP build at a later date, as you only need to recompile the PHP module and not the rest of the Apache Web server. On the flip side, with a dynamically loaded module, performance tends to be lower than with a static module, which is more closely integrated with the server.

- Installing PHP as a static module improves performance because the module is compiled directly into the Apache source tree. However, this close integration has an important drawback: if you ever decide to upgrade your PHP build, you will need to reintegrate the newer PHP module into the Apache source tree and recompile the Apache Web server.

This section shows you how to compile PHP as a dynamic module that is loaded into the Apache server at run time.

1. Ensure that you are logged in as the system's `root` user.

   ```
   [user@host]# su - root
   ```

2. Extract the contents of the Apache source archive to your system's temporary directory.

   ```
   [root@host]# cd /tmp
   [root@host]# tar -xzvf /tmp/apache_1.3.31.tar.gz
   ```

3. To enable PHP to be loaded dynamically, the Apache server must be compiled with Dynamic Shared Object (DSO) support. This support is enabled by passing the `--enable-module=so` option to the Apache *configure* script, as shown here:

   ```
   [root@host]# cd /tmp/apache_1.3.31
   [root@host]# ./configure --prefix=/usr/local/apache ↵
   --enable-module=so
   ```

   You should see a few screens of output (Figure 2-4 has a sample) as *configure* configures and sets up the variables needed for the compilation process.

```
219.65.16.253 - PuTTY                                              _ □ x
root@medusa:/tmp/apache_1.3.31# ./configure --prefix=/usr/local/apache --enable-
module=so
Configuring for Apache, Version 1.3.31
 + using installation path layout: Apache (config.layout)
Creating Makefile
Creating Configuration.apaci in src
Creating Makefile in src
 + configured for Linux platform
 + setting C compiler to gcc
 + setting C pre-processor to gcc -E
 + using "tr [a-z] [A-Z]" to uppercase
 + checking for system header files
 + adding selected modules
 + using system Expat
 + using -ldl for vendor DSO support
 + checking sizeof various data types
 + doing sanity check on compiler and options
Creating Makefile in src/support
Creating Makefile in src/regex
Creating Makefile in src/os/unix
Creating Makefile in src/ap
Creating Makefile in src/main
Creating Makefile in src/modules/standard
root@medusa:/tmp/apache_1.3.31#
```

FIGURE 2-4   Configuring the Apache source tree

4. Now, compile the server using `make` and install it to the system using `make install`.

```
[root@host]# make
[root@host]# make install
```

Figure 2-5 illustrates what you might see during the compilation process.

Apache should now be installed to */usr/local/apache/*.

5. Next, proceed to compile and install PHP. Begin by extracting the contents of the PHP source archive to your system's temporary directory.

```
[root@host]# cd /tmp
[root@host]# tar -xzvf /tmp/php-5.0.1.tar.gz
```

6. This step is the most important in the PHP installation process. It involves sending arguments to the PHP *configure* script to control the final capabilities of the PHP module. These command-line parameters specify which PHP extensions should be activated, and they also tell PHP where to find the supporting libraries needed by those extensions.

```
[root@host]# cd /tmp/php-5.0.1
[root@host]# ./configure --prefix=/usr/local/php5 ↵
--with-apxs=/usr/local/apache/bin/apxs --with-libxml- ↵
```

```
dir=/usr/local/lib --with-zlib --with-zlib-dir=/usr/local/lib ⏎
--with-mysql=/usr/local/mysql
```

Here is a brief explanation of what each of the previous arguments does.

■ The `--with-apxs` argument tells PHP where to find the Apache's APXS (APache eXtenSion) script. This script simplifies the task of building and installing loadable modules for Apache.

■ The `--with-libxml-dir` and `--with-zlib-dir` arguments tell PHP where to find the `libxml2` and `zlib` libraries (the installation procedure for these libraries is discussed in the section entitled "Installing Supporting Libraries").

■ The `--with-mysql` argument activates PHP's MySQL extension and tells PHP where to find the local MySQL installation. The *configure* script uses this information to find the system's MySQL client libraries and to add MySQL support to PHP.

■ The `--with-zlib` argument activates the ZLIB library in the final PHP build, making data compression services available to all extensions.

Figure 2-6 illustrates what you will see during the configuration process.

```
219.65.16.253 - PuTTY
make[2]: Entering directory `/tmp/apache_1.3.31/src'
===> src/regex
sh ./mkh  -p regcomp.c >regcomp.ih
gcc -I.  -I../os/unix -I../include    -DLINUX=22 -DHAVE_SET_DUMPABLE -DUSE_HSREGE
X `../apaci` -DPOSIX_MISTAKE   -c -o regcomp.o regcomp.c
sh ./mkh  -p engine.c >engine.ih
gcc -I.  -I../os/unix -I../include    -DLINUX=22 -DHAVE_SET_DUMPABLE -DUSE_HSREGE
X `../apaci` -DPOSIX_MISTAKE   -c -o regexec.o regexec.c
gcc -I.  -I../os/unix -I../include    -DLINUX=22 -DHAVE_SET_DUMPABLE -DUSE_HSREGE
X `../apaci` -DPOSIX_MISTAKE   -c -o regerror.o regerror.c
gcc -I.  -I../os/unix -I../include    -DLINUX=22 -DHAVE_SET_DUMPABLE -DUSE_HSREGE
X `../apaci` -DPOSIX_MISTAKE   -c -o regfree.o regfree.c
rm -f libregex.a
ar cr libregex.a regcomp.o regexec.o regerror.o regfree.o
ranlib libregex.a
<=== src/regex
===> src/os/unix
gcc -c  -I../../os/unix -I../../include    -DLINUX=22 -DHAVE_SET_DUMPABLE -DUSE_H
SREGEX `../../apaci` os.c
gcc -c  -I../../os/unix -I../../include    -DLINUX=22 -DHAVE_SET_DUMPABLE -DUSE_H
SREGEX `../../apaci` os-inline.c
rm -f libos.a
ar cr libos.a os.o os-inline.o
```

FIGURE 2-5   Compiling Apache

```
219.65.16.253 - PuTTY                                          _ □ X
root@medusa:/tmp/php-5.0.1# ./configure --prefix=/usr/local/php5 --with-apxs=/us
r/local/apache/bin/apxs --with-libxml-dir=/usr/local/lib --with-zlib --with-zlib
-dir=/usr/local/lib --with-mysql=/usr/local/mysql
creating cache ./config.cache
checking host system type... i586-pc-linux-gnu
checking for gcc... gcc
checking whether the C compiler (gcc  ) works... yes
checking whether the C compiler (gcc  ) is a cross-compiler... no
checking whether we are using GNU C... yes
checking whether gcc accepts -g... yes
checking whether gcc and cc understand -c and -o together... yes
checking how to run the C preprocessor... gcc -E
checking for AIX... no
checking if compiler supports -R... no
checking if compiler supports -Wl,-rpath,... yes
checking for re2c... exit 0;
checking for ranlib... ranlib
checking whether ln -s works... yes
checking for mawk... no
checking for gawk... gawk
checking for bison... bison -y
checking bison version... 1.35 (ok)
checking for flex... flex
checking for yywrap in -lfl... yes
```

FIGURE 2-6   Configuring the PHP source tree

The PHP configuration process is extremely sophisticated, enabling you to control many aspects of PHP's behavior. To see a complete list of available options, use the command `./configure --help`*, and visit **http://www.php.net/manual/en/configure.php** for detailed explanations of what each option does.*

7. Next, compile and install PHP using `make` and `make install`:

```
[root@host]# make
[root@host]# make install
```

Figure 2-7 illustrates what you might see during the compilation process.

PHP should now be installed to */usr/local/php5/*.

8. The next step in the installation process consists of configuring Apache to correctly recognize requests for PHP pages. This is accomplished by opening the Apache configuration file, *httpd.conf* (which is found in the *conf/* subdirectory of the Apache installation directory), in a text editor and adding the following line to it.

```
AddType application/x-httpd-php .php
```

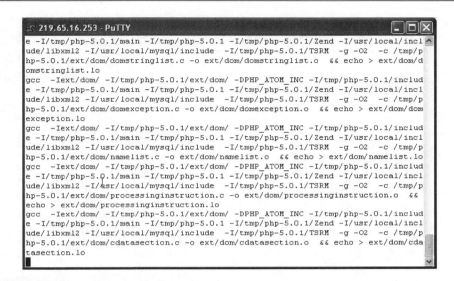

```
219.65.16.253 - PuTTY
e -I/tmp/php-5.0.1/main -I/tmp/php-5.0.1 -I/tmp/php-5.0.1/Zend -I/usr/local/incl
ude/libxml2 -I/usr/local/mysql/include  -I/tmp/php-5.0.1/TSRM  -g -O2  -c /tmp/p
hp-5.0.1/ext/dom/domstringlist.c -o ext/dom/domstringlist.o  && echo > ext/dom/d
omstringlist.lo
gcc  -Iext/dom/ -I/tmp/php-5.0.1/ext/dom/ -DPHP_ATOM_INC -I/tmp/php-5.0.1/includ
e -I/tmp/php-5.0.1/main -I/tmp/php-5.0.1 -I/tmp/php-5.0.1/Zend -I/usr/local/incl
ude/libxml2 -I/usr/local/mysql/include  -I/tmp/php-5.0.1/TSRM  -g -O2  -c /tmp/p
hp-5.0.1/ext/dom/domexception.c -o ext/dom/domexception.o  && echo > ext/dom/dom
exception.lo
gcc  -Iext/dom/ -I/tmp/php-5.0.1/ext/dom/ -DPHP_ATOM_INC -I/tmp/php-5.0.1/includ
e -I/tmp/php-5.0.1/main -I/tmp/php-5.0.1 -I/tmp/php-5.0.1/Zend -I/usr/local/incl
ude/libxml2 -I/usr/local/mysql/include  -I/tmp/php-5.0.1/TSRM  -g -O2  -c /tmp/p
hp-5.0.1/ext/dom/namelist.c -o ext/dom/namelist.o  && echo > ext/dom/namelist.lo
gcc  -Iext/dom/ -I/tmp/php-5.0.1/ext/dom/ -DPHP_ATOM_INC -I/tmp/php-5.0.1/includ
e -I/tmp/php-5.0.1/main -I/tmp/php-5.0.1 -I/tmp/php-5.0.1/Zend -I/usr/local/incl
ude/libxml2 -I/usr/local/mysql/include  -I/tmp/php-5.0.1/TSRM  -g -O2  -c /tmp/p
hp-5.0.1/ext/dom/processinginstruction.c -o ext/dom/processinginstruction.o  &&
echo > ext/dom/processinginstruction.lo
gcc  -Iext/dom/ -I/tmp/php-5.0.1/ext/dom/ -DPHP_ATOM_INC -I/tmp/php-5.0.1/includ
e -I/tmp/php-5.0.1/main -I/tmp/php-5.0.1 -I/tmp/php-5.0.1/Zend -I/usr/local/incl
ude/libxml2 -I/usr/local/mysql/include  -I/tmp/php-5.0.1/TSRM  -g -O2  -c /tmp/p
hp-5.0.1/ext/dom/cdatasection.c -o ext/dom/cdatasection.o  && echo > ext/dom/cda
tasection.lo
```

FIGURE 2-7   Compiling PHP

9. Save the changes to the file. Also, check to make sure this line appears somewhere in the file:

```
LoadModule php5_module libexec/libphp5.so
```

The PHP installation process should automatically add this line to the file, but it has been known to fail. If you don't see it, add it yourself.

10. Start the Apache server by manually running the *apachectl* script.

```
[root@host]# /usr/local/apache/bin/apachectl start
```

Apache should start up normally. Figure 2-8 demonstrates what you will see as the server starts up.

Once installation is successfully completed and the server has started, move down to the section entitled "Testing Apache and PHP" to verify that all is functioning as it should.

Installing on Windows

Compiling applications on Windows is a challenging process, especially for novice developers. With this in mind, it is advisable for Windows users to focus instead on installing and configuring prebuilt binary releases of MySQL, PHP, and Apache,

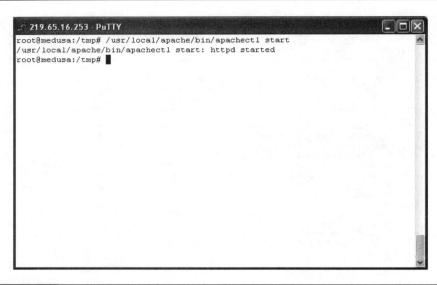

FIGURE 2-8   Apache server startup messages

instead of attempting to compile them from source code. These releases can be downloaded from the web sites listed in the previous section. They are to be installed one after another, as outlined in the following subsections.

Installing MySQL

The binary distribution of MySQL for Windows comes with an automated installer, which enables you to get MySQL up and running on your Windows system in just a few minutes.

1. Log in as an administrator (if you're using Windows NT or Windows 2000) and unzip the distribution archive to a temporary directory on your system. After extraction, your directory should look something like Figure 2-9.

2. Double-click the *setup.exe* file to begin the installation process. You should see a welcome screen (Figure 2-10).

3. Select the directory in which MySQL is to be installed, for example, *c:\program files\mysql* (Figure 2-11).

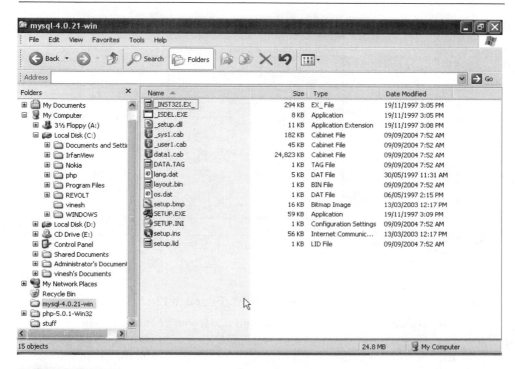

FIGURE 2-9   The directory structure created on unpackaging a MySQL binary distribution for Windows

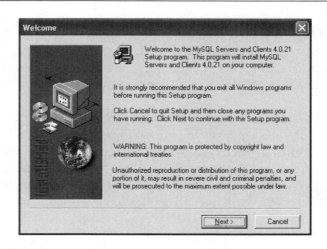

FIGURE 2-10   Beginning MySQL installation on Windows

FIGURE 2-11 Selecting the MySQL installation directory

4. Select the type of installation required (Figure 2-12).

Most often, a Typical Installation will do. If you're the kind who likes tweaking default settings, however, or if you're short of disk space, select the Custom Installation option, and decide which components of the package should be installed (Figure 2-13).

5. MySQL should now begin installing to your system (Figure 2-14).

6. Once installation is complete, you should see a screen like Figure 2-15.

You should now be able to start the MySQL server by diving into the *bin* subdirectory of your MySQL installation and launching the WinMySQLadmin tool (*winmysqladmin.exe*). This tool provides a graphical user interface to MySQL configuration, and is by far the simplest way to configure MySQL on Windows systems.

The first time you start WinMySQLadmin, you will be asked for the name and password of the user the server should run as (Figure 2-16).

Once this information is entered, WinMySQLadmin will automatically create the MySQL configuration file (named *my.ini*) and populate it with appropriate values for your system. You can edit these values at any time using the my.ini Setup section of the WinMySQLadmin application (see Figure 2-17).

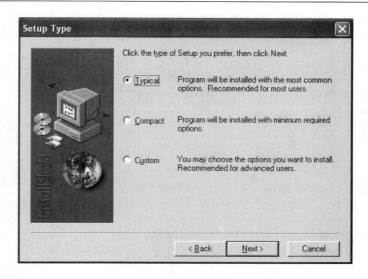

FIGURE 2-12   Selecting the MySQL installation type

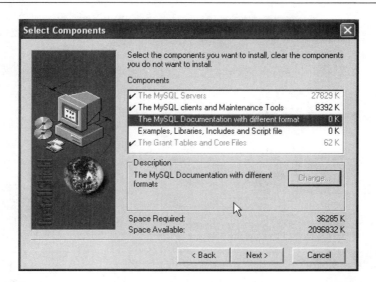

FIGURE 2-13   Selecting components for a custom MySQL installation

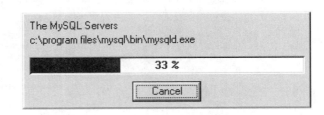

FIGURE 2-14 MySQL installation in progress

You can also start the MySQL server by directly launching the mysqld. exe *or* mysqld-nt.exe *binaries from the* bin\ *subdirectory of your MySQL installation.*

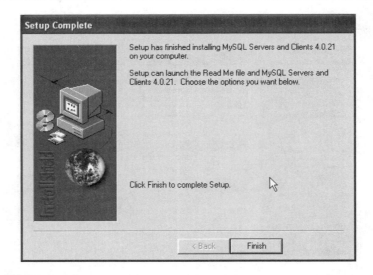

FIGURE 2-15 MySQL installation successfully completed

2

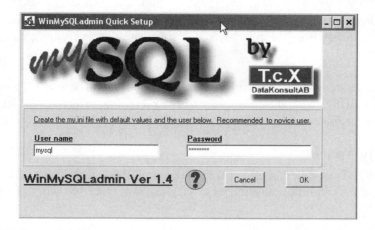

FIGURE 2-16   Setting the WinMySQLadmin username and password

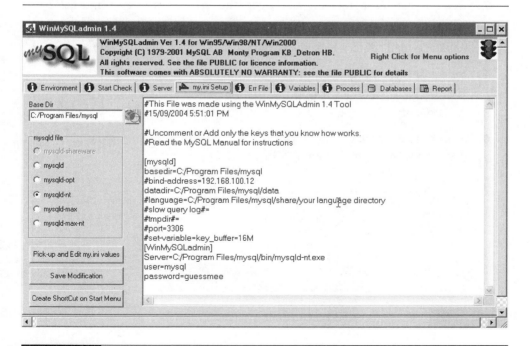

FIGURE 2-17   Editing MySQL configuration on Windows via WinMySQLadmin

Once the server has started, WinMySQLadmin will minimize to a green icon in your Windows taskbar notification area. You can now proceed to test the server, as described in the section "Testing MySQL," to ensure that everything is working as it should.

You can bring the WinMySQLadmin application back to the foreground at any time by right-clicking its taskbar icon and selecting the Show Me option from the menu that pops up (see Figure 2-18).

Installing Apache

Once MySQL is installed, the next step is to install the Apache Web server. On Windows, this is a point-and-click process, similar to that used when installing MySQL.

1. Begin by double-clicking the Apache installer to begin the installation process. You should see a welcome screen (Figure 2-19).

2. Read the license agreement and accept the terms to proceed (Figure 2-20).

3. Read the descriptive information and proceed to enter basic server information and the e-mail address to be displayed on error pages (Figure 2-21).

4. Select the type of installation required (Figure 2-22).

   If you like, select the Custom Installation option to decide which components of the package should be installed (Figure 2-23).

5. Select the location to which Apache should be installed, for example, *c:\program files\apache group* (Figure 2-24).

FIGURE 2-18   Using the WinMySQLadmin system tray icon

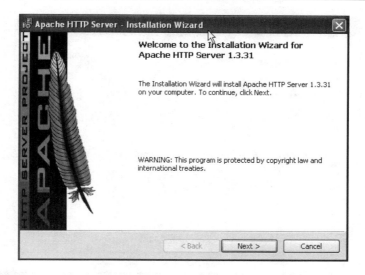

FIGURE 2-19 Beginning Apache installation on Windows

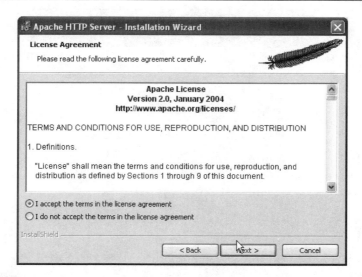

FIGURE 2-20 Apache licensing terms

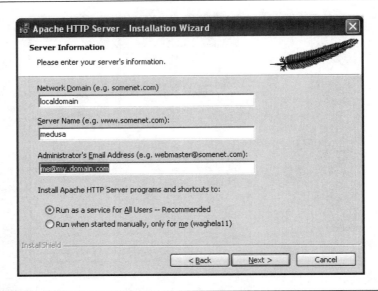

FIGURE 2-21 Entering Apache server information

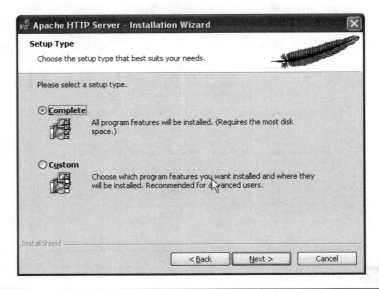

FIGURE 2-22 Selecting the Apache installation type

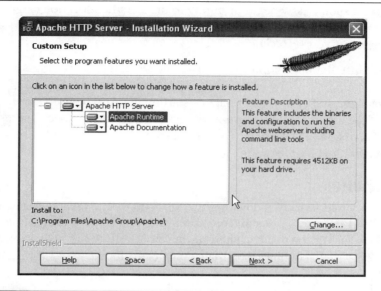

FIGURE 2-23   Selecting components for a custom Apache installation

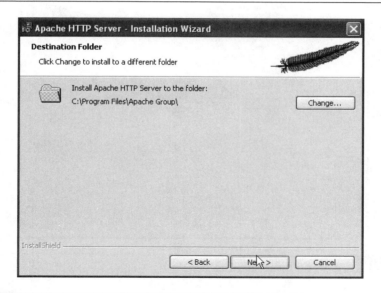

FIGURE 2-24   Selecting the Apache installation directory

6. Apache should now begin installing to the specified location (Figure 2-25). The installation process takes a few minutes to complete, so this is a good time to get yourself a cup of coffee.

7. Once installation is complete, you should see a screen like Figure 2-26.

The Apache installer also takes care of starting the Apache Web server, as the final step of the automated installation process. You can now proceed to test the server as described in the section "Testing Apache," to ensure that the server is correctly handling HTTP requests.

Installing PHP

The PHP binary release for Windows has two versions—a ZIP archive that contains all the bundled PHP extensions and requires manual installation, and an automated Windows Installer-version that contains only the basic PHP binary with no extra extensions. This section outlines the installation process for the PHP 5.0.1 ZIP archive.

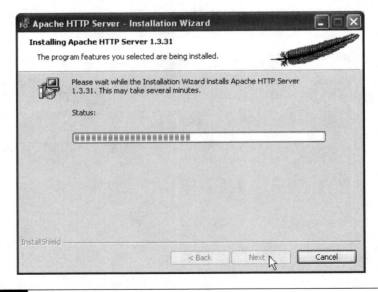

FIGURE 2-25 Apache installation in progress

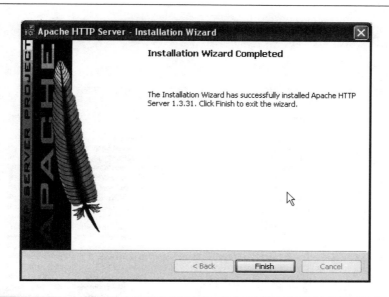

FIGURE 2-26   Apache installation successfully completed

CAUTION

PHP 4.3.0 and better can only be used with Windows 98/Me/NT/2000/ XP/2003. Windows 95 is not supported as of PHP 4.3.0.

1. Log in as an administrator (if you're using Windows NT or Windows 2000) and unzip the distribution archive to a directory on your system, for example, *c:\php*. After extraction, this directory should look something like Figure 2-27.

2. Next, copy the file *php.ini-recommended* from your PHP installation directory to your Windows directory—either *c:\windows* or *c:\winnt*— and rename it to *php.ini*. This file contains configuration settings for PHP, which can be used to alter the way it works. Read the comments within the file to learn more about the available settings.

3. Copy the file *libmysql.dll* from your PHP installation directory to your Windows system directory, usually *c:\windows\system32* or *c:\winnt\ system32*.

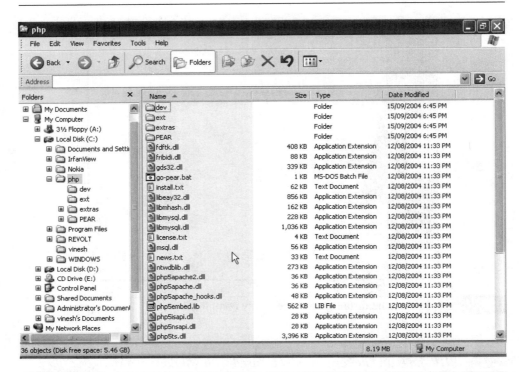

FIGURE 2-27
The directory structure created on unpackaging a PHP binary distribution for Windows

4. Within the *php.ini* file, locate the line,

```
extension_dir = "./"
```

and alter it to read

```
extension_dir = "c:\php\ext\"
```

This tells PHP where to locate the extensions supplied with the package. Remember to replace the path "*c:\php*" with the actual location of your PHP installation.

Next, look for the line,

```
;extension=php_mysql.dll
```

and remove the semicolon at the beginning, so it reads like this:

```
extension=php_mysql.dll
```

This takes care of activating PHP's MySQL extension.

2

5. Open the Apache configuration file, *httpd.conf* (which can be found in the *Apache/conf/* subdirectory of the Apache installation directory), in a text editor, and add the following lines to it.

```
AddType application/x-httpd-php .php
LoadModule php5_module "c:\php\php5apache.dll"
SetEnv PHPRC C:\windows
```

These lines tell Apache how to deal with PHP scripts and where to find the php.ini configuration file. Remember to replace the path *c:\php* with the actual location of your PHP installation and the path *C:\windows* with *C:\winnt* if you're using Windows NT or Windows 2000.

6. When the Apache server is installed, it adds itself to the Start menu. Use this Start menu group to stop and restart the server, as in Figure 2-28.

PHP is now installed and configured to work with Apache. To test it, skip down to the section entitled "Testing Apache and PHP."

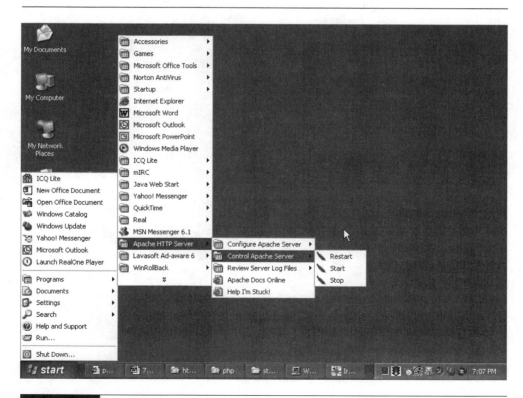

FIGURE 2-28 Apache server controls on Windows

Testing the Software

After you've successfully completed the installation procedure, it is necessary to test the various components to ensure that they're functioning correctly, both individually and with each other. This section shows you how.

Testing MySQL

Once MySQL is successfully installed, the base tables are initialized and the server is started, you can verify that all is working as it should via some simple tests.

First, start up the MySQL command-line client, by changing to the *bin/* sub-directory of your MySQL installation directory and typing

```
prompt# mysql -u root
```

You should be rewarded with a

```
mysql>
```

prompt.

At this point, you are connected to the MySQL server and can begin executing SQL commands or queries to test whether the server is working as it should. Here are a few examples, with their output:

```
mysql> SHOW DATABASES;
+-----------+
| Database  |
+-----------+
| mysql     |
| test      |
+-----------+
2 rows in set (0.13 sec)
mysql> USE mysql;
Reading table information for completion of table and column names
You can turn off this feature to get a quicker startup with -A
Database changed
mysql> SHOW TABLES;
+-----------------+
| Tables_in_mysql |
+-----------------+
```

```
| columns_priv   |
| db             |
| func           |
| host           |
| tables_priv    |
| user           |
+----------------+
6 rows in set (0.00 sec)
mysql> SELECT COUNT(*) FROM user;
+----------+
| count(*) |
+----------+
|        4 |
+----------+
1 row in set (0.00 sec)
```

If you see output similar to the previous, your MySQL installation is working as it should. Exit the command-line client by typing

```
mysql> exit
```

and you'll be returned to your command prompt.

If you don't see output like that previously shown, or if MySQL throws warnings and errors at you, review the installation procedure in the previous section, as well as the documents that shipped with your version of MySQL, to see what went wrong.

The commands sent to the MySQL client in the previous examples are SQL commands. Read more about them in Chapter 8.

Testing Apache

Once you successfully install Apache, test it by popping open your web browser and pointing it to **http://localhost/**. You should see Apache's default It Worked! page, as shown in Figure 2-29.

Testing Apache and PHP

Once you successfully install PHP as an Apache module, you should test it to ensure that the web server can recognize PHP scripts and handle them correctly.

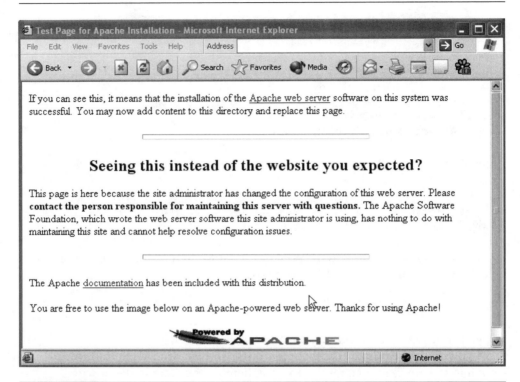

FIGURE 2-29 Testing Apache

To perform this test, create a PHP script in any text editor containing the following lines:

```
<?php
phpinfo();
?>
```

Save this file as *test.php* in your web server document root (the *htdocs/* sub-directory of your Apache installation directory) and point your browser to **http://localhost/test.php**. You should see a page containing information on the PHP build, as in Figure 2-30.

Eyeball the list of extensions to make sure that the MySQL extension is active. If it isn't, review the previous installation procedure, as well as the installation documents that shipped with the software, to see what went wrong.

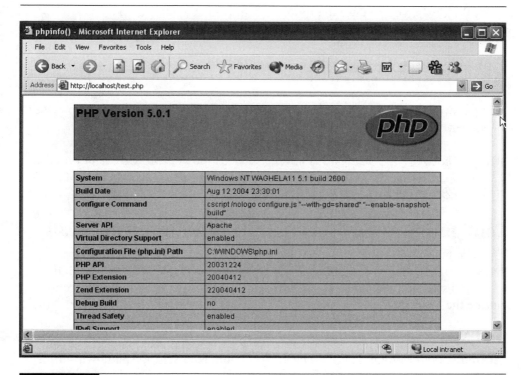

FIGURE 2-30 Viewing the output of the `phpinfo()` command

Performing Postinstallation Steps

Once testing is complete, you should perform two more tasks to complete your MySQL installation.

Setting the MySQL Super-User Password

When MySQL is first installed, access to the database server is restricted to the MySQL administrator, aka `root`. By default, this user is initialized with a null password, which is generally considered a Bad Thing. You should, therefore, rectify this as soon as possible by setting a password for this user via the included `mysqladmin` utility, using the following syntax in UNIX:

```
[root@host]# /usr/local/mysql/bin/mysqladmin ↵
-u root password 'new-password'
```

In Windows, you can use the following equivalent syntax from an MS-DOS prompt:

```
C:\> c:\program files\mysql\bin\mysqladmin ⏎
-u root password 'new-password'
```

This password change goes into effect immediately, with no requirement to restart the server.

 *The MySQL* root *user is not the same as the system* root *user on UNIX. So, altering the system* root *user's password does not affect the MySQL* root *user's password, and vice versa.*

Configuring MySQL and Apache to Start Automatically

If you're going to be doing a lot of development (and if you bought this book, that's a given!), then you should consider configuring the Apache and MySQL servers to start automatically when your system boots up. The following sections outline the process to accomplish this.

On UNIX

On UNIX, both MySQL and Apache servers come with startup/shutdown scripts, which can be used to start and stop them. These scripts are located within the installation hierarchy for each program. Here's an example of how to use the MySQL server control script:

```
[root@host]# /usr/local/mysql/support-files/mysql.server start
[root@host]# /usr/local/mysql/support-files/mysql.server stop
```

And here's an example of how to use the Apache control script:

```
[root@host]# /usr/local/apache/bin/apachectl start
[root@host]# /usr/local/apache/bin/apachectl stop
```

To have MySQL and Apache start automatically at boot time on UNIX, simply invoke their respective control scripts with appropriate parameters from your system's bootup and shutdown scripts in the /etc/rc.d/* hierarchy.

On Windows

On Windows, you can use the `WinMySQLadmin` utility to start and shut down MySQL, and the server controls installed by Apache on the Start menu to control the Apache server. To start MySQL and Apache automatically on Windows, simply add a link to the *mysqld.exe* and *apache.exe* server binaries to your Startup group.

Summary

As popular open-source applications, MySQL, Apache, and PHP are available for a wide variety of platforms and architectures, in both binary and source form. This chapter demonstrated the process of installing and configuring these software components to create a PHP-MySQL development environment on the two most common platforms: UNIX and Windows. It also showed you how to configure your system to launch these components automatically every time the system starts up, and offered some tips on basic MySQL security.

To read more about the installation processes outlined in this chapter, or for detailed troubleshooting advice and assistance, consider visiting the following pages:

- MySQL installation notes, at **http://dev.mysql.com/doc/mysql/en/ Quick_Standard_Installation.html**

- General guidelines for compiling Apache on UNIX, at **http://httpd .apache.org/docs/install.html**

- Windows-specific notes for Apache binary installations, at **http://httpd .apache.org/docs/windows.html**

- Installation instructions for PHP on Windows, at **http://www.php.net/ manual/en/install.windows.php**

- Installation instructions for PHP on UNIX, at **http://www.php.net/manual/ en/install.unix.php**

- Installation instructions for PHP on Mac OS X, at **http://www.php.net/ manual/en/install.macosx.php**

You are now ready to begin working with PHP and MySQL. Turn to the next chapter for an introduction to PHP scripting.

Part II

Learning PHP

Chapter 3

Using Variables, Statements, and Operators

Extremely robust and scalable, PHP can be used for the most demanding of applications, and delivers excellent performance even at high loads. A MySQL extension makes it easy to hook it up to a database, XML support makes it suitable for the new generation of XML-enabled applications, and extensible architecture makes it easy for developers to build their own custom PHP modules. Toss in a great manual, a knowledgeable developer community, and a zero-cost licensing policy, and it's no wonder that more and more web developers are migrating to it.

If you followed the instructions in the last chapter, your development environment should now be installed and ready for use. In this chapter, you'll begin doing something with it.

How to...

- Write and execute a simple PHP script
- Create statements and comments, and name variables
- Use variables to store values
- Choose between PHP's data types
- Understand the special NULL data type
- Read GET and POST form input, and store it in variables
- Perform calculations and comparisons using operators
- Use and override operator precedence rules

Embedding PHP in HTML

One of the nicer things about PHP is that, unlike CGI scripts, which require you to write server-side code to output HTML, PHP lets you embed commands in regular HTML pages. These embedded PHP commands are enclosed within special start and end tags, which are read by the PHP interpreter when it parses the page. Here is an example of what these tags looks like:

```
<?php
... PHP code ...
?>
```

You can also use the short version of the previous, which looks like this:

```
<?
... PHP code
?>
```

To see how this works, create this simple test script, which demonstrates how PHP and HTML can be combined:

```
<html>
<head><basefont face="Arial"></head>
<body>
<h2>Q: This creature can change color to blend in with its surroundings.
What is its name?</h2>

<?php
// print output
echo '<h2><i>A: Chameleon</i></h2>';
?>

</body>
</html>
```

Save the previous script to a location under your web server root as *question.php*, and browse to it. You'll see a page like Figure 3-1.

And here is what the HTML source of the rendered page looks like:

```
<html>
<head><basefont face="Arial"></head>
<body>
<h2>Q: This creature can change color to blend in with ⏎
its surroundings. What is its name?</h2>
<h2><i>A: Chameleon</i></h2>
</body>
</html>
```

When you requested the previous script through your browser, the web server intercepted your request and handed it off to PHP. PHP then parsed the script, executing the code between the <?php...?> marks and replacing it with the resulting output. The result was then handed back to the web server and transmitted to the client. Because the output contained valid HTML, the browser was able to render it for display to the user.

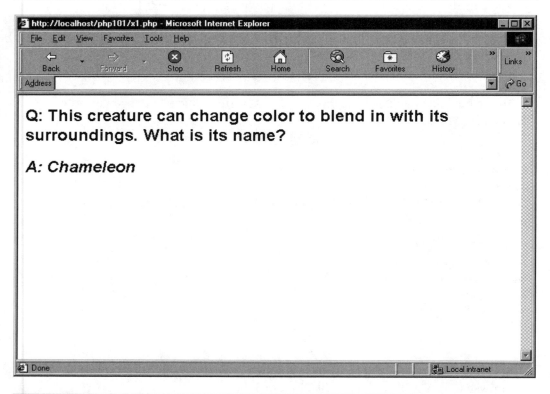

FIGURE 3-1   The HTML page generated by a PHP script

How to Compile or Interpret

PHP is an *interpreted* language (like Perl) and not a *compiled* one (like Java). In case you haven't heard those terms before, they're pretty simple: if you use a compiled language, you need to convert ("compile") your ASCII program code into binary form before you can run it. If, on the other hand, you use an interpreted language, you can run your code as is, without converting it first; the language interpreter reads it and executes it. Thus, with an interpreted language, you don't need to recompile your scripts every time you make a small change, and this can save you some development time. On the other hand, compiled code tends to run faster than interpreted code, because it doesn't have the extra overhead of an interpreter; this can produce better performance.

Writing Statements and Comments

As you can see from the previous example, a PHP script consists of one or more *statements,* with each statement ending in a semicolon. Blank lines within the script are ignored by the parser. Everything outside the tags is also ignored by the parser, and returned as is; only the code between the tags is read and executed.

> **TIP**   *If you're in a hurry, you can omit the semicolon on the last line of a PHP block, because the closing ?> includes an implicit semicolon. Therefore, the line <?php echo 'Hello' ?> is perfectly valid PHP code. This is the only time a PHP statement not ending in a semicolon is still considered valid.*

For greater readability, you should add comments to your PHP code, as I did in the previous example. To do this, simply use one of the comment styles listed here:

```php
<?php
// this is a single-line comment

# so is this

/* and this is a
multiline
comment */
?>
```

Storing Values in Variables

Variables are the building blocks of any programming language. A variable can be thought of as a programming construct used to store both numeric and nonnumeric data. The contents of a variable can be altered during program execution, and variables can be compared and manipulated using operators.

PHP supports a number of different variable types—Booleans, integers, floating point numbers, strings, arrays, objects, resources, and NULLs—and the language can automatically determine variable type by the context in which it is being used. Every variable has a name, which is preceded by a dollar ($) symbol, and it must begin with a letter or underscore character, optionally followed by more letters, numbers, and underscores. For example, $popeye, $one_day, and $INCOME are all valid PHP variable names, while $123 and $48hrs are invalid variable names.

 *Variable names in PHP are case-sensitive; $count is different from $Count or $COUNT.*

To see PHP's variables in action, try out the following script:

```
<html>
<head><basefont face="Arial"></head>
<body>

<h2>Q: This creature has tusks made of ivory. ↵
What is its name?</h2>

<?php
// define variable
$answer = 'Elephant';

// print output
echo "<h2><i>$answer</i></h2>";
?>

</body>
</html>
```

Here, the variable $answer is first defined with a string value, and then substituted in the echo() function call. The echo() function, along with the print() function, is commonly used to print data to the standard output device (here, the browser). Notice that I've included HTML tags within the call to echo(), and they have been rendered by the browser in its output.

Assigning and Using Variable Values

To assign a value to a variable, use the assignment operator, the equality (=) symbol. This operator assigns a value (the right side of the equation) to a variable (the left side). The value being assigned need not always be fixed; it could also be another variable, an expression, or even an expression involving other variables, as here:

```php
<?php
$age = $dob + 15;
?>
```

To use a variable value in your script, simply call the variable by name, and PHP will substitute its value at run time. For example:

```php
<?php
$today = "Jan 05 2004";
echo "Today is $today";
?>
```

Saving Form Input in Variables

Forms have always been one of the quickest and easiest ways to add interactivity to your web site. A form enables you to ask customers if they like your products and casual visitors for comments. PHP can simplify the task of processing web-based forms substantially, by providing a simple mechanism to read user data submitted through a form into PHP variables. Consider the following sample form:

```html
<html>
<head></head>
<body>

<form action="message.php" method="post">
Enter your message: <input type="text" name="msg" size="30">
<input type="submit" value="Send">
</form>

</body>
</html>
```

The most critical line in this entire page is the `<form>` tag:

```
<form method="post" action="message.php">
...
</form>
```

As you probably already know, the `method` attribute of the `<form>` tag specifies the manner in which form data will be submitted (POST), while the `action` attribute specifies the name of the server-side script (*message.php*) that will process the information entered into the form. Here is what *message.php* looks like:

```
<?php
// retrieve form data in a variable
$input = $_POST['msg'];

// print it
echo "You said: <i>$input</i>";
?>
```

To see how this works, enter some data into the form (*"boo"*) and submit it. The form processor should read it and display it back to you (*"you said: boo"*).

Thus, whenever a form is POST-ed to a PHP script, all variable-value pairs within that form automatically become available for use within the script through a special PHP container variable, $_POST. To then access the value of the form variable, use its `name` inside the $_POST container, as in the previous script. If the form uses GET instead of POST, simply retrieve values from $_GET instead of $_POST.

The $_GET and $_POST variables are a special type of animal called an array. Refer to Chapter 5 and to the online manual at **http://www.php .net/manual/en/language.variables.external.php** *for more information on arrays.*

Understanding Simple Data Types

Every language has different types of variables—and PHP has no shortage of choices. The language supports a wide variety of data types, including simple numeric, character, string, and Boolean types, and more complex arrays and objects. Table 3-1 lists the four basic types, with examples:

Data Type	Description	Example
Boolean	The simplest variable type in PHP, a Boolean variable simply specifies a true or false value.	`$auth = true;`
Integer	An integer is a plain-vanilla number like `75`, `-95`, `2000`, or `1`.	`$age = 99;`
Floating-point	A floating-point number is typically a fractional number such as `12.5` or `3.149391239129`. Floating point numbers may be specified using either decimal or scientific notation.	`$temperature = 56.89;`
String	A string is a sequence of characters, like `'hello'` or `'abracadabra'`. String values may be enclosed in either double quotes (`" "`) or single quotes (`' '`).	`$name = 'Harry';`

TABLE 3-1   Simple Data Types in PHP

In many languages, it's essential to specify the variable type before using it; for example, a variable may need to be specified as type `integer` or type `array`. Give PHP credit for a little intelligence, though—the language can *automagically* determine variable type by the context in which it is being used.

Detecting the Data Type of a Variable

To find out what type a particular variable is, PHP offers the `gettype()` function, which accepts a variable or value as argument. The following example illustrates this:

```php
<?php
// define variables
$auth = true;
$age = 27;
$name = 'Bobby';
$temp = 98.6;
```

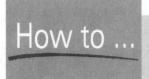

How to ... Explicitly Set the Type of a Variable

To explicitly mark a variable as numeric or string, use the `settype()` function. Read more about this at **http://www.php.net/manual/en/function.settype.php**.

```php
// returns "string"
echo gettype($name);

// returns "boolean"
echo gettype($auth);

// returns "integer"
echo gettype($age);

// returns "double"
echo gettype($temp);
?>
```

PHP also supports a number of specialized functions to check if a variable or value belongs to a specific type. Table 3-2 has a list.

Function	What It Does
is_bool()	Checks if a variable or value is Boolean
is_string()	Checks if a variable or value is a string
is_numeric()	Checks if a variable or value is a numeric string
is_float()	Checks if a variable or value is a floating point number
is_int()	Checks if a variable or value is an integer
is_null()	Checks if a variable or value is NULL
is_array()	Checks if a variable is an array
is_object()	Checks if a variable is an object

TABLE 3-2   Functions to Detect Variable Type in PHP

A Note on String Values

String values enclosed in double quotes are automatically parsed for variable names; if variable names are found, they are automatically replaced with the appropriate variable value. See the following code snippet for an example:

```php
<?php
$identity = 'James Bond';
$car = 'BMW';
// this would contain the string "James Bond drives a BMW"
$sentence = "$identity drives a $car";
// this would contain the string "$identity drives a $car"
$sentence = '$identity drives a $car';
?>
```

Note that if your string contains quotes, carriage returns, or backslashes, it's necessary to escape these special characters with a backslash. The following example illustrates this:

```php
<?php
// will cause an error due to mismatched quotes
$statement = 'It's hot outside';

// will be fine
$statement = 'It\'s hot outside';
?>
```

A Note on NULL Values

PHP 4.x introduced a new data type for empty variables, called NULL. The NULL data type is "special": it means that a variable has no value. A NULL is typically seen when a variable is initialized but not yet assigned a value, or when a variable has been de-initialized with the unset() function.

To see an example of NULL in action, consider the following script:

```php
<?php
// check type of uninitialized variable
// returns NULL
echo gettype($me);
```

```php
// assign a value
$me = 'David';
// check type again
// returns STRING
echo gettype($me);

// deinitialize variable
unset($me);
// check type again
// returns NULL
echo gettype($me);
?>
```

Using Operators to Manipulate and Compare Variables

If variables are the building blocks of a programming language, *operators* are the glue that let you do something useful with them. PHP comes with over 15 operators, including operators for assignment, arithmetic, string, comparison, and logical operations. Table 3-3 has a list.

Using Arithmetic Operators

To perform mathematical operations on variables, use the standard arithmetic operators, as illustrated in the following example:

```php
<?php
// define variables
$num1 = 101;
$num2 = 5;

// add
$sum = $num1 + $num2;

// subtract
$diff = $num1 - $num2;

// multiply
$product = $num1 * $num2;
```

```
// divide
$quotient = $num1 / $num2;

// modulus
$remainder = $num1 % $num2;
?>
```

To perform an arithmetic operation simultaneously with an assignment, use the two operators together. The following two code snippets are equivalent:

```
<?php
$a = $a + 10;
?>
```

```
<?php
$a += 10;
?>
```

Operator	What It Does
=	Assignment
+	Addition
–	Subtraction
*	Multiplication
/	Division; returns quotient
%	Division; returns modulus
.	String concatenation
==	Equal to
===	Equal to and of the same type
!==	Not equal to or not of the same type
<> aka !=	Not equal to
<	Less than
<=	Less than or equal to
>	Greater than
>=	Greater than or equal to
&&	Logical AND
||	Logical OR
xor	Logical XOR
!	Logical NOT
++	Addition by 1
--	Subtraction by 1

TABLE 3-3 Operators in PHP

Using String Operators

To add strings together, use the string concatenation operator, represented by a period (.). The following example illustrates this:

```php
<?php
$username = 'john';
$domain = 'example.com';

// combine them using the concatenation operator
$email = $username . '@' . $domain;
?>
```

You can concatenate and assign simultaneously, as in the following:

```php
<?php
// define string
$str = 'the';

// add and assign
$str .= 'n';

// $str now contains "then"
?>
```

Using Comparison Operators

To test whether two variables are different, use any one of PHP's many comparison operators. The following listing demonstrates most of the important ones:

```php
<?php
// define some variables
$mean = 29;
$median = 40;
$mode = 29;

// less-than operator
// returns true if left side is less than right
// returns true here
$result = ($mean < $median);
```

```php
// greater-than operator
// returns true if left side is greater than right
// returns false here
$result = ($mean > $median);

// less-than-or-equal-to operator
// returns true if left side is less than or equal to right
// returns false here
$result = ($median <= $mode);

// greater-than-or-equal-to operator
// returns true if left side is greater than or equal to right
// returns true here
$result = ($median >= $mode);

// equality operator
// returns true if left side is equal to right
// returns true here
$result = ($mean == $mode);

// not-equal-to operator
// returns true if left side is not equal to right
// returns false here
$result = ($mean != $mode);

// inequality operator
// returns true if left side is not equal to right
// returns false here
$result = ($mean <> $mode);
?>
```

The result of a comparison test is always a Boolean value (either true or false). This makes comparison operators a critical part of your toolkit, as you can use them in combination with a conditional statement to send a script down any of its multiple action paths.

The === Operator

An important comparison operator in PHP 4.0 is the === operator, which enables you to test both for equality and type. The following listing demonstrates this:

```php
<?php
// define two variables
```

```
$str = '14';
$int = 14;

// returns true
// since both variables contain the same value
$result = ($str == $int);

// returns false
// since the variables are not of the same type
// even though they have the same value
$result = ($str === $int);
?>
```

Using Logical Operators

To link together related conditions in a simple and elegant manner, use one of PHP's four logical operators—logical AND, logical OR, logical XOR, and logical NOT—as illustrated in the following listing:

```
<?php
// define some variables
$user = 'joe';
$pass = 'trym3';
$saveCookie = 1;
$status = 1;

// logical AND
// returns true if all conditions are true
// returns true here
$result = (($user == 'joe') && ($pass == 'trym3'));

// logical OR
// returns true if any condition is true
// returns false here
$result = (($status < 1) || ($saveCookie == 0));

// logical NOT
// returns true if the condition is false and vice-versa
// returns false
$result = !($saveCookie == 1);
```

```
// logical XOR
// returns true if any of the two conditions are true
// returns false if both conditions are true
// returns false here
$result = (($status == 1) xor ($saveCookie == 1));
?>
```

Using the Auto-Increment and Auto-Decrement Operators

The *auto-increment* operator is a PHP operator designed to automatically increment the value of the variable it is attached to by 1. It is represented by a double addition symbol (++). To see it in action, run the following script:

```
<?php
// define $total as 10
$total = 10;
// increment it
$total++;
// $total is now 11
?>
```

Thus, `<?php $total++; ?>` is functionally equivalent to `<?php $total = $total + 1; ?>`.

There's also a corresponding auto-decrement operator (- -), which does exactly the opposite:

```
<?php
// define $total as 10
$total = 10;
// decrement it
$total--;
// $total is now 9
?>
```

These operators are frequently used in loops to update the value of the loop counter. See Chapter 4 for examples of these operators in action.

Understanding Operator Precedence

When it comes to evaluating operators, PHP does not necessarily process them in the order in which they appear; rather, the language has its own set of rules about which operators have precedence over others. The following list illustrates the important PHP precedence rules. (Operators on the same line have the same level of precedence.)

- `'!'  '++'  '--'`
- `'*'  '/'  '%'`
- `'+'  '-'  '.'`
- `'<'  '<='  '>'  '>='`
- `'=='  '!='  '==='  '!=='`
- `'&&'`
- `'||'`
- `'?'  ':'`

If in doubt, remember that you can—in fact, should—override these rules with parentheses, as some of the examples in this chapter do. This reduces ambiguity and ensures that operators are evaluated in the order that you specify. For example, the expression `10 * 10 + 1` would return `101`, while the expression `10 * (10 + 1)` would return `110`. The difference lies in the fact that the second version uses parentheses to clearly indicate the order in which operations are to be performed.

Summary

This chapter focused on getting you started with PHP, by teaching you the basic things you need to know about PHP scripting. It showed you how to embed PHP code inside HTML documents using the special `<?php...?>` PHP tags, and taught you the basic syntactical rules for statements, comments, and variables. It showed you how to assign values to variables and use PHP to easily store user input from an HTML form in one or more PHP variables. It introduced you to some of PHP's data types and operators, illustrating how operators can be used to perform calculations, comparisons, and string manipulation operations. And, finally, it wrapped things up with a brief look at PHP's precedence rules, which define the order in which operators are evaluated, and showed you how to use parentheses to override the default order.

If you're interested in learning more about the topics in this chapter, these web links have more information:

- The official PHP.net tutorial, at **http://www.php.net/manual/en/ tutorial.php**

- Basic language syntax, at **http://www.php.net/manual/en/language.basic- syntax.php**

- Variables in PHP, at **http://www.php.net/manual/en/language .variables.php**

- The PHP string manipulation API, at **http://www.melonfire.com/ community/columns/trog/article.php?id=88**

- Form variables and PHP, at **http://www.php.net/manual/en/tutorial .forms.php**

- Simple and complex data types in PHP, at **http://www.php.net/manual/en/ language.types.php**

- The special NULL type, at **http://www.php.net/manual/en/language .types.null.php**

- PHP operators, at **http://www.php.net/manual/en/language .operators.php**

- The PHP 101 series, at **http://www.everythingphpmysql.com/**

Chapter 4

Using Conditional Statements and Loops

The previous chapter introduced you to the basics of PHP scripting, showing you how to create and execute PHP scripts, capture form input, assign values to variables, and use operators to manipulate variables. This chapter introduces you to conditional statements, which make your scripts respond intelligently to different situations, and loops, which enable you to repeatedly perform a series of actions.

How to...

- Use conditional tests to control program flow
- Perform "either-or" actions with the ternary operator
- Nest conditional statements inside each other for more sophisticated flow control
- Combine a form and its result page into a single script with a conditional statement
- Repeatedly execute a set of statements a fixed or variable number of times
- Use the increment and decrement operators, and the `break` and `continue` keywords, to control loop iteration

Adding Decision-Making Capabilities with Conditional Statements

One of the more interesting things you can do with a programming language like PHP involves adding decision-making routines to your scripts. These decision-making routines can be used to add intelligence to your PHP scripts, allowing it to perform different tasks on the basis of user-defined conditions. In the previous chapter, you've already seen how PHP allows you to perform comparisons using its comparison and logical operators; in this section, you will learn to use this capability to perform conditional tests and make your scripts perform different actions depending on the results of those tests.

A conditional statement enables you to test whether a specific condition is true or false, and to perform different actions on the basis of the test result. PHP comes with two basic types of conditional statements, both of which are discussed in the following sections.

Using the `if()` Statement

In PHP, the simplest form of conditional statement is the `if()` statement, which looks like this:

```php
<?php
if (conditional test)

{
    do this;
}
?>
```

4

Here's an example:

```php
<?php
if ($temp >= 100)
{
    echo 'Very hot!';
}
?>
```

The argument to `if()` here is a conditional expression, which evaluates to either true or false. If the statement evaluates to true, all PHP code within the curly braces is executed; if not, the code within the curly braces is skipped and the lines following the `if()` construct are executed.

In addition to the `if()` statement, PHP also offers the `if-else()` construct, used to define an alternate block of code that gets executed when the conditional expression in the `if()` statement evaluates as false. This is good for "either-or" situations, as illustrated in the following:

```php
<?php
if (conditional test)
{
    do this;
}
else
{
    do this;
}
?>
```

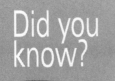

More Than One Way to Skin a Cat

PHP also supports an alternative syntax for the various control structures discussed so far. For example, the following two snippets are equivalent:

```php
<?php
if ($elvis == 0) {
    echo 'Elvis has left the building!';
} else {
    echo 'Elvis is still backstage!';
}
?>
```

```php
<?php
if ($elvis == 0):
    echo 'Elvis has left the building!';
else:
    echo 'Elvis is still backstage!';
endif;
?>
```

The second alternative is equivalent to the first, and simply involves replacing the first curly brace of every pair with a colon (:), removing the second curly brace, and ending the block with `endif`.

Here is an example:

```php
<?php
if ($temp >= 100)
{
    echo 'Very hot!';
}
else
{
    echo 'Within tolerable limits';
}
?>
```

Finally, PHP also provides you with a way of handling multiple possibilities—the `if-elseif-else()` construct. This construct consists of listing a number of possible results, one after another, and specifying the action to be taken for each. It looks like this:

```php
<?php
if (conditional test #1)
{
    do this;
}
elseif (conditional test #2)
{
    do this;
}
...
elseif (conditional test #n)
{
    do this;
}
else
{
    do this;
}
?>
```

Here is an example:

```php
<?php
if ($country == 'UK')
{
        $capital = 'London';
}
elseif ($country == 'US')
{
        $capital = 'Washington';
}
elseif ($country == 'FR')
{
        $capital = 'Paris';
}
else
{
        $capital = 'Unknown';
}
?>
```

Here, the `if-elseif-else()` control structure assigns a different value to the `$capital` variable, depending on the country code. As soon as one of the `if()` branches within the block is found to be true, PHP will execute the corresponding code, skip the remaining `if()` statements in the block, and jump immediately to the lines following the entire `if-elseif-else()` block.

Using the `switch()` Statement

An alternative to the `if-else()` family of control structures is PHP's `switch-case()` statement, which does almost the same thing. Here, a `switch()` statement evaluates a conditional expression or decision variable; depending on the result of the evaluation, an appropriate `case()` block is executed. If no matches can be found, a default block is executed instead.

Here is what the syntax of this construct looks like:

```php
<?php
switch (condition variable)
{
    case possible result #1:
        do this;
    case possible result #2:
        do this;
        ...
    case possible result #n:
        do this;
    case default;
        do this;
}
?>
```

Here's a rewrite of the last example using `switch-case()`:

```php
<?php
switch ($country)
{
    case 'UK':
        $capital = 'London';
        break;
    case 'US':
        $capital = 'Washington';
        break;
```

```
    case 'FR':
        $capital = 'Paris';
        break;
    default:
        $capital = 'Unknown';
        break;
}
?>
```

A couple of important keywords are here: the `break` keyword is used to break out of the `switch()` statement block and move immediately to the lines following it, while the `default` keyword is used to execute a default set of statements when the variable passed to `switch()` does not satisfy any of the conditions listed within the block. Read more about the `break` keyword in the section entitled "Controlling Loop Iteration with `break` and `continue`" later in this chapter.

If you forget to break out of a `case()` block, PHP will continue executing the code in each subsequent `case()` block until it reaches the end of the `switch()` block.

The Ternary Operator

PHP's *ternary operator*, represented by a question mark (?), is aptly named: the first time you see it, you're sure to wonder what exactly it's for. The ternary operator provides shortcut syntax for creating a single-statement `if-else()` block. The following two code snippets, which are equivalent, illustrate how it works:

```
<?php
if ($dialCount > 10)
{
    $msg = 'Cannot connect after ⤶
10 attempts';
}
else
{
    $msg = 'Dialing....';
}
?>
```

```
<?php
$msg = $dialCount > 10 ? 'Cannot connect after ⤶
10 attempts' : 'Dialing...';
?>
```

Nesting Conditional Statements

To handle multiple conditions, you can "nest" conditional statements inside each other. For example, this is perfectly valid PHP code:

```php
<?php
if ($country == 'India')
{
    if ($state == 'Maharashtra')
    {
        if ($city == 'Bombay')
        {
            $home = true;
        }
    }
}
?>
```

However, a better idea (and also more elegant) is to use logical operators wherever possible, instead of a series of nested conditional statements. This next snippet illustrates by rewriting the previous example in terms of logical operators:

```php
<?php
if ($country == 'India' && $state == 'Maharashtra' && $city == 'Bombay')
{
    $home = true;
}
?>
```

Merging Forms and Their Result Pages with Conditional Statements

Normally, when creating and processing forms in PHP, you would place the HTML form in one file, and handle form processing through a separate PHP script. That's the way all the examples you've seen so far have worked. However, with the power of conditional statements at your disposal, you can combine both pages into one.

To do this, assign a name to the form's submit control, and then check whether the special $_POST container variable contains that name when the script first loads up. If it does, it means that the form has already been submitted, and you can process the data. If it does not, it means that the user has not submitted the form and you, therefore, need to generate the initial, unfilled form. Thus, by testing for the presence or absence of this `submit` variable, you can use a single PHP script to generate both the initial form and the postsubmission output.

To see how this technique works in the real world, consider the following example:

```
<html>
<head></head>
<body>

<?php
// if the "submit" variable does not exist
// form has not been submitted
// display initial page
if (!$_POST['submit'])
{
?>

    <form action="<?=$_SERVER['PHP_SELF']?>" method="post">
    Enter a number: <input name="number" size="2">
    <input type="submit" name="submit" value="Go">
    </form>

<?php
}
else
{
    // if the "submit" variable exists
    // the form has been submitted
    // look for and process form data
    // display result
    $number = $_POST['number'];
    if ($number > 0)
    {
        echo 'You entered a positive number';
    }
    elseif ($number < 0)
    {
        echo 'You entered a negative number';
    }
    else
    {
        echo 'You entered 0';
    }
}
?>

</body>
</html>
```

Taking a Shortcut

The `<?=$variable?>` syntax is a shortcut for quickly displaying the value of a variable in a PHP script. It is equivalent to `<?php echo $variable; ?>`.

As you can see, the script contains two pages: the initial, empty form and the result page generated after pressing the submit button. When the script is first called, it tests for the presence of the `$_POST['submit']` key. Because the form has not been submitted, the key does not exist and so an empty form is displayed. Once the form has been submitted, the same script is called again; this time, the `$_POST['submit']` key will exist, and so PHP will process the form data and display the result.

The `$_SERVER` array is a special PHP array that holds the values of important server variables: the server version number, the path to the currently executing script, the server port and IP address, and the document root. For more on arrays, see the section entitled "Using Arrays to Group Related Values," in Chapter 5.

Repeating Actions with Loops

A *loop* is a control structure that enables you to repeat the same set of statements or commands over and over again; the actual number of repetitions may be dependent on a number you specify, or on the fulfillment of a certain condition or set of conditions.

Using the `while()` Loop

The first—and simplest—loop to learn in PHP is the so-called `while()` loop. With this loop type, so long as the conditional expression specified evaluates to true, the loop will continue to execute. When the condition becomes false, the loop will be broken and the statements following it will be executed.

Here is the syntax of the `while()` loop:

```php
<?php
while (condition is true)
{
    do this;
}
?>
```

Here is a simple example that illustrates how a while() loop works by creating a multiplication table for a specified number:

```php
<?php
// define number and limits for multiplication tables
$num = 11;
$upperLimit = 10;
$lowerLimit = 1;

// loop and multiply to create table
while ($lowerLimit <= $upperLimit)
{
    echo "$num x $lowerLimit = " . ($num * $lowerLimit);
    $lowerLimit++;
}
?>
```

This script uses a while() loop to count forwards from 1 until the values of $lowerLimit and $upperLimit are equal.

Using the do() Loop

A while() loop executes a set of statements while a specified condition is true. If the condition evaluates as false on the first iteration of the loop, the loop will never be executed. In the previous example, if the lower limit is set to a value greater than the upper limit, the loop will not execute even once.

However, sometimes you might need to execute a set of statements *at least once,* regardless of how the conditional expression evaluates. For such situations, PHP offers the do-while() loop. The construction of the do-while() loop is such that the statements within the loop are executed first, and the condition to be tested is checked after. This implies that the statements within the loop block will be executed at least once.

```php
<?php
do
{
    do this;
} while (condition is true)
?>
```

Thus, the construction of the `do-while()` loop is such that the statements within the loop are executed first, and the condition to be tested is checked after.

Let's now revise the previous PHP script so that it runs at least once, regardless of how the conditional expression evaluates the first time:

```php
<?php
// define number and limits for multiplication tables
$num = 11;
$upperLimit = 10;
$lowerLimit = 12;

// loop and multiply to create table
do
{
    echo "$num x $lowerLimit = " . ($num * $lowerLimit);
    $lowerLimit++;
} while ($lowerLimit <= $upperLimit)
?>
```

Using the `for()` Loop

Both the `while()` and `do-while()` loops continue to iterate for so long as the specified conditional expression remains true. But there often arises a need to execute a certain set of statements a fixed number of times, for example, printing a series of ten sequential numbers, or displaying a particular set of values five times. For such nails, the `for()` loop is the most appropriate hammer.

Here is what the `for()` loop looks like:

```php
<?php
for (initialize counter; conditional test; update counter)
{
    do this;
}
?>
```

PHP's `for()` loop uses a counter that is initialized to a numeric value, and keeps track of the number of times the loop is executed. Before each execution of the loop, a conditional statement is tested. If it evaluates to true, the loop will execute once more and the counter will be incremented by 1 (or more) positions. If it evaluates to false, the loop will be broken and the lines following it will be executed instead.

To see how this loop can be used, create the following script, which lists all the numbers between 2 and 100:

```php
<?php
for ($x = 2; $x <= 100; $x++)
{
    echo "$x ";
}
?>
```

To perform this task, the script uses a `for()` loop with `$x` as the counter variable, initializes it to 2, and specifies that the loop should run until the counter hits 100. The auto-increment operator (discussed in Chapter 3) automatically increments the counter by 1 every time the loop is executed. Within the loop, the value of the counter is displayed each time the loop runs.

For a more realistic example of how a `for()` loop can save you coding time, consider the following example, which accepts user input to construct an HTML table using a double `for()` loop:

```php
<html>
<head></head>
<body>

<?php
if (!$_POST['submit'])
{
?>
    <form method="post" action="<?=$_SERVER['PHP_SELF']?>">
    Enter number of rows ↵
    <input name="rows" type="text" size="4"> ↵
    and columns ↵
    <input name="columns" type="text" size="4"> ↵
    <input type="submit" name="submit" value="Draw Table">
    </form>
<?php
}
else
{
?>
    <table border="1" cellspacing="5" cellpadding="0">
<?php
```

```php
    // set variables from form input
    $rows = $_POST['rows'];
    $columns = $_POST['columns'];

    // loop to create rows
    for ($r = 1; $r <= $rows; $r++)
    {
        echo "<tr>";
        // loop to create columns
        for ($c = 1; $c <= $columns; $c++)
        {
            echo "<td> </td>\n";
        }
        echo "</tr>\n";
    }
?>
    </table>
<?php
}
?>

</body>
</html>
```

As you'll see if you try coding the same thing by hand, PHP's for() loop just saved you a whole lot of work!

Controlling Loop Iteration with break and continue

The break keyword is used to exit a loop when it encounters an unexpected situation. A good example of this is the dreaded "division by zero" error—when dividing one number by another one (which keeps decreasing), it is advisable to check the divisor and use the break statement to exit the loop as soon as it becomes equal to zero. Here's an example:

```php
<?php
for ($x=-10; $x<=10; $x++)
{
    if ($x == 0) { break; }
    echo '100 / ' . $x . ' = ' . (100/$x);
}
?>
```

The `continue` keyword is used to skip a particular iteration of the loop and move to the next iteration immediately. This statement can be used to make the execution of the code within the loop block dependent on particular circumstances. The following example demonstrates by printing a list of only those numbers between 10 and 100 that are divisible by 12:

```php
<?php
for ($x=10; $x<=100; $x++)
{
    if (($x % 12) == 0)
    {
        echo "$x ";
    }
    else
    {
        continue;
    }
}
?>
```

Summary

This chapter built on the basic constructs taught earlier to increase your knowledge of PHP scripting and language constructs. In this chapter, you learned how to use PHP's comparison and logical operators to build conditional statements, and use those conditional statements to control the flow of a PHP program. Because conditional statements are also frequently used in loops, to perform a certain set of actions while the condition remains true, this chapter discussed the loop types available in PHP, together with examples of how and when to use them

If you're interested in learning more about the topics in this chapter, these web links have more information:

- Control structures in PHP, at **http://www.php.net/manual/en/language.control-structures.php**

- The break and continue statements, at **http://www.php.net/manual/en/control-structures.break.php** and **http://www.php.net/manual/en/control-structures.continue.php**

Loops are frequently used in combination with one of PHP's complex data types: the array. Because that's a whole topic in itself, I'm going to discuss it in detail in the next chapter. And, once you know how it works, I'm going to show you how arrays, loops, and forms all work together to make creating complex web forms as easy as pie.

Chapter 5

Using Arrays and Custom Functions

Now that you know the basics of variables, operators, conditional statements, and loops, and you can read and understand simple PHP scripts, it's time to move into murkier territory. As your familiarity with PHP increases, and your scripts become more and more complex, you'll soon find yourself wishing for more sophisticated variables and data types. You'll also wish for a way to simplify common tasks, so as to reduce code duplication and make your scripts more efficient and reusable.

How to...

- Use a complex PHP data type—the array—to group and manipulate multiple values at once

- Create and access array values by number or name

- Process the values in an array with the foreach() loop

- Use arrays to group related form values

- Split, combine, extract, remove, and add array elements with PHP's built-in functions

- Define your own functions to create reusable code fragments

- Pass arguments to your functions and accept return values

- Understand the difference between global and local variables in a function

- Store function definitions in a separate file and import them as needed

Using Arrays to Group Related Values

Thus far, the variables you've used contain only a single value—for example,

```
<?php
$i = 5;
?>
```

Often, however, this is not enough. Sometimes, what you need is a way to store multiple related values in a single variable, and act on them together. With the simple data types discussed thus far, the only way to do this is by creating a group of variables sharing similar nomenclature and acting on them together, or perhaps by storing multiple values as a comma-separated string in a single string variable and splitting the string into its constituents when required. Both these approaches are inefficient, prone to errors and—most important to a programmer—lack elegance.

That's where arrays come in. An *array* is a complex variable that enables you to store multiple values in a single variable; it comes in handy when you need to store and represent related information. An array variable can best be thought of as a "container" variable, which can contain one or more values. Here is an example:

```php
<?php
// define an array
$flavors = array('strawberry', 'grape', ↵
'vanilla', 'caramel', 'chocolate');
?>
```

Here, `$flavors` is an array variable, which contains the values *strawberry, grape, vanilla, caramel,* and *chocolate.*

The various elements of the array are accessed via an index number, with the first element starting at zero. So, to access the value *grape,* use the notation `$flavors[1]`, while *chocolate* would be `$flavors[4]`—basically, the array variable name followed by the index number in square braces.

PHP also enables you to replace indices with user-defined "keys" to create a slightly different type of array. Each key is unique, and corresponds to a single value within the array. Keys may be made up of any string of characters, including control characters.

```php
<?php
// define associative array
$fruits = array('red' => 'apple', 'yellow' => 'banana', ↵
'purple' => 'plum', 'green' => 'grape');
?>
```

In this case, `$fruits` is an array variable containing four key-value pairs. The `=>` symbol is used to indicate the association between a key and its value. To access the value *banana,* use the notation `$fruits['yellow']`, while the value *grape* would be accessible via the notation `$fruits['green']`. This type of array is sometimes referred to as a *hash* or *associative array.*

True Colors

If you want to look inside an array, head straight for the print_r() function, which X-rays the contents of any PHP variable or structure. Try running it on any of the arrays in this tutorial, and you'll see exactly what I mean!

Creating an Array

To define an array variable, name it using standard PHP variable naming rules and populate it with elements using the array() function, as illustrated in the following:

```php
<?php
// define an array
$flavors = array('strawberry', 'grape', ↵
'vanilla', 'caramel', 'chocolate');
?>
```

An alternative way to define an array is by specifying values for each element using index notation, like this:

```php
<?php
// define an array
$flavors[0] = 'strawberry';
$flavors[1] = 'grape';
$flavors[2] = 'vanilla';
$flavors[3] = 'caramel';
$flavors[4] = 'chocolate';
?>
```

To create an associative array, use keys instead of numeric indices:

```php
<?php
// define an associative array
$fruits['red'] = 'apple';
$fruits['yellow'] = 'banana';
$fruits['purple'] = 'plum';
$fruits['green'] = 'grape';
?>
```

Modifying Array Elements

To add an element to an array, assign a value using the next available index number or key:

```php
<?php
// add an element to a numeric array
$flavors[5] = 'mango';

// if you don't know the next available index
// this will also work
$flavors[] = 'mango';
// add an element to an associative array
$fruits['pink'] = 'peach';
?>
```

To modify an element of an array, assign a new value to the corresponding scalar variable. If you wanted to replace the flavor "strawberry" with "blueberry" in the $flavors array created previously, you'd use the following:

```php
<?php
// modify an array
$flavors[0] = 'blueberry';
?>
```

To remove an array element, use the array_pop() or array_push() function, discussed in the section entitled "Using Array Functions."

Some unique features of arrays are in the context of both loops and forms. The following sections discuss these unique features in greater detail.

Processing Arrays with Loops

To iteratively process the data in a PHP array, loop over it using any of the loop constructs discussed in Chapter 4. To better understand this, create and run the following script:

```
<html>
<head></head>
<body>

Today's shopping list:
<ul>
<?php
// define array
$shoppingList = array('eye of newt', ↵
'wing of bat', 'tail of frog');

// loop over it
// print array elements
for ($x = 0; $x < sizeof($shoppingList); $x++)
{
    echo "<li>$shoppingList[$x]";
}
?>
</ul>

</body>
</html>
```

Here, the `for()` loop is used to iterate through the array, extract the elements from it using index notation, and display them one after the other in an unordered list.

Note the `sizeof()` function used in the previous script. This function is one of the most important and commonly used array functions, and it returns the size of (number of elements within) the array. The `sizeof()` function is mostly used in loop counters to ensure that the loop iterates as many times as there are elements in the array.

The foreach() Loop

While on the topic of arrays and loops, it is worthwhile to spend a few minutes discussing the new loop type introduced in PHP 4.0 for the purpose of iterating over an array: the `foreach()` loop. This loop runs once for each element of the array, moving forward through the array on each iteration. On each run, the statements within the curly braces are executed, and the currently selected array element is made available through a temporary loop variable. Unlike a `for()` loop, a `foreach()` loop doesn't need a counter or a call to `sizeof()`; it keeps track of its position in the array automatically.

To better understand how this works, rewrite the previous example using the `foreach()` loop:

```
<html>
<head></head>
<body>

Today's shopping list:
<ul>
<?php
// define array
$shoppingList = array('eye of newt', 'wing of bat', ↵
'tail of frog');

// loop over it
foreach ($shoppingList as $item)
{
    echo "<li>$item";
}
?>
</ul>
</body>
</html>
```

You can process an associative array with a `foreach()` loop as well, although the manner in which the temporary variable is constructed is a little different to accommodate the key-value pairs. Try the following script to see how this works:

```
<html>
<head></head>
<body>

I can see:
<ul>
<?php
```

```php
// define associative array
$animals = array ('dog' => 'Tipsy', 'cat' => 'Tabitha', ↵
'parrot' => 'Polly');
// iterate over it
foreach ($animals as $key => $value)
{
    echo "<li>a $key named $value";
}
?>
</ul>
</body>
</html>
```

Grouping Form Selections with Arrays

In addition to their obvious uses, arrays and loops also come in handy when processing forms in PHP. For example, if you have a group of related checkboxes or a multiselect list, you can use an array to capture all the selected form values in a single variable for greater ease in processing. To see how this works, create and run the following script:

```php
<html>
<head></head>
<body>

<?php
// check if form has been submitted
if (!$_POST['submit'])
{
    // if not, display form
?>
    Select from the items below: <br />
    <form action="<?=$_SERVER['PHP_SELF']?>" method="POST">
        <select name="options[]" multiple>
            <option value="power steering">Power steering</option>
            <option value="rear wiper">Rear windshield wiper</option>
            <option value="cd changer">6 CD changer</option>
            <option value="fog lamps">Fog lamps</option>
            <option value="central locking">Central locking</option>
            <option value="onboard navigation"> ↵
```

```
Computer-based navigation</option>
        </select>
    <input type="submit" name="submit" value="Select">
    </form>
<?php
}
else
{
    // form has been submitted
    // check if any items were selected
    // if so, display them
    if (is_array($_POST['options']))
    {
        echo 'Here is your selection: <br />';
        // use a foreach() loop to read and display array elements
        foreach ($_POST['options'] as $o)
        {
            echo "<i>$o</i><br />";
        }
    }
    else
    {
        echo 'Nothing selected';
    }
}
?>

</body>
</html>
```

Notice in this script that the `name` of the `<select>` control contains the square braces used when defining a PHP array. The result is this: when the form is submitted, PHP will automatically create an array variable to hold the selected items. This array can then be processed with a `foreach()` loop, and the selected items retrieved from it.

TIP

You can do this with checkboxes also, simply by using array notation in the checkbox's name. For example, `<input type="checkbox" name="ingredients[]" value="tomatoes">`.

Using Array Functions

If you're using an associative array, the `array_keys()` and `array_values()` functions come in handy to get a list of all the keys and values within the array. The following example illustrates this:

```php
<?php
// define an array
$menu = array('breakfast' => 'bacon and eggs', ↵
'lunch' => 'roast beef', 'dinner' => 'lasagna');

// returns the array ('breakfast', 'lunch', 'dinner')
$result = array_keys($menu);

// returns the array ('bacon and eggs', 'roast beef', 'lasagna')
$result = array_values($menu);
?>
```

To check if a variable is an array, use the `is_array()` function, as in the following:

```php
<?php
// create array
$desserts = array('chocolate mousse', 'tiramisu');

// returns 1 (true)
echo is_array($desserts);
?>
```

You can convert array elements into regular PHP variables with the `list()` and `extract()` functions. The `list()` function assigns array elements to variables, as in the following example:

```php
<?php
// define an array
$flavors = array('strawberry', 'grape', 'vanilla');

// extract values into variables
list ($flavor1, $flavor2, $flavor3) = $flavors;

// returns "strawberry"
echo $flavor1;
?>
```

The `extract()` function iterates through a hash, converting the key-value pairs into corresponding variable-value pairs. Here's how:

```php
<?php
// define associative array
$fruits = array('red' => 'apple', 'yellow' => 'banana', ↵
'purple' => 'plum', 'green' => 'grape');

// extract values into variables
extract ($fruits);

// returns "banana"
echo $yellow;
?>
```

You can add an element to the end of an existing array with the `array_push()` function, and remove an element from the end with the interestingly named `array_pop()` function. If you need to pop an element off the top of the array, you can use the `array_shift()` function, while the `array_unshift()` function takes care of adding elements to the beginning of the array. The following example demonstrates all these functions:

```php
<?php
// define array
$students = array('Tom', 'Jill', 'Harry');

// remove an element from the beginning
array_shift($students);

// remove an element from the end
array_pop($students);

// add an element to the end
array_push($students, 'John');

// add an element to the beginning
array_unshift($students, 'Ronald');

// array now looks like ('Ronald', 'Jill', 'John')
print_r($students);
?>
```

The `explode()` function splits a string into smaller components on the basis of a user-specified pattern, and then returns these elements as an array. This function is particularly handy if you need to take a string containing a list of items (for example, a comma-delimited list) and separate each element of the list for further processing. Here's an example:

```php
<?php
// define string
$string = 'English Latin Greek Spanish';

// split on whitespace
$languages = explode(' ', $string);

// $languages now contains ('English', 'Latin', 'Greek', 'Spanish')
?>
```

Obviously, you can also do the reverse: the `implode()` function creates a single string from all the elements of an array, joining them together with a user-defined separator. Revising the previous example, you have the following:

```php
<?php
// define string
$string = 'English Latin Greek Spanish';

// split on whitespace
$languages = explode(' ', $string);

// create new string
// returns "English and Latin and Greek and Spanish"
$newString = implode(" and ", $languages);
?>
```

Creating User-Defined Functions

A *function* is simply a set of program statements that perform a specific task, and that can be called, or executed, from anywhere in your program. Every programming language comes with its own functions, and typically also enables developers to define their own. For example, if you had a series of numbers, and you wanted to reduce each of them by 20 percent, you could pull out your calculator and do it manually . . . or you could write a simple PHP function called `cheatTheTaxman()`, send it the numbers one by one, and have it do the heavy lifting for you.

Functions are a Good Thing for three important reasons:

■ User-defined functions enable developers to extract commonly used pieces of code into separate packages, thereby reducing unnecessary code repetition and redundancies. This separation of code into independent subsections also makes the code easier to understand and debug.

■ Because functions are defined once (but used many times), they are easy to maintain. A change to the function code need only be implemented in a single place—the function definition—with no changes needed anywhere else. Contrast this with the nonabstracted approach, where implementing a change means tracking down and manually changing every occurrence of the earlier version of the code.

■ Because functions force developers to think in abstract terms (define input and output values, set global and local scope, and turn specific tasks into generic components), they encourage better software design and help in creating extensible applications.

NOTE   *While PHP has always offered developers a well-thought-out framework for basic software abstractions like functions and classes, PHP 5.0 improves this framework significantly with a redesigned object framework. Read more about these improvements at **http://www.zend.com/manual/migration5.oop.php**.*

The following sections discuss how to create and use functions, arguments, and return values in a PHP script.

Defining and Invoking Functions

To understand how custom functions work, examine the following script:

```php
<?php
// define a function
function displayShakespeareQuote()
{
    echo 'Some are born great, some achieve greatness, ⏎
and some have greatness thrust upon them';
}

// invoke a function
displayShakespeareQuote();
?>
```

The Name Game

Function invocations are case-insensitive—PHP will find and execute the named function even if the case of the function invocation doesn't match that of the definition—but to avoid confusion and add to the readability of your scripts, a good idea is to invoke functions as they are defined.

In PHP, functions are defined using the special `function` keyword. This keyword is followed by the name of the function (which must conform to the standard naming rules for variables in PHP), a list of arguments (optional) in parentheses, and the function code itself, enclosed in curly braces. This function code can be any legal PHP code—it can contain loops, conditional statements, or calls to other functions. In the previous example, the function is named `displayShakespeareQuote()` and only contains a call to PHP's `echo()` function.

Calling a user-defined function is identical to calling a built-in PHP function like `sizeof()` or `die()`—simply invoke it by using its name. If the function is designed to accept input values, the values can be passed to it during invocation in parentheses. In PHP 3.x, functions could only be invoked after they had been defined. In PHP 4.x and PHP 5.0, functions can be invoked even if their definitions appear further down in the program.

Using Arguments and Return Values

Because functions are supposed to be reusable code fragments (remember my discussion at the beginning of this section about why they are Good Things?), it doesn't make sense for them to always return the same value. Thus, it is possible to create functions that accept different values from the main program and operate on those values to return different, more pertinent results on each invocation. These values are called *arguments*, and they add a whole new level of power and flexibility to your code.

Typically, you tell your function which arguments it can accept through an *argument list* (one or more variables) in the function definition. When a function is invoked with arguments, the variables in the argument list are replaced with the actual values passed to the function and manipulated by the statements inside the function block to obtain the desired result.

To illustrate, consider the next example, which uses a function with a single-argument list. Depending on the value passed to the function, conversion is performed between two different measurement scales:

```php
<?php
// define a function
// with a single-argument list
function convertMilesToKilometres($miles)
{
    echo "$miles miles = " . $miles * 1.60 . " km";
}

// invoke a function
// pass it a single argument
convertMilesToKilometres(50);
?>
```

Usually, when a function is invoked, it generates a *return value*. This return value is explicitly set within the function with the `return` statement. To see how this works, consider the following example:

```php
<?php
// define a function
function getTriangleArea($base, $height)
{
    $area = $base * $height * 0.5;
    return $area;
}

// invoke a function
echo 'The area of a triangle with base 10 and height 50 ⏎
is ' . getTriangleArea(10, 50);
?>
```

Here, when the `getTriangleArea()` function is invoked with two arguments, it performs a calculation and assigns the result to the `$area` variable. This result is then returned to the main program through the `return` statement. It is important to note that when PHP encounters a `return` statement within a function, it stops processing the function and returns control to the statement that invoked the function.

5

 *If you invoke a function with an incorrect number of arguments, PHP will generate a warning, but still attempt to process the function. To avoid this, either make arguments optional by setting default values for them or define your function with support for variable-length argument lists.*

Using Arrays with Argument Lists and Return Values

PHP fully supports passing arrays to functions in the argument list and returning arrays from functions with the `return` statement. To see how this works, try the following script:

```php
<?php
// define a function
// with a single-argument list
function addDomainToUsername($u, $d)
{
    // create empty result array
    $resultArray = array();
    // process input array
    // add domain to username and place in result array
    foreach ($u as $element)
    {
        $resultArray[] = $element . '@' . $d;
    }
    // return result array
    return $resultArray;
}

// define variables
$users = array('john', 'jim', 'harry');

// send array as argument to function
// receive result array
$newUsers = addDomainToUsername($users, 'guess.me.domain');
?>
```

Defining Global and Local Variables

Unless you specify otherwise, the variables used within a function are *local*—that is, the values assigned, and the changes made to them, are restricted to the function space alone. This insulates function variables from the main program space, reducing the risk of variable clashes and corruption of data. To use a variable from the main program inside a function (or vice versa), use the `global` keyword before the variable name inside the function definition.

The following example explains this clearly:

```php
<?php
// define two variables
$itemCount = 65;
$employeeCount = 125;

// write a function
// that alters the global $itemCount variable
function addItems()
{
    global $itemCount;
    $itemCount = $itemCount + 100;
}

// write a function that alters a local variable
// with the same name as a global variable
// note that the global keyword is not used
function addEmployees()
{
    $employeeCount = 2000;
}

// returns 65
echo "Initial number of items: $itemCount";
addItems();
// returns 165
echo "Items after addItems(): $itemCount";

// returns 125
echo "Initial number of employees: $employeeCount";
addEmployees();
// returns 125
echo "Employees after addEmployees(): $employeeCount";
?>
```

Super-Duper Variables

The $_SERVER, $_POST, $_GET, $_REQUEST, $GLOBALS, $_FILE, $_SESSION, and $_COOKIE arrays are what the PHP manual calls *superglobal variables,* because you can access them from anywhere in a PHP program. Regardless of whether you're inside a function or outside it in the main program, these arrays (together with a few others) are always available to you.

Importing Function Definitions

Thus far, all the examples you've seen have had the function definitions embedded in the same script as their invocation. This goes against the original raison d'être of functions, as expounded upon in great length in the introduction to this section. In the real world, it's more common to store function definitions in an external file, and to import it into your script when required.

PHP also offers two useful functions to import files into a PHP script: the include() and require() functions. These functions can be used to suck external files lock, stock, and barrel into a PHP script, so they come in handy if you have a modular application with functions placed in a separate file from the main program code.

Here's an example of how to use the include() function:

```php
<?php
// import file
include("/path/to/user/defined/functions.php");

// invoke functions here
?>
```

The include() function generates a warning if the file cannot be found, although script processing continues. However, the require() function forces a file to be included in the script and generates a fatal error that stops script processing if the file cannot be found.

> TIP
>
> *Classify your custom functions into different categories (example categories might be authentication, input validation, error handling, and math/ scientific calculations), and keep functions related to each category in a separate file. This enables you to import specific types of functions into your applications on an "as-needed" basis, is neater than dumping all definitions in a single file, and also reduces overhead, because PHP only has to read a subset instead of* all *the functions you've ever created.*

Summary

5

This chapter moved your PHP skills up a notch, by introducing you to two of the language's more sophisticated constructs: arrays and user-defined functions. Arrays are extremely useful to group-related data values, and PHP comes with a wide range of functions to define them, create and manipulate array elements, and process them with loops. User-defined functions make it possible for you to package your code into reusable blocks, to make your scripts more efficient and maintainable.

This chapter also introduced you to the applications of these new language constructs, showing you how to use arrays to group-related form controls together, and how to create custom functions and abstract them into separate files that can be imported into your scripts on an as-needed basis. If you're interested in learning more about these topics, these web links have additional information:

- Creating and using arrays, at **http://www.php.net/manual/en/language .types.array.php**

- Array manipulation functions, at **http://www.melonfire.com/community/ columns/trog/article.php?id=95** and **http://www.php.net/manual/en/ref .array.php**

- PHP's special built-in arrays, at **http://www.php.net/manual/en/language .variables.predefined.php**

- Creating and using user-defined functions, at **http://www.php.net/manual/ en/language.functions.php**

- References, at **http://www.php.net/manual/en/language.references.php**

Chapter 6

Using Files, Sessions, Cookies, and External Programs

Now that you know the basics of variables, operators, conditional statements, loops, and arrays, you should be able to read, understand. and create relatively complex PHP scripts. It's time to begin using everything you've learned for real-world programming. This chapter builds on the previous one to teach you common techniques and functions you'll find yourself using regularly in your PHP development.

How to...

- Read and write files, and check file permissions
- Obtain and parse a directory listing in PHP
- Use sessions to maintain client state
- Store information in cookies
- Retrieve the current date and time, and create UNIX timestamps
- Execute external programs from your PHP script

Reading and Writing Files

PHP comes with a powerful and flexible file manipulation API, which enables developers to view and modify file attributes, read and list directory contents, alter file permissions, retrieve file contents into a variety of native data structures, and search for files based on specific patterns. The following sections discuss reading and writing files, and retrieving file information.

Reading Data from a File

To begin with, let's consider the process of opening a file and reading its contents. Create and run the following PHP script (remember to alter the value of the $file variable to an actual file on your system that is readable by the web server):

```php
<?php
// set file to read
$file = '/home/web/projects.txt';
```

```
// open file
$fh = fopen($file, 'r') or die('Could not open file!');

// read file contents
$data = fread($fh, filesize($file)) or die('Could not read file!');

// close file
fclose($fh);

// print file contents
echo $data;
?>
```

A review of the previous script will reveal the three basic steps to reading data from a file:

1. Open the file and assign it a file handle: PHP needs a file handle to read data from a file. This file handle can be created with the fopen() function, which accepts two arguments: the name and path to the file, and a string indicating the mode in which the file is to be opened ('r' for read).

2. Interact with the file via its handle and extract its contents into a PHP variable. If the fopen() function is successful, it returns a file handle—$fh—which can be used for further interaction with the file. This file handle is used by the fread() function, which reads the file and places its contents into a variable.

   The second argument to fread() is the number of bytes to be read. You can usually obtain this information through the filesize() function, which returns the size of the file in bytes.

3. Close the file. Once you're done with the file, it's a good idea to close it with fclose(), to avoid using up memory. This last step is not strictly necessary, but it's a good habit to develop.

An alternative method of reading data from a file is the file() function, which reads the entire file into an array with a single function call. Each element of the array then contains one line from the file. To display the contents of the file, simply iterate over the array in a foreach() loop and print each element (line).

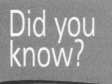

Read or Write?

You can use any one of three different modes with the fopen() function: 'r' (opens a file in read mode), 'w' (opens a file in write mode, destroying existing file contents) and 'a' (opens a file in append mode, preserving existing file contents). You can also add the 'b' modifier to force the file to open in binary mode, and the 't' modifier to control how the line-ending character is handled on different platforms. Read **http://www.php.net/manual/en/ function.fopen.php** for more information.

The following example demonstrates this:

```php
<?php
// set file to read
$file = '/home/web/projects.txt';

// read file into array
$data = file($file) or die('Could not read file!');

// loop through array and print each line
foreach ($data as $line)
{
    echo $line;
}
?>
```

How to ... Create a Primitive Error Handler

PHP's die() function is mostly used as a primitive error-handling mechanism. In the event of a fatal error, die() can be used to terminate script processing with an explanatory user-specified error message indicating the reason why.

Did you know?

No Pain, No Gain

The `fopen()`, `fwrite()`, and `fread()` functions are all binary-safe, which means you can use them on binary files without worrying about damage to the file contents. Read more about many of the issues related to binary-safe file manipulation on different platforms at **http://www.php.net/manual/en/ function.fopen.php**.

6

Another way to do this is with the `file_get_contents()` function, new in PHP 4.3.0 and PHP 5.0, which reads the entire file into a string. Here's an example:

```php
<?php
// set file to read
$file = '/home/web/projects.txt';

// read file into string
$data = file_get_contents($file) or die('Could not read file!');

// print contents
echo $data;
?>
```

Writing Data to a File

The steps involved in writing data to a file are almost identical to those involved in reading it: open the file and obtain a file handle, use the file handle to write data to it, and close the file. There are two differences:

1. You must `fopen()` the file in write mode (`'w'` for write).

2. Instead of using the `fread()` function to read from the file handle, use the `fwrite()` function to write to it.

To try this out yourself, create and run the following script:

```php
<?php
// set file to write
$file = '/tmp/dummy.txt';

// open file
$fh = fopen($file, 'w') or die('Could not open file!');

// write to file
fwrite($fh, 'Hello, file!') or die('Could not write to file');

// close file
fclose($fh);
?>
```

An alternative here is the `file_put_contents()` function, new in PHP 5.0, which takes a string and writes it to a file in a single line of code. The next example illustrates this:

```php
<?php
// set file to write
$file = '/tmp/dump.txt';

// write to file
file_put_contents($file, 'Hello, file!') ↵
or die('Could not write to file');
?>
```

Bear in mind that the directory in which you're trying to create the file must exist before you can write to it. Forgetting this important step is a common cause of script errors.

Testing File Attributes

PHP also comes with a bunch of functions that enable you to test the status of a file—for example, find out whether it exists, whether it's empty, whether it's readable or writable, and whether it's a binary or a text file. Table 6-1 has a list of the more interesting functions in this category.

Function	What It Does
file_exists()	Returns a Boolean indicating whether the file exists
is_dir()	Returns a Boolean indicating whether the specified path is a directory
is_file()	Returns a Boolean indicating whether the specified file is a regular file
is_link()	Returns a Boolean indicating whether the specified file is a symbolic link
is_executable()	Returns a Boolean indicating whether the specified file is executable
is_readable()	Returns a Boolean indicating whether the specified file is readable
is_writable()	Returns a Boolean indicating whether the specified file is writable
filesize()	Gets file size, in bytes
filemtime()	Gets last modification time of file
fileatime()	Gets last access time of file
fileowner()	Gets file owner
filegroup()	Gets file group
fileperms()	Gets file permissions
filetype()	Gets file type

TABLE 6-1   Useful PHP File Functions

And here is an example that demonstrates some of these functions:

```php
<?php
// set file
$file = $_GET['file'];

// check if file exists
echo file_exists($file) ? 'File exists' : 'File does not exist';

// check if file is executable
echo is_executable($file) ? 'File is executable' :
'File is not executable';
```

```php
// check if file is readable
echo is_readable($file) ? 'File is readable' : ↵
'File is not readable';

// check if file is writable
echo is_writable($file) ? 'File is writable' : ↵
'File is not writable';

// print file size
echo 'File size is ' . filesize($file) . ' bytes';

// print file owner
echo 'File owner is ' . fileowner($file);

// print file type
echo 'File type is ' . filetype($file);
?>
```

Obtaining Directory Listings

Thus far, most of the examples you've seen have dealt with individual files.
However, you often find yourself faced with the task of iterating over one or more
directories and processing the file list within each. To meet this requirement, PHP
offers a comprehensive set of directory manipulation functions, which enable
developers to read and parse an entire directory listing.

To demonstrate, consider the following simple example, which lists all the files
in the directory /bin:

```php
<?php

// initialize counter
$count = 0;

// set directory name
$dir = "/bin";

// open directory and parse file list
if (is_dir($dir))
{
        if ($dh = opendir($dir))
        {
                // iterate over file list
```

```
            // print filenames
            while (($filename = readdir($dh)) !== false)
            {
                if (($filename != ".") && ($filename != ".."))
                {
                    $count++;
                    echo $dir . "/" . $filename . "\n";
                }
            }
        // close directory
        closedir($dh);
        }
}

echo "-- $count FILES FOUND --";
?>
```

Here, the `opendir()` function first retrieves a handle to the named directory; this handle serves as the primary point of contact for all subsequent operations. The `readdir()` function then uses the file handle to read the contents of the directory, and return a list of file names one after another. Once the complete contents of the directory have been retrieved, `readdir()` returns a false value, and the `closedir()` function is used to destroy the directory handle.

Notice the manner in which entries for the current (.) and parent directory (..) are excluded from the list—with an `if()` conditional statement.

Managing Sessions and Using Session Variables

You may have heard that HTTP, the protocol on which the Web runs, is a "stateless" protocol and, therefore, treats each request for a web page as a unique and independent transaction, with no relationship whatsoever to the transactions that preceded it. While this doesn't present a problem for most web users, it throws a massive wrench in the works of transaction-based sites, which need to track the activities of each user.

Consider, for example, the common shopping cart used in web storefronts: in a "stateless" environment, it is impossible to keep track of the items each user has short listed for purchase, as the stateless nature of the HTTP protocol makes it impossible to identify which transactions belong to which client or user.

Consequently, what is required is a method that makes it possible to "maintain state," something that allows client connections to be tracked and connection-specific data to be maintained. A common solution to the problem is to use *sessions* to store information about each client and track its activities. This session data is preserved for the duration of the visit, and is usually destroyed on its conclusion.

PHP has included built-in session support since PHP 4.0. Client transactions are identified through unique numbers; these identifiers are used to re-create each client's prior session environment whenever required. The *session identifier* may be stored on the client in a cookie or it may be passed from page to page in the URL.

The following sections discuss the PHP functions to create sessions, register and use session variables, and destroy sessions.

Creating a Session and Registering Session Variables

In PHP, the `session_start()` function is used to create a client session and generate a session ID. Once a session has been created, it becomes possible to register any number of *session variables;* these are regular variables which can store textual or numeric information and can be manipulated by standard PHP functions, but are unique to each client. In a PHP script, session variables may be registered as key-value pairs in the special `$_SESSION` associative array.

 *When cookies are used to store session data—the most common case— the `session_start()` function must be called before any output is generated by the script (and that includes the starting `<html>` tag). This is because of restrictions in the HTTP protocol that require cookies and other headers to be sent before any script output.*

To see how sessions and session variables work, examine the following script, which creates a new client session and registers two session variables:

```php
<?php
// first page

// create a session
session_start();

// register some session variables
$_SESSION['username'] = 'deathsbane';
$_SESSION['role'] = 'admin';
?>
```

On subsequent pages, calls to the `session_start()` function re-create the prior session environment by restoring the values of the `$_SESSION` associative array. This can be tested by attempting to access the values of the session variables registered in the previous example:

```php
<?php
// second page

// re-create the previous session
session_start();

// print the value of the session variable
// returns 'deathsbane'
echo $_SESSION['username'];
?>
```

CAUTION *On Windows, you typically need to edit the PHP configuration file, php.ini, and edit the session.save_path variable to reflect your system's temporary directory. The default value for this variable is /tmp, a directory that does not exist on Windows. Using this default value as is will cause your sessions to fail.*

Destroying a Session

To destroy an extant session—for example, on user logout—reset the $_SESSION array, and then use the session_destroy() function to erase session data.

```php
<?php
// re-create session
session_start();

// reset session array
$_SESSION = array();

// destroy session
session_destroy();
?>
```

NOTE *Before you can destroy a session with session_destroy(), you need to first re-create the session environment (so there is something to destroy) with session_start(). This probably seems counterintuitive, and it is, but there isn't much you can do except grin and bear it.*

Storing Data in Cookies

Cookies allow web sites to store client-specific information in a file on the client system, and retrieve this information on an as-needed basis. Cookies are typically used to bypass the stateless nature of the HTTP protocol, by using the client's disk as a storage area for persistent data; however, they're dependent on the client browser being configured to accept cookies.

PHP has included support for cookie generation and retrieval since PHP 3.x. Using PHP's built-in functions, you can create client-side cookies, store values in them, and delete them after a specified period has passed.

When dealing with cookies, you should be aware of some ground rules:

1. Because cookies are used to record information about your activities on a particular site, they can only be read by the site that created them.

2. A single domain cannot set more than 20 cookies, and each cookie is limited to a maximum size of 4KB.

3. A cookie usually possesses five types of attributes. Table 6-2 lists them.

4. Of all the five attributes, only the first is not optional.

 Because cookies are stored on the user's hard drive, you as the developer have little control over them. If a user decides to turn off cookie support in his or her browser, your cookies will simply not be saved. Therefore, if data persistence is an important feature of your web site, have a backup plan (such as server-side cookies or sessions) ready as well.

Attribute	What It Does
Name	Sets the name and value of the cookie
Expires	Sets the date and time at which the cookie expires
path	Sets the top-level directory on the domain from which cookie data can be accessed
domain	Sets the domain for which the cookie is valid
secure	Sets a Boolean flag indicating that the cookie should be transmitted only over a secure HTTP connection

TABLE 6-2   Cookie Attributes

The following sections discuss the PHP functions for setting cookies, using cookie data, and deleting cookies.

Setting Cookies

In PHP, cookies are set with the setcookie() function, which accepts six arguments: the cookie name, its value, its expiry date (in UNIX timestamp format), its path and domain, and a Boolean flag indicating its security status. Only the first argument is required, all the rest are optional. To better understand this, try out the following example script:

```php
<?php
// set a cookie called 'username' with value 'admin'
// expiring after 1 day
setcookie('username', 'admin', mktime()+86400, '/');
?>
```

The setcookie() function returns true if successful. By checking for this, you can verify if the cookie was sent to the browser or not.

```php
<?php
// set a cookie called 'username' with value 'admin'
// expiring after 1 day
$ret = setcookie('username', 'admin', mktime()+86400, '/');

// check if cookie was set
// display error if not
if (!$ret)
{
    echo "Unable to set cookie";
}
?>
```

You can set multiple cookies, simply by calling setcookie() once for each cookie. Consider the following example, which sets three cookies for the same domain, each with different expiry dates:

```php
<?php
setcookie('username', 'admin', mktime()+86400, '/');
setcookie('role', '2', mktime()+1800, '/secure/web/');
setcookie('country', 'UK', 0, '/');
?>
```

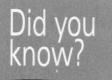

2 PM by Any Other Name...

The mktime() function accepts a series of date and time parameters, and converts them into a UNIX timestamp.

Retrieving Cookie Data

Once a cookie has been set for a domain, it becomes available in the special $_COOKIE associative array, and its value may be accessed using standard array notation. Here's an example:

```php
<?php
// if cookie present, use it
// else display generic message
if ($_COOKIE['username'])
{
    echo "Welcome back, " . $_COOKIE['username'];
}
else
{
    echo "Is this your first time here? Take our guided tour!";
}
?>
```

TIP *To check whether your cookies are working correctly, use the statement `<?php print_r($_COOKIE); ?>` to look inside PHP's special $_COOKIE array.*

Deleting Cookies

To delete a cookie, simply use setcookie() with its name to set the cookie's expiry date to a value in the past.

```php
<?php
setcookie('username', ''NULL, mktime()-10000, '/');
?>
```

Dealing with Dates and Times

Calculating and formatting date and time values is par for the course when creating web applications. And PHP comes with some fairly powerful functions to create and format time- and date-stamps. The following sections discuss some of the more common tasks in this context.

Retrieving the Current Date and Time

The most basic thing you can do with PHP's date and time functions is retrieve the current date and time. And the easiest way to do this is with the getdate() function, which returns an associative array containing the current date and time. To try it out, create and run the following script:

```php
<?php
// get current date and time
$current = getdate();

// turn it into a string
$current_time = $current['hours'] . ':' . $current['minutes']
. ':' . $current['seconds'];
$current_date = $current['mday'] . '.' . $current['mon'] . '.'
    . $current['year'];

// print it
// this would generate output of the form
// "It is now 13:22:45 on 19.6.2004"
echo "It is now $current_time on $current_date";
?>
```

As should be clear from the script above, the getdate() function returns an associative array containing keys for the current hour, minute, second, day, date, month, and year. These values can be accessed using standard array notation.

Obtaining Timestamps for Arbitrary Dates and Times

Most of PHP's date functions work on the basis of timestamps. This timestamp is a unique numeric representation of a particular date, calculated as the number of seconds between January 1, 1970 and the date and time specified. In PHP, UNIX timestamps are created via the mktime() function, which accepts a series of date and time parameters and converts them into a timestamp. Here's an example:

```php
<?php
// get a timestamp for 08:45:00 June 17 2004
// returns a long integer like 1150485300
echo mktime(08, 45, 00, 6, 17, 2006);
?>
```

To obtain a timestamp for an arbitrary date or time, pass the mktime() function six parameters: the hour, minute, second, month, day, and year. To obtain a timestamp for the current moment in time, call mktime() without any arguments.

Executing External Programs

To run an external program from your PHP script, place the program command line within backticks (``). The output of the command can also be assigned to a variable for further use within the script. Try the following example, which runs the UNIX du command (to calculate disk usage) and places the resulting output in a PHP variable:

```php
<?php
$output = `/bin/du -s /tmp/`;
echo $output;
?>
```

If user input is required for the command you're executing, it is recommended that you "defang" that input by removing or escaping illegal characters from it before running it. PHP can do this for you automatically with its escapeshellarg() and escapeshellcmd() functions. To illustrate, consider the following script, which asks the user for a directory path, and then uses the system's du command to return the total space occupied by that directory on disk:

```html
<html>
<head></head>
<body>
```

6

```php
<?php
if (!$_POST['submit'])
{
?>
    <form action="<?=$_SERVER['PHP_SELF']?>" method="post">
        Enter path: <input type="text" name="path">
        <input type="submit" name="submit" value="Go!">
    </form>
<?php
}
else
{
    // escape user input
    $path = escapeshellarg($_POST['path']);

    // run external command
    $output = `/bin/du -s $path`;

    // extract size from output and print
    $outputArray = explode("\t", $output);
    $size = $outputArray[0];
    echo "$path occupies $size bytes";
}
?>
</body>
</html>
```

In this example, the `escapeshellarg()` command escapes the user's input with quotes to nullify harmful code that may be embedded within it.

 *Using external programs from within a PHP script, especially if those programs require privileges greater than those normally possessed by the web server, is a risky proposition. You should only attempt such an exercise after you're comfortable with the security issues surrounding such external program execution.*

Summary

This chapter offered a grab-bag of different techniques, using the concepts taught in previous techniques in practical usage examples. Among the items covered were reading files into an array and processing them, writing new files or appending data to existing files, testing file attributes, using sessions and cookies for persistent storage on a client, and executing external programs from inside a PHP script.

If you're interested in learning more about these topics, these web links have more information:

- File manipulation in PHP, at **http://www.melonfire.com/community/ columns/trog/article.php?id=208** and **http://www.php.net/manual/en/ ref.filesystem.php**

- Reading directory entries with PHP, at **http://www.php.net/manual/en/ ref.dir.php**

- Sessions and PHP, at **http://www.melonfire.com/community/columns/ trog/article.php?id=3** and **http://www.php.net/manual/en/ref .session.php**

- The Netscape cookie specification, at **http://www.netscape.com/newsref/ std/cookie_spec.html**

- Cookies and PHP, at **http://www.php.net/manual/en/features .cookies.php**

- Program execution functions in PHP, at **http://www.php.net/manual/en/ ref.exec.php**

Chapter 7

Sample Application: Session-Based Shopping Cart

Now that you can find your way around a PHP script, it's time to start writing your own. This chapter brings the basic PHP course taught over the last few chapters to a logical conclusion, by attempting to use as many of the constructs and techniques taught over the previous pages to create a working application. This example is, of necessity, somewhat contrived, but I hope you find it interesting.

How to...

- Create a web-based shopping cart
- Read and display a product catalog from a text file
- Store item quantities in a session, and perform calculations on them

Understanding Requirements

The application here is a web-based shopping cart that uses PHP's built-in session-management support to track the items selected for purchase by a user. Items are listed in a product catalog, and the user has the ability to select custom quantities of each item using an HTML form. The selected items then appear in the user's "cart," with item subtotals automatically calculated from the quantity and unit price. Users can clear their carts of all selected items, or selectively update the quantities to be purchased of each item; the totals are recalculated automatically. The catalog itself is read from a text file; this file contains a list of product IDs, descriptions, and unit prices.

If all this seems somewhat daunting, fear not—it's pretty simple, once you break it down.

Retrieving Catalog Data

Let's begin with the catalog file itself and examine the format in which catalog data is stored:

```
101:AA batteries (pack of 2):2.99
102:AA batteries (pack of 4):5.49
103:Backpack (black): 69.99
104:Money belt with 6 compartments (black):13.49
105:Haversack (red):199.99
106:Swiss Army knife (6 blades including can opener and scissors):24.99
107:Duffel bag (steel gray):28.50
```

This is fairly easy to understand: each product is listed on a separate line, with colons used to demarcate the product code or SKU, its description, and its price. It's easy to parse this file and store its contents in a PHP array using the `file()` and `explode()` functions. And this next snippet of code does exactly that:

```php
<?php
// look for catalog file
$catalogFile = "catalog.dat";
// file is available, extract data from it
// place into $CATALOG array, with SKU as key
if (file_exists($catalogFile))
{
    $data = file($catalogFile);
    foreach ($data as $line)
    {
        $lineArray = explode(':', $line);
        $sku = trim($lineArray[0]);
        $CATALOG[$sku]['desc'] = trim($lineArray[1]);
        $CATALOG[$sku]['price'] = trim($lineArray[2]);
    }
}
else
{
    die("Could not find catalog file");
}
?>
```

The end result of this is an associative array called `$CATALOG`, which uses the product codes as keys. Each key further points to a nested associative array with two keys—`desc` and `price`—which the product's description and price, respectively. This `$CATALOG` array, once created, becomes available for use by other components within the script. Obviously, in the event that the catalog file cannot be found, the user must be notified with an error message, hence, the `if (file_exists(...))` test and subsequent call to `die()` if the test proves false.

Once the catalog data is successfully imported into a PHP variable, the next step is to print it. Because the data is in an array, it's logical to reach for the `foreach()` loop to process it. Here's the code:

```php
<table border="0" cellspacing="10">
<?php
// print items from the catalog for selection
```

```
foreach ($CATALOG as $k => $v)
{
    echo "<tr><td colspan=2>";
    echo "<b>" . $v['desc'] . "</b>";
    echo "</td></tr>\n";
    echo "<tr><td>";
    echo "Price per unit: " . $CATALOG[$k]['price'];
    echo "</td><td>Quantity: ";
    echo "<input size=4 type=text name=\"a_qty[" . $k . "]\">";
    echo "</td></tr>\n";
}
?>
<tr>
<td colspan="2">
<input type="submit" name="add" value="Add items to cart">
</td>
</tr>
</table>
```

Notice that each item in the product catalog contains an empty text field next to it, which can be used to input quantities. The data entered into these fields is submitted back to the same script, by means of a POST-ed array called $a_qty. The keys of this array are the product codes, and its values are the corresponding quantities selected.

Creating the Shopping Cart

On submission, the items and quantities selected need to find their way into the "shopping cart"—essentially, a session variable that remains available throughout the user's session. This shopping cart is an associative array called $_SESSION['cart']. Its keys are the product codes of the selected items, and its values are the corresponding quantities entered by the user.

```
<?php
session_start();
if ($_POST['add'])
{
    foreach ($_POST['a_qty'] as $k => $v)
    {
        $_SESSION['cart'][$k] = $_SESSION['cart'][$k] + $v;
    }
}
?>
```

Note that for items already in the cart, submitting the form with new numbers adds to the existing quantities, instead of replacing them.

Calculating Costs

Once items have been stored in the shopping cart, it's a simple matter to display them. All you need to do is iterate over the $_SESSION['cart'] array and print its values. Because $_SESSION['cart'] only stores product codes with quantities, it's necessary to cross-reference the product codes with the data in the $CATALOG array to retrieve the human-readable descriptions and prices (these prices are also used to calculate subtotals and the grand total).

```
<table width="100%" border="0" cellspacing="10">
<?php
// initialize a variable to hold total cost
$total = 0;
// check the shopping cart
// if it contains values
// look up the SKUs in the $CATALOG array
// get the cost and calculate subtotals and totals
if (is_array($_SESSION['cart']))
{
    foreach ($_SESSION['cart'] as $k => $v)
    {
        if ($v > 0)
        {
            $subtotal = $v * $CATALOG[$k]['price'];
            $total += $subtotal;
            echo "<tr><td>";
            echo "<b>$v unit(s) of " . $CATALOG[$k]['desc'] ↵
. "</b>";
            echo "</td><td>";
            echo "New quantity: <input size=4 type=text ↵
name=\"u_qty[" . $k . "]\">";
            echo "</td></tr>\n";
            echo "<tr><td>";
            echo "Price per unit: " . $CATALOG[$k]['price'];
            echo "</td><td>";
            echo "Sub-total: " . sprintf("%0.2f", $subtotal);
            echo "</td></tr>\n";
        }
    }
}
```

Sprinting Ahead

In case you were wondering, the `sprintf()` function is used to massage numbers into user-defined formats. It enables you to format the padding, alignment, and precision of a number using predefined format specifiers, in a manner similar to the `date()` function. Read more about it at **http://www.php.net/manual/en/function.sprintf.php**.

```
?>
<tr>
<td><b>TOTAL</b></td>
<td><b><?=sprintf("%0.2f", $total)?></b></td>
</tr>

<tr>
<td><input type="submit" name="update" value="Update Cart"></td>
<td><input type="submit" name="clear" value="Clear Cart"></td>
</tr>
</table>
```

Handling Cart Updates

This display contains a text field next to each item, for the user to update the quantities of each item in the cart. Values are submitted to the form processor through the $u_qty array (similar in structure to the $a_qty array explained earlier). This update operation differs from the add operation in that submitting the form with new values replaces the existing quantities (instead of adding to them). The user also has the option of "emptying" the cart with a single click; essentially, this destroys the session data and presents the user with an empty $_SESSION['cart'] array.

Here's the code to perform the previous logic:

```
<?php
if ($_POST['update'])
```

```
    foreach ($_POST['u_qty'] as $k => $v)
    {
        $_SESSION['cart'][$k] = $v;
    }
}
// if this is a clear operation
// reset the session and the cart
// destroy all session data
if ($_POST['clear'])
{
    $_SESSION = array();
    session_destroy();
}
?>
```

7

Putting It All Together

And now that you've seen how the various pieces interact with each other, here's the complete script:

```php
<?php
// start session
session_start();

// initialize session shopping cart
if (!isset($_SESSION['cart']))
{
    $_SESSION['cart'] = array();
}

// look for catalog file
$catalogFile = "catalog.dat";
// file is available, extract data from it
// place into $CATALOG array, with SKU as key
if (file_exists($catalogFile))
{
    $data = file($catalogFile);
    foreach ($data as $line)
    {
        $lineArray = explode(':', $line);
        $sku = trim($lineArray[0]);
```

```php
        $CATALOG[$sku]['desc'] = trim($lineArray[1]);
        $CATALOG[$sku]['price'] = trim($lineArray[2]);
    }
}
// file is not available
// stop immediately with an error
else
{
    die("Could not find catalog file");
}


// check to see if the form has been submitted
// and which submit button was clicked

// if this is an add operation
// add to already existing quantities in shopping cart
if ($_POST['add'])
{
    foreach ($_POST['a_qty'] as $k => $v)
    {
        // if the value is 0 or negative
        // don't bother changing the cart
        if ($v > 0)
        {
            $_SESSION['cart'][$k] = $_SESSION['cart'][$k] + $v;
        }
    }
}
// if this is an update operation
// replace quantities in shopping cart with values entered
else if ($_POST['update'])
{
    foreach ($_POST['u_qty'] as $k => $v)
    {
        // if the value is empty, 0 or negative
        // don't bother changing the cart
        if ($v != "" && $v >= 0)
        {
            $_SESSION['cart'][$k] = $v;
        }
    }
}
```

```php
    // if this is a clear operation
    // reset the session and the cart
    // destroy all session data
    else if ($_POST['clear'])
    {
        $_SESSION = array();
        session_destroy();
    }

?>
<html>
<head></head>
<body>

<h2>Catalog</h2>
Please add items from the list below to your shopping cart.

<form action="<?=$_SERVER['PHP_SELF']?>" method="post">
<table border="0" cellspacing="10">
<?php
// print items from the catalog for selection
foreach ($CATALOG as $k => $v)
{
    echo "<tr><td colspan=2>";
    echo "<b>" . $v['desc'] . "</b>";
    echo "</td></tr>\n";
    echo "<tr><td>";
    echo "Price per unit: " . $CATALOG[$k]['price'];
    echo "</td><td>Quantity: ";
    echo "<input size=4 type=text name=\"a_qty[" . $k . "]\">";
    echo "</td></tr>\n";
}
?>
<tr>
<td colspan="2">
<input type="submit" name="add" value="Add items to cart">
</td>
</tr>
</table>

<hr />
<hr />
```

```php
<h2>Shopping cart</h2>

<table width="100%" border="0" cellspacing="10">
<?php
// initialize a variable to hold total cost
$total = 0;
// check the shopping cart
// if it contains values
// look up the SKUs in the $CATALOG array
// get the cost and calculate subtotals and totals
if (is_array($_SESSION['cart']))
{
    foreach ($_SESSION['cart'] as $k => $v)
    {
        // only display items that have been selected
        // that is, quantities > 0
        if ($v > 0)
        {
            $subtotal = $v * $CATALOG[$k]['price'];
            $total += $subtotal;
            echo "<tr><td>";
            echo "<b>$v unit(s) of " . $CATALOG[$k]['desc'] ↵
. "</b>";
            echo "</td><td>";
            echo "New quantity: <input size=4 type=text ↵
name=\"u_qty[" . $k . "]\">";
            echo "</td></tr>\n";
            echo "<tr><td>";
            echo "Price per unit: " . $CATALOG[$k]['price'];
            echo "</td><td>";
            echo "Sub-total: " . sprintf("%0.2f", $subtotal);
            echo "</td></tr>\n";
        }
    }
}
?>
<tr>
<td><b>TOTAL</b></td>
<td><b><?=sprintf("%0.2f", $total)?></b></td>
</tr>
```

```
<tr>
<td><input type="submit" name="update" value="Update Cart"></td>
<td><input type="submit" name="clear" value="Clear Cart"></td>
</tr>
</table>
</form>

</body>
</html>
```

Pop it into your browser, and see how it works. When you first load it up, you'll see a list of items, like in Figure 7-1.

Select a few items by attaching quantities to them, and submit the form. The page will refresh and display those items to you in your shopping cart, together with unit and total costs. Figure 7-2 shows what this might look like.

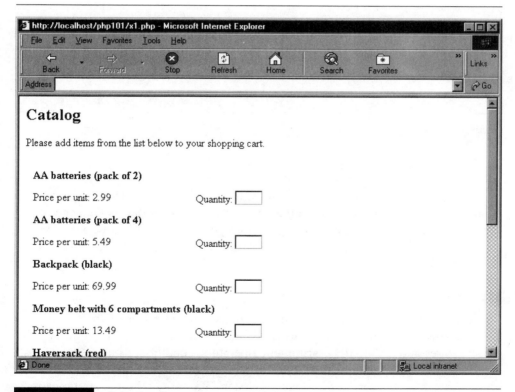

FIGURE 7-1   Selection list

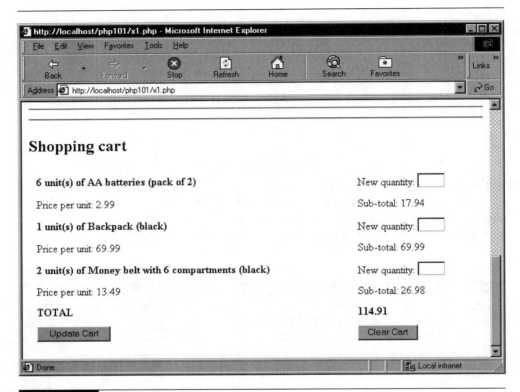

FIGURE 7-2   Your shopping cart

Because the shopping cart is maintained in a session, your selection will be "remembered" even if you visit another site, and then come back to the page. The session will only be destroyed if you close your browser window, or if you explicitly empty your cart by calling the `session_destroy()` function.

Summary

This chapter was designed to demonstrate a practical application of PHP: creating a simple session-based shopping-cart application. This application used many of the structures and techniques—arithmetic operators, conditional statements, loops, arrays, sessions, file manipulation, and form processing—taught in earlier sections of the chapter, and if you were able to understand it, you're all set to start creating your own PHP scripts.

Two great ways of improving your knowledge of PHP scripting are by reading case studies and analyzing the code of your peers. To this end, consider visiting the following links, all of which contain case studies and sample PHP code from real-world applications:

- A polling system, at **http://www.melonfire.com/community/columns/trog/article.php?id=59**

- Web-based file management systems, at **http://www.melonfire.com/community/columns/trog/article.php?id=64** and **http://www.horde.org/gollem/**

- A web-based e-mail client, at **http://www.melonfire.com/community/columns/trog/article.php?id=100**

- An advertiser/banner management system for web sites, at **http://www.phpadsnew.com/**

- A threaded discussion forum, at **http://www.sporum.org/**

- A content management and personalization system for web sites, at **http://www.php-nuke.org/**

- Articles and tutorials on PHP, at **http://www.melonfire.com/community/columns/trog/archives.php?category=PHP**

The next few chapters look at the other half of the PHP-MySQL combo, teaching you what MySQL is, and how to use it for data storage and retrieval.

7

Part III

Learning MySQL

Chapter 8

Understanding an RDBMS

According to its official web site, MySQL is "the world's most popular open-source database." That's no small claim, but the numbers seem to back it up: today, over five million sites are creating, using, and deploying MySQL or MySQL-based applications. There are numerous reasons for this popularity: the server is fast and scalable, offers all the features and reliability of commercial-grade competitors, comes with a customer-friendly licensing policy, and is simple to learn and use. It's also well suited for development—the PHP programming language has supported MySQL since its early days, and the PHP-MySQL combination has become extremely popular for building database-driven web applications.

The previous chapters showed you the basics of PHP scripting, with discussions of PHP syntax and examples of common techniques you'll use when building PHP-based applications. This chapter focuses on the other half of the PHP-MySQL combo, giving you a crash course in basic RDBMS concepts and introducing you to the MySQL command-line client. In case you've never used a database before or the thought of learning another language scares you, don't worry, because MySQL is quite friendly and you should have no trouble learning how to use it.

How to...

- Organize data into fields, records, and tables
- Identify records uniquely with primary keys
- Connect records in different tables through common fields
- Understand the three components of Structured Query Language (SQL)
- Write simple SQL statements
- Gain the benefits of normalized databases
- Send commands to, and receive responses from, MySQL with the command-line MySQL client

Understanding a Relational Database

You may remember from the introductory notes in Chapter 1 that an electronic database management system (DBMS) is a tool that helps you organize information efficiently, so it becomes easier to find exactly what you need. A relational database management system (RDBMS) like MySQL takes things a step further, by enabling you to create links between the various pieces of data in a database, and then use the relationships to analyze the data in different ways.

Now, while this is wonderful theory, it is still just that: theory. To truly understand how a database works, you need to move from abstract theoretical concepts to practical real-world examples. This section does just that, by creating a sample database and using it to explain some of the basic concepts you must know before proceeding further.

Understanding Tables, Records, and Fields

Every database is composed of one or more *tables*. These tables, which structure data into rows and columns, are what lend organization to the data.

Here's an example of what a typical table looks like:

```
+-----+----------------------+-------+
| mid | mtitle               | myear |
+-----+----------------------+-------+
|   1 | Rear Window          |  1954 |
|   2 | To Catch A Thief     |  1955 |
|   3 | The Maltese Falcon   |  1941 |
|   4 | The Birds            |  1963 |
|   5 | North By Northwest   |  1959 |
|   6 | Casablanca           |  1942 |
|   7 | Anatomy Of A Murder  |  1959 |
+-----+----------------------+-------+
```

As you can see, a table divides data into rows, with a new entry (or *record*) on every row. The data in each row is further broken down into columns (or *fields*), each of which contains a value for a particular attribute of that data. For example, if you consider the record for the movie *Rear Window,* you'll see that the record is clearly divided into separate fields for the row number, the movie title, and the year in which it was released.

> TIP
>
> *Think of a table as a drawer containing files. A record is the electronic representation of a file in the drawer.*

Understanding Primary and Foreign Keys

Records within a table are not arranged in any particular order—they can be sorted alphabetically, by ID, by member name, or by any other criteria you choose to specify. Therefore, it becomes necessary to have some method of identifying a specific record in a table. In the previous example, each record is identified by a unique number and this unique field is referred to as the *primary key* for that table. Primary keys don't appear automatically; you have to explicitly mark a field as a primary key when you create a table.

Think of a primary key as a label on each file, which tells you what it contains. In the absence of this label, the files would all look the same and it would be difficult for you to identify the one(s) you need.

With a relational database system like MySQL, it's also possible to link information in one table to information in another. When you begin to do this, the true power of an RDBMS becomes evident. So let's add two more tables, one listing important actors and directors, and the other linking them to movies.

```
+-----+--------------------+------+------------+
| pid | pname              | psex | pdob       |
+-----+--------------------+------+------------+
|   1 | Alfred Hitchcock   | M    | 1899-08-13 |
|   2 | Cary Grant         | M    | 1904-01-18 |
|   3 | Grace Kelly        | F    | 1929-11-12 |
|   4 | Humphrey Bogart    | M    | 1899-12-25 |
|   5 | Sydney Greenstreet | M    | 1879-12-27 |
|   6 | James Stewart      | M    | 1908-05-20 |
+-----+--------------------+------+------------+
```

```
+-----+-----+------+
| mid | pid | role |
+-----+-----+------+
|   1 |   1 | D    |
|   1 |   3 | A    |
|   1 |   6 | A    |
|   2 |   1 | D    |
|   2 |   2 | A    |
|   2 |   3 | A    |
|   3 |   4 | A    |
|   3 |   5 | A    |
|   4 |   1 | D    |
|   5 |   1 | D    |
|   5 |   2 | A    |
|   6 |   4 | A    |
+-----+-----+------+
```

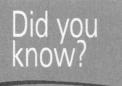

Invasion of the Foreign Keys

Referential integrity is a basic concept with an RDBMS, and one that becomes important when designing a database with more than one table. When foreign keys are used to link one table to another, referential integrity, by its nature, imposes constraints on inserting new records and updating existing records. For example, if a table only accepts certain types of values for a particular field, and other tables use that field as their foreign key, this automatically imposes certain constraints on the dependent tables. Similarly, referential integrity demands that a change in the field used as a foreign key—a deletion or new insertion—must immediately be reflected in all dependent tables.

Many of today's databases take care of this automatically—if you've worked with Microsoft Access, for example, you'll have seen this in action—but some don't. In the case of the latter, the task of maintaining referential integrity becomes a manual one, in which the values in all dependent tables have to be manually updated whenever the value in the primary table changes. Because using foreign keys can degrade the performance of your RDBMS, MySQL leaves the choice of activating such automatic updates (and losing some measure of performance) or deactivating foreign keys (and gaining the benefits of greater speed) to the developer, by making it possible to choose a different type for each table.

8

If you take a close look at the third table, you'll see that it links each movie with the people who participated in it, and it also indicates if they were actors (A) or directors (D). Thus, you can see that *Rear Window* (movie #1) was directed by Alfred Hitchcock (person #1), with Grace Kelly (person #3) and James Stewart (person #6) as actors. Similarly, you can see that Cary Grant (person #2) acted in two movies in the list, *To Catch A Thief* (movie #2) and *North By Northwest* (movie #5).

To understand these relationships visually, look at Figure 8-1.

The third table sets up a relationship between the first and second table, by linking them together using common fields. Such relationships form the foundation of a relational database system. The common fields used to link the tables together

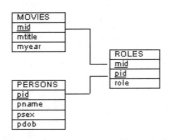

FIGURE 8-1   The interrelationships among movies, actors, and directors

are called *foreign keys,* and when every foreign key value is related to a field in another table, this relationship being unique, the system is said to be in a state of *referential integrity.* In other words, if the mid field is present once and only once in each table that uses it, and if a change to the mid field in any single table is reflected in all other tables, referential integrity is said to exist.

Once one or more relationships are set up between tables, it is possible to extract a subset of the data (a *data slice*) to answer specific questions. The act of pulling out this data is referred to as a *query,* and the resulting data is referred to as a *result set.* And it's in creating these queries, as well as in manipulating the database itself, that SQL truly comes into its own.

Understanding SQL and SQL Queries

Putting data into a database is only half the battle—the other half involves using it effectively. This section tells you a little bit about SQL, which is the primary means of communicating with a database and extracting the data you require.

SQL began life as SEQUEL, the Structured English Query Language; the name was later changed to SQL for legal reasons. SEQUEL was a part of System/R, a prototype of the first relational database system created by IBM in 1974. In the late 1970s, SQL was selected as the query language for the Oracle RDBMS. This put it on the map and, by the 1980s, SQL was used in almost all commercial RDBMS. In 1989, SQL became an ANSI standard. The latest version of this standard, referred to as SQL92 or SQL2, is currently used on most of today's commercial RDBMSs (including MySQL).

SQL statements resemble spoken English and can broadly be classified into three categories:

- **Data Definition Language (DDL)**   DDL consists of statements that define the structure and relationships of a database and its tables. Typically, these statements are used to create, delete, and modify databases and tables; specify field names and types; set indexes; and establish relationships between tables.

- **Data Manipulation Language (DML)**   DML statements are related to altering and extracting data from a database. These statements are used to add records to, and delete records from, a database; perform *queries;* retrieve table records matching one or more user-specified criteria; and join tables together using their common fields.

- **Data Control Language (DCL)**   DCL statements are used to define access levels and security privileges for a database. You would use these statements to grant or deny user privileges, assign roles, change passwords, view permissions, and create rulesets to protect access to data.

> TIP   *When creating applications with PHP and MySQL, you'll mostly be using DML statements.*

Here are a few examples of valid SQL statements:

```
CREATE DATABASE addressbook;
DESCRIBE catalog;
SELECT title FROM books WHERE targetAge > 3;
DELETE FROM houses WHERE area < 100;
```

As the previous examples demonstrate, SQL syntax is close to spoken English, which is why most novice programmers find it easy to learn and use. Every SQL statement begins with an "action word" and ends with a semicolon. White space, tabs, and carriage returns are ignored. This makes the following two commands equivalent:

```
DELETE FROM houses WHERE monthlyRent > 25000;
DELETE FROM
     houses
WHERE monthlyRent >

25000;
```

Understanding Database Normalization

An important part of designing a database is a process known as normalization. *Normalization* refers to the activity of streamlining a database design by eliminating redundancies and repeated values. Most often, redundancies are eliminated by placing repeating groups of values into separate tables and linking them through foreign keys. This not only makes the database more compact and reduces the disk space it occupies, but it also simplifies the task of making changes. In nonnormalized databases, because values are usually repeated in different tables, altering them is a manual (and error-prone) find-and-replace process. In a normalized database, because values appear only once, making changes is a simple one-step UPDATE.

The normalization process also includes validating the database relationships to ensure that there aren't any crossed wires and to eliminate incorrect dependencies. This is a worthy goal, because when you create convoluted table relationships, you add greater complexity to your database design … and greater complexity translates into slower query time as the optimizer tries to figure out how best to handle your table joins.

A number of so-called normal forms are defined to help you correctly normalize a database. A *normal form* is simply a set of rules that a database must conform to. Five such normal forms exist, ranging from the completely nonnormalized database to the fully normalized one.

*To see an example of how to go about turning a badly designed database into a well-designed one, visit Chapter 12, or look online at **http://dev .mysql.com/tech-resources/articles/intro-to-normalization.html** for a primer on the topic.*

Using the MySQL Command-Line Client

The MySQL RDBMS consists of two primary components: the MySQL database server itself, and a suite of client-side programs, including an interactive client and utilities to manage MySQL user permissions, view and copy databases, and import and export data. If you installed and tested MySQL according to the procedure outlined in Chapter 2 of this book, you've already met the MySQL command-line client. This client is your primary means of interacting with the MySQL server and, in this section, I'll be using it to demonstrate how to communicate with the server.

To begin, ensure that your MySQL server is running, and then connect to it with the `mysql` command-line client. Remember to send a valid password with your username, or else MySQL will reject your connection attempt. (Throughout this section and the ones that follow, boldface type is used to indicate commands that you should enter at the prompt.)

```
[user@host]# mysql -u root -p
Password: ******
```

If all went well, you'll see a prompt like this:

```
Welcome to the MySQL monitor.  Commands end with ; or \g.
Your MySQL connection id is 134 to server version: 4.0.12
Type 'help;' or '\h' for help. Type '\c' to clear the buffer.
mysql>
```

The `mysql>` you see is an interactive prompt, where you enter SQL statements. Statements entered here are transmitted to the MySQL server using a proprietary client-server protocol, and the results are transmitted back using the same manner.

Try this out by sending the server a simple statement:

```
mysql> SELECT 5+5;
+-----+
| 5+5 |
+-----+
|  10 |
+-----+
1 row in set (0.06 sec)
```

Here, the `SELECT` statement is used to perform an arithmetic operation on the server and return the results to the client (you can do a lot more with the `SELECT` statement, and it's all covered in Chapter 10). Statements entered at the prompt must be terminated with either a semicolon or a `\g` signal, followed by a carriage return to send the statement to the server. Statements can be entered in either uppercase or lowercase type.

The response returned by the server is displayed in tabular form, as rows and columns. The number of rows returned, as well as the time taken to execute the command, are also printed. If you're dealing with extremely large databases, this information can come in handy to analyze the speed of your queries.

8

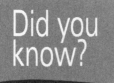

Version Control

Different MySQL server versions support different functions. MySQL 3.*x* included support for joins; MySQL 4.*x* added support for transactions; MySQL 4.1.*x* introduced subqueries, prepared statements and multiple character sets; and the upcoming MySQL 5.*x* promises to support views, stored procedures, and triggers. To find out which version of the MySQL server you're running, look in the message text displayed by the client when it first connects, or use the SELECT VERSION() command.

As noted previously, white space, tabs, and carriage returns in SQL statements are ignored. In the MySQL command-line client, typing a carriage return without ending the statement correctly simply causes the client to jump to a new line and wait for further input. The continuation character - > is displayed in such situations to indicate that the statement is not yet complete. This is illustrated in the next example, which splits a single statement over three lines:

```
mysql> SELECT 100
    -> *
    -> 9 + (7*2);
+-----------------+
| 100
*
9 + (7*2)         |
+-----------------+
|             914 |
+-----------------+
1 row in set (0.00 sec)
```

Notice that the SQL statement in the previous example is only transmitted to the server once the terminating semicolon is entered.

Most of the time, you'll be using SQL to retrieve records from one or more MySQL tables. Consider, for example, the following simple SQL query, which counts all the records in the `user` table from the `mysql` database (this database comes preinstalled with MySQL):

```
mysql> SELECT COUNT(*) FROM mysql.user;
+----------+
| COUNT(*) |
+----------+
|        4 |
+----------+
1 row in set (0.11 sec)
```

To obtain help on using the MySQL client, type **help** at the `mysql>` prompt.

```
mysql> help
List of all MySQL commands:
   (Commands must appear first on line and end with ';')

help    (\h)    Display this help.
?       (\?)    Synonym for `help'.
clear   (\c)    Clear command.
connect (\r)    Reconnect to the server. Optional arguments are db and host.
ego     (\G)    Send command to mysql server, display result vertically.
exit    (\q)    Exit mysql. Same as quit.
go      (\g)    Send command to mysql server.
...
```

To close the connection to the server and exit the client, type **quit** at the `mysql>` prompt.

```
mysql> quit
Bye
```

Interacting with MySQL Through a Graphical Client

If using the command line isn't your style, don't lose heart—a number of good graphical clients also exist for MySQL. Here's a list of the better ones:

- **MySQL Control Center (http://www.mysql.com/products/mysqlcc/ index.html)** is an excellent front-end query and database management tool for MySQL. Currently, Windows, UNIX, and Linux versions are available, with a Mac OS X version under development.

8

- **SQLyog (http://www.webyog.com/sqlyog/)** is a Windows-based front-end for MySQL administration. It offers a graphical interface that supports copying and pasting query results, syntax highlighting, and datagrid display, and it includes a synchronization tool to synchronize databases on different servers.

- **phpMyAdmin (http://www.phpmyadmin.net/)** is a web-based tool to manage MySQL databases and tables, input records, and execute queries. It is written entirely in PHP, is licensed under the GNU GPL, and is currently available in 47(!) languages.

Summary

This chapter focused on getting you started with MySQL, by teaching you the basic concepts you need to know to use MySQL efficiently. It showed you how a database structures data into tables, records, and fields; how it identifies records with primary keys; and how it connects records in different tables with each other through foreign keys. This chapter also introduced you to SQL, giving you a brief look at some SQL commands—these commands will be discussed in greater detail over the next few chapters. Finally, an introduction to database normalization and a few examples of using the MySQL command-line client wrapped things up.

If you're interested in learning more about the topics in this chapter, these web links have more information:

- The official MySQL tutorial, at **http://dev.mysql.com/doc/mysql/en/ Tutorial.html**

- The origins of MySQL, at **http://dev.mysql.com/doc/mysql/en/ History.html**

- A detailed discussion of basic RDBMS concepts, at **http://www.melonfire .com/community/columns/trog/article.php?id=52**

- The normal forms of a database design, at **http://en.wikipedia.org/wiki/ Database_normalization**

- The MySQL command-line client, at **http://dev.mysql.com/doc/mysql/en/ Client-Side_Scripts.html**

Chapter 9

Working with Databases and Tables

Now that you know the big-picture view of how an RDBMS works, it's time to get into the details. This chapter focuses on the first component of SQL, the Data Definition Languages (DDL), by discussing the SQL commands to create (and delete) databases and tables, and view database, table, and field information.

A large part of this chapter is focused on a single command: the CREATE TABLE command. When designing a database, this is one of the most important commands you must know, because it enables you to decide the fundamental structure of your database. With the CREATE TABLE command, you can control, for example, how many fields each record must contain, which of those fields are optional, and what type of data can be entered into each field. MySQL lets you use different types of tables depending on your storage and data retrieval requirements. The CREATE TABLE command enables you to specify this information as well.

How to...

- Name and create a MySQL database
- Add tables to a database
- Decide the names and default values for the fields in a table
- Select the appropriate data type for a field
- Use enumerations to limit field input to a predefined list of values
- Specify which fields are optional and which are mandatory
- Select the table's primary and foreign key(s)
- Index frequently used fields for better performance
- Choose between MySQL's different table types (and select the one best suited for your needs)
- Alter a table definition after it's been created
- Back up and restore a table or a database
- View the structure and contents of a database or table
- Empty a table of its records
- Delete a database or table

Creating Databases

Because all tables are stored in a database, the first command you need to know is the CREATE DATABASE command, which initializes an empty database. Try it out by creating a database called db2:

```
mysql> CREATE DATABASE db2;
Query OK, 1 row affected (0.05 sec)
```

Databases in MySQL are represented as directories on the disk, and tables are represented as files within those directories. Therefore, database names must comply with the operating system's (OS) restrictions on which characters are permissible within directory names. Database names cannot exceed 64 characters and names that contain special characters or consist entirely of digits or reserved words must be quoted with the backtick (`) operator.

Generally, it's considered good practice to start database names with an alphabetic character and to ensure they consist of only alphanumeric and underscore characters. Try to avoid using reserved MySQL keywords as database names.

You can select a particular database for use with the USE command. Select the db2 database you just created to try this:

```
mysql> USE db2;
Database changed
```

Once you select a database with the USE command, it becomes the default database for all operations.

Creating Tables

Because this is a new database, no tables are in it yet. To create a table, use the CREATE TABLE command, as in the following:

```
mysql> CREATE TABLE movies (
    -> mid int(10) UNSIGNED NOT NULL AUTO_INCREMENT,
    -> mtitle varchar(255) NOT NULL default '',
    -> myear year(4) NOT NULL default '0000',
    -> PRIMARY KEY (mid)
    -> ) TYPE=MyISAM;
Query OK, 0 rows affected (0.10 sec)
```

9

The CREATE TABLE statement begins with the table name, followed by a set of parentheses. These parentheses enclose one or more *field definitions,* separated by commas. Each field definition contains the field name, its data type, and any special modifiers or constraints that apply. Following the closing parenthesis is an optional *table type specifier,* which tells MySQL which storage engine to use for this table.

Table and field names must conform to the same rules that apply to database names. MySQL tables are stored as files within the database directory and, as such, are subject to the host operating system's rules on file names.

 *To simplify moving your databases and tables between different operating systems, lowercase all your table names, and use underscores instead of spaces.*

Specifying Field Data Types

When creating a MySQL table, specifying a data type for every field is necessary. This data type plays an important role in enforcing the integrity of the data in a MySQL database, and in making this data easier to use and manipulate. MySQL offers a number of different data types, which are summarized in Table 9-1.

The following sections examine each of these types in greater detail.

Numeric Types

For integer values, MySQL offers you a choice of the TINYINT, SMALLINT, MEDIUMINT, INT, and BIGINT types, which differ from each other only in the size of values they can store. Use the TINYINT and SMALLINT type for small integer values, the INT type for larger integer values, and the BIGINT type for extremely large values. For floating-point values, use the FLOAT and DOUBLE types for single-precision and double-precision floating point values, respectively. And, finally, for decimal values, use the DECIMAL data type.

When defining an integer field, you can include a width specifier in parentheses. This *width specifier* controls the padding MySQL applies to the field when retrieving it from the database. For a field defined as BIGINT (20), MySQL will automatically pad the value to 20 characters before displaying it.

When defining floating-point and decimal fields, MySQL enables you to include both a width specifier and a *precision specifier*. For example, the declaration FLOAT (7, 4) specifies that displayed values will not contain more than seven digits, with four digits after the decimal point.

Type	Used For
TINYINT, SMALLINT, MEDIUMINT, INT, BIGINT	Integer values
FLOAT	Single-precision floating-point values
DOUBLE	Double-precision floating-point values
DECIMAL	Decimal values
CHAR	Fixed-length strings up to 255 characters
VARCHAR	Variable-length strings up to 255 characters
TINYBLOB, BLOB, MEDIUMBLOB, LONGBLOB	Large blocks of binary data
TINYTEXT, TEXT, MEDIUMTEXT, LONGTEXT	Longer blocks of text data
DATE	Date values
TIME	Time values or durations
YEAR	Year values
DATETIME	Combined date and time values
TIMESTAMP	Timestamps
ENUM	Fields that must contain one of a set of predefined mutually exclusive values
SET	Fields that can contain zero, one, or more of a set of predefined values

TABLE 9-1 MySQL Data Types

CAUTION *If you try to use a value that's too big for the field you're placing it in, MySQL will automatically truncate or round the value down to the maximum allowed value for that field.*

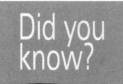

Zero-ing In

You can add two optional attributes to numeric type definitions: the ZEROFILL attribute, which pads a value with leading zeroes, and the UNSIGNED attribute, which forces a field to only accept positive values.

Character and String Types

MySQL lets you store strings up to 255 characters in length as either CHAR or VARCHAR types. The difference between these two types is simple: CHAR fields are fixed to the length specified at the time of definition, while VARCHAR fields can grow and shrink dynamically, based on the data entered into them. This makes VARCHAR fields more suitable for fields that accept variable-length data, and CHAR fields better for fields that always contain values of the same length.

Both CHAR and VARCHAR type definitions must include a width specifier in parentheses, as with numeric type definitions. Thus, the definition CHAR (10) creates a field whose length remains *exactly 10 characters* regardless of what is entered into it, while the definition VARCHAR (10) creates a field whose length can range *anywhere between 0 and 10 characters* depending on what is entered into it.

Text and Binary Types

MySQL enables you to store strings greater than 255 characters in length as either TEXT or BLOB types. The difference between TEXT and BLOB types is minimal at best: TEXT types are compared in a case-insensitive manner, while BLOB types are compared in a case-sensitive manner. For this reason, BLOBs are usually used to store binary data, while TEXT fields are used to store ASCII data.

Depending on the size of the string you're trying to store, MySQL offers you a choice of the TINYTEXT, TEXT, MEDIUMTEXT, and LONGTEXT types (for ASCII text blocks) and the TINYBLOB, BLOB, MEDIUMBLOB, and LONGBLOB types (for binary data).

Date and Time Types

For simple date and time values, MySQL offers the intelligently named DATE and TIME data types. The DATE type is used to store date values consisting of year, month, and day components, while the TIME type is used for time values or durations consisting of house, minute, and second components. Both DATE and TIME types can be used for values in either numeric (YYYYMMDD and HHMMSS) or string ('YYYY-MM-DD' and 'HH:MM:SS') format.

If what you need is a combination of the two, consider using the DATETIME or TIMESTAMP types, both of which let you specify both date and time values in a single field. The difference between the two lies in how the values are stored: DATETIME fields are stored in the form 'YYYY-MM-DD HH:MM:SS', and TIMESTAMP fields are stored in the form YYYYMMDDHHMMSS.

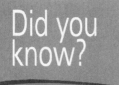

Time Out!

When inserting records into a table containing a TIMESTAMP field, MySQL automatically fills that field with the current date and time (assuming no other value was specified, of course). To accomplish the same thing with DATETIME fields, manually specify a value for the field with the NOW() function, which returns the current date and time.

Finally, for simple applications that only need to store the year, MySQL offers the special YEAR type, which accepts a 4-digit year value. It's worthwhile to use this value if your application deals mostly with the year component of a date value, because a field marked as YEAR occupies 1 byte on disk (as compared to a DATETIME or DATE field, which can occupy up to 8 bytes). MySQL is completely Y2K-compliant, and YEAR fields can accept any value in the range 1901 to 2155.

Enumerations

For situations where a field value must be selected from a predefined list of values, MySQL offers the ENUM and SET data types. For both these types, a list of predefined values must be included as part of the type definition. An ENUM field definition can contain up to 65,536 elements, while a SET field definition can hold up to 64 elements.

For a field marked as an ENUM field, only one of the predefined values may be selected, whereas for a field marked as a SET field, zero, one, or more than one of the predefined values may be selected. So, ENUM fields are best suited for mutually exclusive values, while SET fields are best suited for independent values. As an example, the definition ENUM ('red', 'green', 'yellow') forces entry of any one of the three values, while the definition SET ('sugar', 'salt', 'pepper', 'mustard') allows entry of none, one, or all of the four values.

With both ENUM and SET types, attempting to insert a value that does not exist in the predefined list of values will cause MySQL to insert either an empty string or a zero.

Selecting the Most Appropriate Data Type

Choosing the data type best suited to the values you expect to enter into the corresponding field is extremely important. When making this decision, take into account the following factors:

- The range and type of values that the field will hold

- The types of calculations you expect to perform on those values

- The manner in which the data is to be formatted for display purposes

- The manner in which the data is to be sorted and compared against other fields

- The available subtypes for each field and their storage efficiencies

By taking all these factors into consideration at the time of designing your database, you reduce the chance of incompatibilities and storage inefficiencies later.

Using the wrong data type can affect both the performance of your RDBMS and the types of operations you can perform on that field. For example, using a VARCHAR type on a field that is meant for numeric or date values could result in unexpected behavior when you perform calculations on it, just as using a large TEXT field for small string values could lead to a waste of space and inefficient indexing.

Adding Field Modifiers and Keys

You can apply a number of additional constraints, or modifiers, to a field to increase the consistency of the data that will be entered into it, and to mark it as "special" in some way. These modifiers can either appear as part of the field definition if they apply only to that specific field (for example, a default value for a field) or after all the field definitions if they relate to multiple fields (for example, a multicolumn primary key).

- You can specify whether the field is allowed to be empty or if it must necessarily be filled with data by placing the NULL and NOT NULL modifiers after each field definition.

- You can specify a default value for a field with the DEFAULT modifier. This default value is used if no value is specified for that field when inserting a record. In the absence of a DEFAULT modifier for NOT NULL fields, MySQL automatically inserts a nonthreatening default value into the field.

■ You can have MySQL automatically generate a number for a field (by incrementing the previous value by 1) with the AUTO_INCREMENT modifier. This is particularly useful when you need to generate row numbers for each record in the table. However, the AUTO_INCREMENT modifier can only be applied to numeric fields that are both NOT NULL and belong to the PRIMARY KEY. A table may only contain one AUTO_INCREMENT field.

■ For fields that accept string values, you can specify the character set for these values with the CHARACTER SET modifier (new in MySQL 4.1.1). However, this feature is only supported in MySQL's MyISAM, MERGE, and InnoDB table types (see the section entitled "Selecting a Table Type" for more on MySQL's table types).

■ You can *index* a field with the INDEX modifier. When a field is indexed in this manner, MySQL no longer needs to scan each row of the table for a match when performing queries; instead, it can simply look up the index. This speeds up searches and reduces query response time. Indexing is recommended for fields that frequently appear in the WHERE, ORDER BY, and GROUP BY clauses of SELECT queries, and for fields used to join tables together.

■ You can specify that values entered into a field must be either unique—that is, not duplicated—or NULL with the UNIQUE modifier.

NOTE   *The UNIQUE modifier is actually a special type of index.*

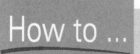

How to ... **Create a Primary Key Consisting of Multiple Fields**

In some tables, it is the combination of two or more fields, rather than a single field, that uniquely identifies a row. This is called a composite primary key; to create it, simply use a comma-separated field list instead of a single field in the PRIMARY KEY modifier.

- You can specify a primary key for the table with the PRIMARY KEY modifier. The PRIMARY KEY constraint can best be thought of as a combination of the NOT NULL and UNIQUE constraints because it requires values in the specified field to be neither NULL nor repeated in any other row. It thus serves as a unique identifier for each record in the table, and it should be selected only after careful thought has been given to the inter-relationships between tables.

- You can specify a foreign key for a table with the FOREIGN KEY modifier. The FOREIGN KEY modifier links a field in one table to a field (usually a primary key) in another table, setting up a base for relationships. However, foreign keys are only supported in MySQL's InnoDB table type; the FOREIGN KEY modifier is simply ignored in all other table types (see the section entitled "Selecting a Table Type" for more on MySQL's table types).

Selecting a Table Type

Following the field definitions and modifiers come one or more table modifiers, which specify table-level attributes. Of these, the most frequently used one is the TYPE modifier, which tells MySQL which table type to use. A number of such types are available, each with different advantages. Here is a list:

- **MyISAM** The MyISAM format is optimized for speed and reliability, it supports tables in excess of 4GB in size, and it can be compressed to save space. This is MySQL's default table type and, as such, contains numerous MySQL-specific optimizations and features.

  Select this table type by adding TYPE = MYISAM to your CREATE TABLE statement.

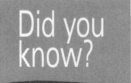

What's in a Name?

In MySQL, the terms *key* and *index* are synonymous. PRIMARY KEY fields are automatically indexed by MySQL, while FOREIGN KEY fields must be explicitly indexed by the user.

- **InnoDB** The successor to the MyISAM format, the InnoDB format, is the most sophisticated table type available in MySQL. It supports transactions and foreign keys (the only MySQL table type to do both), and allows multiple simultaneous users to execute SELECT statements; this improves performance and query response times. InnoDB tables are fully portable between different operating systems, and include crash recovery features to avoid data corruption or loss.

  Select this table type by adding TYPE = INNODB to your CREATE TABLE statement.

- **HEAP** A HEAP table is stored in memory, making it extremely fast. This format is optimized for temporary tables and it is rarely used for other purposes. This is because the data in a HEAP table is available only while the server is running, and is automatically erased when the server shuts down and the memory is flushed.

  Select this table type by adding TYPE = HEAP to your CREATE TABLE statement.

- **BerkeleyDB** The BerkeleyDB format is one of the more advanced table formats supported by MySQL. It supports transactions, checkpoints, crash recovery, and page-level locking. However, it also has certain disadvantages: BerkeleyDB tables are not easily portable between different operating systems and they lack many of the optimizations of the MyISAM format, making them slower and less memory efficient.

  Select this table type by adding TYPE = BDB to your CREATE TABLE statement.

- **MERGE** The MERGE table format makes it possible for a collection of MyISAM tables to be treated as one, by combining them into a single "virtual" table. This table format makes improving performance or increasing query efficiency possible in certain situations; however, it can only be used for tables that are completely identical in their internal structure.

  Select this table type by adding TYPE = MERGE to your CREATE TABLE statement.

- **ISAM** The forerunner of the newer MyISAM format, the ISAM format is primarily offered for compatibility with older MySQL tables. It lacks many of the features of the MyISAM format, cannot handle large tables, and is more prone to fragmentation (which degrades performance).

  Select this table type by adding TYPE = ISAM to your CREATE TABLE statement.

Most of the time, you won't need to look further than the default MyISAM table type. Use the InnoDB table type only if you want to use advanced features like transactions and foreign keys, use the MERGE table type if you need to query multiple similar tables simultaneously, and use the HEAP table type if you need a temporary data storage area.

Now that you know what the various components of a CREATE TABLE statement are, try it out for yourself by revisiting the tables in Chapter 8 and writing the corresponding CREATE TABLE statement for each. Here's how:

```
mysql> CREATE TABLE persons (
    -> pid int(11) NOT NULL auto_increment,
    -> pname varchar(255) NOT NULL default '',
    -> PRIMARY KEY  (pid)
    -> ) TYPE=MyISAM;
Query OK, 0 rows affected (0.09 sec)
mysql> CREATE TABLE roles (
    -> mid int(11) NOT NULL default '0',
    -> pid int(11) NOT NULL default '0',
    -> role enum('A','D') NOT NULL default 'A',
    -> PRIMARY KEY mid (mid,pid,role)
    -> ) TYPE=MyISAM;
Query OK, 0 rows affected (0.11 sec)
```

The CREATE TABLE statement can be one of the most complex statements in the SQL lexicon. Because you'll use it frequently when designing a database, you should spend some time reading about it in detail in the MySQL manual, at **http://dev.mysql.com/doc/mysql/en/CREATE_TABLE.html**.

It Was Here Just a Second Ago...

MySQL also lets you create temporary tables in memory with the CREATE TEMPORARY TABLE command. These tables remain in existence only for the duration of a single MySQL session and are automatically deleted when the client that created them closes its connection with the MySQL server. Temporary tables come in handy for transient, session-based data or calculations. And, because they're session-dependant, two different sessions can use the same table name without conflicting.

Altering Tables

Table definitions created with the CREATE TABLE command are not set in stone—you're free to alter them at a later date as well. The SQL command to do this is the ALTER TABLE command. It lets you add or delete fields; alter field types; add, remove, or modify keys; alter the table type; and change the table name (among other things). The following sections discuss these capabilities in greater detail.

Altering Table and Field Names

To alter a table name, use an ALTER TABLE command with a supplementary RENAME clause. The following example demonstrates, by renaming table bills to invoices:

```
mysql> ALTER TABLE bills RENAME TO invoices;
Query OK, 0 rows affected (0.11 sec)
```

An alternative is to use the RENAME TABLE command, which does the same thing:

```
mysql> RENAME TABLE bills TO invoices;
Query OK, 0 rows affected (0.06 sec)
```

You can just as easily alter a field name. Here's an example, which uses the ALTER TABLE command with a CHANGE clause to modify the name of field address to address1:

```
mysql> ALTER TABLE users CHANGE address address1 VARCHAR(255);
Query OK, 0 rows affected (0.17 sec)
```

Notice that you must include the column definition when changing a field name in this manner, or else MySQL will generate an error and disallow the operation.

Altering Field Properties

You can use the CHANGE clause discussed in the previous section to alter a field's type and properties as well, simply by using a new column definition instead of the

9

original one. Here's an example, which changes the field named `tel` defined as `VARCHAR(30)` to a field named `age` with definition `TINYINT(2)`:

```
mysql> ALTER TABLE users CHANGE tel age TINYINT(2);
Query OK, 0 rows affected (0.05 sec)
```

When you `CHANGE` a field from one type to another, MySQL will automatically attempt to convert the data in that field to the new type. If the data in the field is inconsistent with the new field definition—for example, a field defined as `NOT NULL` contains `NULL` values, or a field marked as `UNIQUE` contains duplicate values—MySQL will generate an error. You can alter this default behavior by adding an `IGNORE` clause to the `ALTER TABLE` command that tells MySQL to ignore such inconsistencies.

Adding and Removing Fields and Keys

You can add a new field to a table by including an `ADD` clause in your `ALTER TABLE` command. The following example demonstrates, by adding a field named `salary` to the `employees` table:

```
mysql> ALTER TABLE employees ADD salary INT(7) NOT NULL;
Query OK, 0 rows affected (0.06 sec)
```

You can also do the reverse—delete an existing field from a table—by using a `DROP` clause instead of an `ADD` clause. The following example removes the field added in the previous operation (together with any data it might have contained):

```
mysql> ALTER TABLE employees DROP salary;
Query OK, 0 rows affected (0.05 sec)
```

You can delete a table's primary key with the `DROP PRIMARY KEY` clause, as illustrated here:

```
mysql> ALTER TABLE users DROP PRIMARY KEY;
Query OK, 0 rows affected (0.06 sec)
```

and add a new primary key with the `ADD PRIMARY KEY` clause, as illustrated here:

```
mysql> ALTER TABLE users ADD PRIMARY KEY (id);
Query OK, 0 rows affected (0.05 sec)
```

TIP *A table's primary key must always be NOT NULL.*

Altering Table Types

You can alter the table type by adding a `TYPE` clause to the `ALTER TABLE` command, as in the following example:

```
mysql> ALTER TABLE data TYPE = INNODB;
Query OK, 6 rows affected (0.11 sec)
```

Backing Up and Restoring Databases and Tables

The MySQL distribution comes with a powerful tool for backing up and restoring databases and tables: the `mysqldump` utility. When run on a database (or table), this command-line utility creates a text file containing all the SQL commands needed to re-create that database (or table) from scratch. The text file created by `mysqldump` can contain table definitions, table contents, or both, and it comes in handy both to create backups of your MySQL databases and to copy tables from one database or platform to another.

Backing Up Databases and Tables

To use the `mysqldump` utility to back up a database, invoke it from your command prompt and pass it a valid username, password, and database name. The following example illustrates, by using `mysqldump` on the `db2` database:

```
$ /usr/local/mysql/bin/mysqldump -u root -p hidden db2
```

The Need for Speed

When you issue an `ALTER TABLE` command, MySQL first creates a copy of the original table, changes it, and then deletes the original table and replaces it with the changed copy. For this reason, `ALTER TABLE` operations on large tables may take a fair amount of time.

9

When `mysqldump` is invoked in this manner, it will connect to the MySQL server and retrieve the contents of the named database. The output of `mysqldump` is a series of SQL statements, which can be used to re-create the contents of the database. Because `mysqldump` sends everything to the screen by default, redirect the output to a file with the standard > redirection operator:

```
$ /usr/local/mysql/bin/mysqldump -u root ↵
-p hidden db2 > db2backup.sql
```

To back up only a specific table from the database, add the table name after the database name in the `mysqldump` command line. The following command backs up only the `movies` table from the `db2` database:

```
$ /usr/local/mysql/bin/mysqldump -u root ↵
-p hidden db2 movies > movies.sql
```

By default, `mysqldump` backs up both the table definitions and their contents. To only back up table definitions—useful if, for example, you're attempting to re-create the empty tables in another database or platform—append the `--no-data` option to the `mysqldump` command line, as follows:

```
$ /usr/local/mysql/bin/mysqldump -u root -p hidden ↵
--no-data db2 movies > movies.sql
```

With the `--no-data` option, `mysqldump` stores the CREATE TABLE statement for the table, but none of its records.

Restoring Databases and Tables from Backup

Restoring a database or table from the text file created by `mysqldump` is extremely simple. All you need to do is pipe the file to the `mysql` command-line client, so that the SQL commands inside it are read and executed by the server. For example, to re-create the table previously backed up to the file `movies.sql` in the database `newdb`, use the following command:

```
$ mysql -u root -p secret -D newdb < movies.sql
```

More Than One Way...

In MySQL 4.1, you can create an empty copy of a table by using the new LIKE clause in a CREATE TABLE command. Here is an example, which creates a new, empty copy of the grades table and the names it marks:

```
mysql> CREATE TABLE grades LIKE marks;
Query OK, 0 rows affected (0.01 sec)
```

Notice that the database into which the table is restored must already exist and must be named on the mysql command line with the -D option. If you now inspect the newdb database with the SHOW TABLES command (as discussed in the section "Viewing Database, Table, and Field Information"), you will see the table in it.

Dropping Databases and Tables

To delete a database, use the DROP DATABASE command, which deletes the named database and all its tables permanently. Try this out by creating and dropping a database:

```
mysql> CREATE DATABASE music;
Query OK, 1 row affected (0.05 sec)
mysql> DROP DATABASE music;
Query OK, 0 rows affected (0.49 sec)
```

Similarly, you can delete a table with the DROP TABLE command. Try this out by creating and dropping a table:

```
mysql> CREATE TABLE members ( memberId INT NOT NULL );
Query OK, 0 rows affected (0.00 sec)
mysql> DROP TABLE members;
Query OK, 0 rows affected (0.00 sec)
```

The DROP TABLE command will immediately wipe out the specified table, together with all the data it contains—so use it with care!

If what you wanted was to empty the table of all records, use the TRUNCATE TABLE command instead, which internally DROP-s the table, and then re-creates it. The AUTO_INCREMENT counter, if one exists, is automatically reset in TRUNCATE TABLE operations (this does not happen if you simply delete all the records in the table with a DELETE command).

Here is an example:

```
mysql> TRUNCATE TABLE movies;
Query OK, 0 rows affected (0.01 sec)
```

Viewing Database, Table, and Field Information

You can view all available databases with the SHOW DATABASES command:

```
mysql> SHOW DATABASES;
+----------+
| Database |
+----------+
| db2      |
| mysql    |
| test     |
+----------+
3 rows in set (0.00 sec)
```

You can view available tables in a database with the SHOW TABLES command, as in the following:

```
mysql> SHOW TABLES FROM db2;
+---------------+
| Tables_in_db2 |
+---------------+
| movies        |
| persons       |
| roles         |
+---------------+
3 rows in set (0.06 sec)
```

You can omit the FROM clause in the SHOW TABLES command if you've already selected the database with the USE command.

To see the structure of a particular table, use the DESCRIBE command, as in the following:

```
mysql> DESCRIBE movies;
+--------+-------------------+------+-----+---------+----------------+
| Field  | Type              | Null | Key | Default | Extra          |
+--------+-------------------+------+-----+---------+----------------+
| mid    | int(10) unsigned  |      | PRI | NULL    | auto_increment |
| mtitle | varchar(255)      |      |     |         |                |
| myear  | year(4)           |      |     | 0000    |                |
+--------+-------------------+------+-----+---------+----------------+
3 rows in set (0.05 sec)
```

You can also

- Retrieve the SQL commands originally used to create the table with the SHOW CREATE TABLE command

- View a list of table indexes with the SHOW INDEX command

- Retrieve a list of table types supported by the server with the SHOW ENGINES command (in MySQL 4.1.2 and better)

- View a list of active connections to the server, as well as what each one is doing, with the SHOW PROCESSLIST command

- View a list of errors and warnings generated by the server with the SHOW ERRORS and SHOW WARNINGS commands (in MySQL 4.1.0 and better)

- Obtain server status (including information on server uptime, number of queries processed, and number of connections) with the SHOW STATUS command

- Obtain detailed information on the tables in a database (including information on the table type, the number of rows, the date and time of the last table update, and the lengths of indexes and rows) with the SHOW TABLE STATUS command, and

- View a list of available character sets (in MySQL 4.1.1 and better) with the SHOW CHARACTER SET command

9

The output of these commands cannot be reproduced here due to page-width considerations. Try them out for yourself to see how they work.

Summary

You should now have a clear understanding of how to work with MySQL's databases and tables. This chapter discussed most of the important aspects of the DDL, including how to create and delete databases, define table structures, work with field data types and modifiers, choose a MySQL table type, and use primary and foreign keys. It also showed you how to alter a table after it's been created, and how to back up and restore an existing table structure and/or its contents.

With your database(s) and table(s) defined, the next step is to begin adding data to them. That's what the next chapter is all about, but before you begin reading, take some time to learn more about the topics covered in this chapter by visiting the following links:

- A complete list of options to the CREATE TABLE statement, at **http://dev.mysql.com/doc/mysql/en/CREATE_TABLE.html**

- Detailed descriptions of MySQL's numerous data types, at **http://dev.mysql.com/doc/mysql/en/Column_types.html**

- Detailed descriptions of MySQL's table types and guidelines on how to choose among them, at **http://dev.mysql.com/doc/mysql/en/Table_types.html**

- More information on altering tables, at **http://dev.mysql.com/doc/mysql/en/ALTER_TABLE.html**

- More information on the mysqldump utility, at **http://dev.mysql.com/doc/mysql/en/mysqldump.html**

- A complete list of SHOW... commands, with output samples, at **http://dev.mysql.com/doc/mysql/en/SHOW.html**

Chapter 10

Editing Records and Performing Queries

Once you have your databases and tables defined, the next step is to begin using them, by populating them with records and performing queries on the data stored inside them. To do this, you need to master the Data Manipulation Languages (DML) component of SQL. That's why this chapter discusses the SQL commands to add, edit, and delete records to a table, and then perform different types of queries on that data to retrieve a result set of records that satisfy the query.

How to...

- Use the INSERT command to add records to a table

- Edit and delete records with the UPDATE and DELETE commands

- Retrieve table records with the SELECT command

- Use the WHERE clause to restrict the scope of your actions to a subset of records

- Use functions and operators to manipulate and compare field values

- Sort result sets and eliminate duplicate values

- Set a limit on the number of records in a result set

- Group records in a result set using common attributes (and then perform operations on these groups)

- Join tables together using foreign keys

- Use the results of one query inside another

Inserting Records

Once you've created a table, it's time to begin entering data into it-and the SQL command to accomplish this is the INSERT command. The syntax of the INSERT command is illustrated in the following example:

```
mysql> INSERT INTO movies (mtitle, myear) VALUES ('Rear Window', 1954);
Query OK, 1 row affected (0.06 sec)
```

The INSERT command is followed by the optional keyword INTO, a table name, and a field list, in parentheses, which indicates which fields the values are to be inserted into. A VALUES clause completes the command, by specifying the values to be inserted into the previously named fields.

You can also use an abbreviated form of the INSERT command, in which the field list is left unspecified. The following example, which is equivalent to the previous one illustrates the following:

```
mysql> INSERT INTO movies VALUES (NULL, 'Rear Window', 1954);
Query OK, 1 row affected (0.06 sec)
```

When using this shorter format, the order in which values are inserted must correspond to the sequence of fields in the table (you can determine the field order with a quick call to the DESCRIBE command, described in Chapter 9).

Normally, the first version of the INSERT command is preferable, because it offers you the flexibility of inserting values in any order you please and protects you from structural changes in the table. Because of this, the following statements are equivalent:

```
mysql> INSERT INTO movies (mtitle, myear) VALUES ('Rear Window', 1954);
Query OK, 1 row affected (0.06 sec)
```

```
mysql> INSERT INTO movies (myear, mtitle) VALUES (1954, 'Rear Window');
Query OK, 1 row affected (0.06 sec)
```

In MySQL, you can insert multiple records into a table at once, by using multiple VALUES () clauses within the same INSERT statement. To see how this works, try running the following command:

```
mysql> INSERT INTO movies (mtitle, myear) VALUES ('Rear Window', 1954), ↵
('To Catch A Thief', 1955), ('The Maltese Falcon', 1941);
Query OK, 3 rows affected (0.12 sec)
Records: 3  Duplicates: 0  Warnings: 0
```

Fields that are not specified in the INSERT command will either be set to NULL or to their default values, depending on how they have been defined. MySQL comes with built-in intelligence to automatically deal with conflicts between the values entered into a field and the field's data type, or with missing values, and so can automatically perform the following operations:

■ For AUTO_INCREMENT fields, entering a NULL value automatically increments the previously generated field value by 1.

■ For the first TIMESTAMP field in a table, entering a NULL value automatically inserts the current date and time.

■ For UNIQUE or PRIMARY KEY fields, entering a value that already exists causes MySQL to generate an error.

When inserting string and some date values into a table, enclose them in quotation marks, so that MySQL doesn't confuse them with variable or field names. Quotation marks within the values themselves can be "escaped" by preceding them with the backslash (\ ) symbol.

Now that you know how to insert records, try inserting some sample records for the three tables created in the previous section, using the sample data in Chapter 8 as a reference. You can start with these samples:

```
mysql> INSERT INTO movies VALUES (1,'Rear Window',1954);
Query OK, 1 row affected (0.06 sec)
mysql> INSERT INTO persons VALUES (1,'Alfred Hitchcock','M','1899-08-13');
Query OK, 1 row affected (0.06 sec)
mysql> INSERT INTO roles VALUES (1,1,'D'), (1,3,'A');
Query OK, 2 rows affected (0.06 sec)
```

Editing and Deleting Records

Just as you INSERT records into a table, you can also DELETE records with the DELETE command, which is illustrated in the following:

```
mysql> DELETE FROM movies;
Query OK, 0 rows affected (0.06 sec)
```

The previous command would delete all the records from the movies table.

You can select a specific subset of rows to be deleted by adding the WHERE clause to the DELETE statement. The following example would only delete records for those persons born after 1960:

```
mysql> DELETE FROM movies WHERE myear > 1960;
Query OK, 1 row affected (0.05 sec)
```

CAUTION   *It is not possible to reverse a DELETE operation in MySQL (unless you're in the middle of a InnoDB transaction which hasn't yet been committed). Therefore, be extremely careful when using DELETE commands, both with and without WHERE clauses-a small mistake and the contents of your entire table will be lost for good.*

TIP   *To delete all the records in a table, consider using the TRUNCATE TABLE command, described in Chapter 9.*

Data in a database usually changes over time, which is why SQL includes an UPDATE command designed to change existing values in a table. As with the DELETE command described previously, you can use the UPDATE command to change all the values in a particular column, or change only those values matching a particular condition.

To illustrate how this works, consider the following example, which changes the value of the field 'The Maltese Falcon' to 'Maltese Falcon, The'.

```
mysql> UPDATE movies SET mtitle = 'Maltese Falcon, The' ↵
WHERE mtitle = 'The Maltese Falcon';
Query OK, 1 row affected (0.05 sec)
Rows matched: 1  Changed: 1  Warnings: 0
```

You can update multiple fields at once, simply by using multiple SET clauses. The following example illustrates, by updating record #7 with a new movie title and year:

```
mysql> UPDATE movies SET mtitle = 'Vertigo', myear = 1958 WHERE mid = 7;
Query OK, 1 row affected (0.06 sec)
Rows matched: 1  Changed: 1  Warnings: 0
```

Thus, the SET clause specifies the field name, as well as the new value for the field. The WHERE clause is used to identify which rows of the table to change. In the absence of this clause, all the rows of the table are updated with the new value. Try this out by entering the following command, which updates the psex field in the persons table:

```
mysql> UPDATE persons SET psex = 'M';
Query OK, 1 row affected (0.06 sec)
Rows matched: 6  Changed: 1  Warnings: 0
```

10

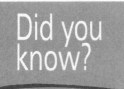

Multitasking with MySQL

Newer versions of MySQL enable you to update and delete records in multiple tables simultaneously with a single query.

If you look at the table now, you will see that all the records in the table sport the value M for their psex field. Correct it by again using an UPDATE command with a WHERE clause:

```
mysql> UPDATE persons SET psex = 'F' WHERE pname = 'Grace Kelly';
Query OK, 1 row affected (0.00 sec)
Rows matched: 1  Changed: 1  Warnings: 0
```

 *Forgetting the WHERE clause in an UPDATE command is a common newbie mistake, and it can lead to widespread data corruption. Always use a WHERE clause to restrict the effect of the UPDATE to relevant fields only.*

Performing Queries

Just as you can add records to a table with the INSERT command, you can retrieve them with the SELECT command. The SELECT command is one of the most versatile and useful commands in SQL. It offers tremendous flexibility in extracting specific subsets of data from a table.

In its most basic form, the SELECT statement can be used to evaluate expressions and functions, or as a "catch-all" query that returns all the records in a specific table. Here is an example of using SELECT to evaluate mathematical expressions:

```
mysql> SELECT 75 / 15, 61 + (3 * 3);
+---------+---------------+
| 75 / 15 | 61 + (3 * 3) |
+---------+---------------+
|    5.00 |           70 |
+---------+---------------+
1 row in set (0.05 sec)
```

And here is an example of using SELECT to retrieve all the records in a table:

```
mysql> SELECT * FROM movies;
+-----+----------------------+-------+
| mid | mtitle               | myear |
+-----+----------------------+-------+
|   1 | Rear Window          |  1954 |
|   2 | To Catch A Thief     |  1955 |
|   3 | The Maltese Falcon   |  1941 |
|   4 | The Birds            |  1963 |
|   5 | North By Northwest   |  1959 |
|   6 | Casablanca           |  1942 |
|   7 | Anatomy Of A Murder  |  1959 |
+-----+----------------------+-------+
7 rows in set (0.00 sec)
```

Retrieving Specific Columns

The asterisk (*) in the previous example indicates that you'd like the output of SELECT to contain all the columns present in the table. If, instead, you'd prefer to see one or two specific columns only in the result set, you can specify the column name(s) in the SELECT statement, like this:

```
mysql> SELECT mtitle FROM movies;
+---------------------+
| mtitle              |
+---------------------+
| Rear Window         |
| To Catch A Thief    |
| The Maltese Falcon  |
| The Birds           |
| North By Northwest  |
| Casablanca          |
| Anatomy Of A Murder |
+---------------------+
7 rows in set (0.00 sec)
```

Filtering Records with a WHERE Clause

You can also restrict which records appear in the result set, by adding a WHERE clause to your SELECT statement. This WHERE clause lets you define specific criteria used to filter records from the result set. Records that do not meet the specified criteria will not appear in the result set.

10

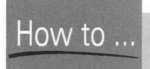

Refer to Fields Clearly

When dealing with multiple tables, a good idea is to prefix the field name with the table name so it is immediately clear which table each field belongs to. This is of particular importance when joining tables to each other through common fields. For example, the query SELECT a.name, b.dob from a,b where a.id = b.id makes it clear that the name field belongs to table a and the dob field belongs to table b. See the section entitled "Joining Tables" to see many more examples of this in practice.

For example, suppose you want to find out which year *Casablanca* was released:

```
mysql> SELECT myear FROM movies WHERE mtitle = 'Casablanca';
+-------+
| myear |
+-------+
|  1942 |
+-------+
1 row in set (0.11 sec)
```

Using Operators

The = symbol previously used is an equality operator, used to test whether the left side of the expression is equal to the right side. MySQL comes with numerous such operators that can be used in the WHERE clause for comparisons and calculations. Table 10-1 lists the important operators in MySQL, by category.

Here is an example of using a comparison operator in the WHERE clause, to list all movies released after 1950:

```
mysql> SELECT myear, mtitle FROM movies WHERE myear > 1950;
+-------+--------------------+
| myear | mtitle             |
+-------+--------------------+
```

```
|  1954 | Rear Window        |
|  1955 | To Catch A Thief   |
|  1963 | The Birds          |
|  1959 | North By Northwest |
|  1959 | Anatomy Of A Murder |
+-------+--------------------+
5 rows in set (0.00 sec)
```

Operator	What It Does
Arithmetic operators	
+	Addition
–	Subtraction
*	Multiplication
/	Division; returns quotient
%	Division; returns modulus
Comparison operators	
=	Equal to
<> aka !=	Not equal to
<=>	NULL-safe equal to
<	Less than
<=	Less than or equal to
>	Greater than
>=	Greater than or equal to
BETWEEN	Exists in specified range
IN	Exists in specified set
IS NULL	Is a NULL value
IS NOT NULL	Is not a NULL value
LIKE	Wildcard match
REGEXP aka RLIKE	Regular expression match
Logical operators	
NOT aka !	Logical NOT
AND aka &&	Logical AND
OR aka ||	Logical OR
XOR	Exclusive OR

TABLE 10-1 MySQL Operators

You can combine multiple conditions by using the AND or OR logical operators. This next example lists all movies released between 1955 and 1965:

```
mysql> SELECT mtitle FROM movies WHERE myear >= 1955 AND myear <= 1965;
+---------------------+
| mtitle              |
+---------------------+
| To Catch A Thief    |
| The Birds           |
| North By Northwest  |
| Anatomy Of A Murder |
+---------------------+
4 rows in set (0.06 sec)
```

Another way to perform this comparison is with the BETWEEN operator:

```
mysql> SELECT mtitle FROM movies WHERE myear BETWEEN 1955 AND 1965;
+---------------------+
| mtitle              |
+---------------------+
| To Catch A Thief    |
| The Birds           |
| North By Northwest  |
| Anatomy Of A Murder |
+---------------------+
4 rows in set (0.06 sec)
```

The LIKE operator can be used to perform queries using wildcards, and comes in handy when you're not sure what you're looking for. Two types of wildcards are allowed when using the LIKE operator: the % wildcard, which is used to signify zero or more occurrences of a character, and the _ wildcard, which is used to signify exactly one occurrence of a character.

This next example uses the LIKE operator with the logical OR operator to list all movie titles containing the letters *m* or *n*:

```
mysql> SELECT mtitle FROM movies WHERE mtitle LIKE '%m%' ↵
OR mtitle LIKE '%n%';
+---------------------+
| mtitle              |
+---------------------+
| Rear Window         |
```

```
| The Maltese Falcon  |
| North By Northwest  |
| Casablanca          |
| Anatomy Of A Murder |
+---------------------+
5 rows in set (0.06 sec)
```

Sorting Records and Eliminating Duplicates

If you'd like to see the data from your table ordered by a specific field, SQL offers the ORDER BY clause. This clause enables you to specify both the column name and the direction in which you would like to see data (ASCending or DESCending).

Here is an example of sorting the persons table by name, in ascending order:

```
mysql> SELECT * FROM persons ORDER BY pname ASC;
+-----+---------------------+------+------------+
| pid | pname               | psex | pdob       |
+-----+---------------------+------+------------+
|   1 | Alfred Hitchcock    | M    | 1899-08-13 |
|   2 | Cary Grant          | M    | 1904-01-18 |
|   3 | Grace Kelly         | F    | 1929-11-12 |
|   4 | Humphrey Bogart     | M    | 1899-12-25 |
|   6 | James Stewart       | M    | 1908-05-20 |
|   5 | Sydney Greenstreet  | M    | 1879-12-27 |
+-----+---------------------+------+------------+
6 rows in set (0.00 sec)
```

And here is the same table sorted by date of birth, in descending order:

```
mysql> SELECT * FROM persons ORDER BY pdob DESC;
+-----+---------------------+------+------------+
| pid | pname               | psex | pdob       |
+-----+---------------------+------+------------+
|   3 | Grace Kelly         | F    | 1929-11-12 |
|   6 | James Stewart       | M    | 1908-05-20 |
|   2 | Cary Grant          | M    | 1904-01-18 |
|   4 | Humphrey Bogart     | M    | 1899-12-25 |
|   1 | Alfred Hitchcock    | M    | 1899-08-13 |
|   5 | Sydney Greenstreet  | M    | 1879-12-27 |
+-----+---------------------+------+------------+
6 rows in set (0.00 sec)
```

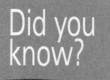

Need for Speed

MySQL 4.0 includes a query cache, which can substantially improve performance by caching the results of common queries and returning this cached data to the caller without having to reexecute the query each time.

To eliminate duplicate records in a table, add the DISTINCT keyword. Consider the following example, which illustrates the use of this keyword by printing a list of all the unique year values in the movies table:

```
mysql> SELECT DISTINCT myear FROM movies;
+--------+
| myear |
+--------+
|  1954 |
|  1955 |
|  1941 |
|  1963 |
|  1959 |
|  1942 |
+--------+
6 rows in set (0.06 sec)
```

Limiting Results

You can limit the number of records returned by MySQL with the LIMIT clause, as illustrated in the following:

```
mysql> SELECT mtitle FROM movies LIMIT 0,4;
+---------------------+
| mtitle              |
+---------------------+
| Rear Window         |
| To Catch A Thief    |
| The Maltese Falcon  |
| The Birds           |
+---------------------+
4 rows in set (0.00 sec)
```

You can even combine the ORDER BY and LIMIT clauses to return a sorted list restricted to a certain number of values. The following example illustrates, by listing the three oldest people (as per their birth dates) in the persons table:

```
mysql> SELECT pname FROM persons ORDER BY pdob LIMIT 0,3;
+--------------------+
| pname              |
+--------------------+
| Sydney Greenstreet |
| Alfred Hitchcock   |
| Humphrey Bogart    |
+--------------------+
3 rows in set (0.00 sec)
```

Using Built-In Functions

MySQL comes with over 100 built-in functions to help you perform calculations and process the records in a result set. These functions can be used in a SELECT statement, either to manipulate field values or in the WHERE clause. The following example illustrates, by using MySQL's COUNT() function to return the total number of records in the movies table:

```
mysql> SELECT COUNT(*) FROM movies;
+----------+
| COUNT(*) |
+----------+
|        7 |
+----------+
1 row in set (0.00 sec)
```

You can calculate string length with the LENGTH() function, as in the following:

```
mysql> SELECT pname, LENGTH(pname) FROM persons;
+--------------------+---------------+
| pname              | LENGTH(pname) |
+--------------------+---------------+
| Alfred Hitchcock   |            16 |
| Cary Grant         |            10 |
| Grace Kelly        |            11 |
| Humphrey Bogart    |            15 |
| Sydney Greenstreet |            18 |
| James Stewart      |            13 |
+--------------------+---------------+
6 rows in set (0.00 sec)
```

10

You can use the DATE() function to format date and time values into a human-readable form, as illustrated in the following:

```
mysql> SELECT pname, DATE_FORMAT(pdob, '%W %d %M %Y') FROM persons;
+--------------------+----------------------------------+
| pname              | DATE_FORMAT(pdob, '%W %d %M %Y')  |
+--------------------+----------------------------------+
| Alfred Hitchcock   | Sunday 13 August 1899            |
| Cary Grant         | Monday 18 January 1904          |
| Grace Kelly        | Tuesday 12 November 1929        |
| Humphrey Bogart    | Monday 25 December 1899         |
| Sydney Greenstreet | Saturday 27 December 1879       |
| James Stewart      | Wednesday 20 May 1908           |
+--------------------+----------------------------------+
6 rows in set (0.00 sec)
```

You can even use functions in the WHERE clause of a SELECT statement. The following example illustrates, by listing all those people who would be more than 100 years old today if they were still alive:

```
mysql> SELECT pname FROM persons WHERE YEAR(NOW()) - YEAR(pdob) > 100;
+--------------------+
| pname              |
+--------------------+
| Alfred Hitchcock   |
| Humphrey Bogart    |
| Sydney Greenstreet |
+--------------------+
3 rows in set (0.06 sec)
```

Grouping Records

You can group records on the basis of a specific field with MySQL's GROUP BY clause. Each group created in this manner is treated as a single row, even though it internally contains multiple records. Consider the following example, which groups the records in the persons table on the basis of their sex:

```
mysql> SELECT * FROM persons GROUP BY psex;
+-----+-------------------+------+------------+
| pid | pname             | psex | pdob       |
```

```
+-----+-----------------+------+------------+
|   1 | Alfred Hitchcock | M    | 1899-08-13 |
|   3 | Grace Kelly      | F    | 1929-11-12 |
+-----+-----------------+------+------------+
2 rows in set (0.00 sec)
```

A number of specialized functions are available when grouping records in this manner. The most commonly used one in this context is the COUNT() function, which you saw earlier. In the context of a GROUP BY clause, this function can be used to count the number of records in each group. The following example illustrates by counting the number of males and females in the persons table:

```
mysql> SELECT psex, COUNT(psex) FROM persons GROUP BY psex;
+------+-------------+
| psex | COUNT(psex) |
+------+-------------+
| M    |           5 |
| F    |           1 |
+------+-------------+
2 rows in set (0.00 sec)
```

Here's another example, this one returning the number of persons linked to each movie in the roles table:

```
mysql> SELECT mid, COUNT(pid) FROM roles GROUP BY mid;
+-----+------------+
| mid | COUNT(pid) |
+-----+------------+
|   1 |          3 |
|   2 |          3 |
|   3 |          2 |
|   4 |          1 |
|   5 |          2 |
|   6 |          1 |
+-----+------------+
6 rows in set (0.06 sec)
```

You can further filter the groups by adding a HAVING clause to the GROUP BY clause. This HAVING clause works much like a regular WHERE clause, letting you further filter the grouped data by a specific condition. The following example revises the previous one to only return those movies having two or more persons linked to them:

```
mysql> SELECT mid, COUNT(pid) FROM roles GROUP BY mid ↵
HAVING COUNT(pid) >= 2;
+------+------------+
| mid  | COUNT(pid) |
+------+------------+
|    1 |          3 |
|    2 |          3 |
|    3 |          2 |
|    5 |          2 |
+------+------------+
4 rows in set (0.00 sec)
```

Joining Tables

So far, all the queries you've seen have been concentrated on a single table. But SQL also enables you to query two or more tables at a time, and to display a combined result set. This is technically referred to as a *join,* because it involves "joining" different tables at specific points to create new views of the data. MySQL has supported joins well right from its inception, and today boasts support for standard SQL2-compliant join syntax, which makes it possible to combine table records in a variety of sophisticated ways.

When using a join, the recommendation is that you prefix each field name with the name of the table it belongs to. For example, you would use `movies.mid` to refer to the field named `mid` in the table `movies`, and `roles.pid` to refer to the `pid` field in the roles table.

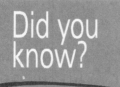

Playing the Numbers

In addition to the COUNT() function, MySQL also offers the MIN() and MAX() functions to retrieve the minimum and maximum of a group, the AVG() function to return the average of a group of values, and the SUM() function to return the total of a group of values.

Inner Joins

Here's an example of a simple join:

```
mysql> SELECT * FROM movies, roles WHERE movies.mid = roles.mid;
+------+---------------------+--------+------+------+------+
| mid  | mtitle              | myear  | mid  | pid  | role |
+------+---------------------+--------+------+------+------+
|    1 | Rear Window         |  1954  |   1  |   1  | D    |
|    1 | Rear Window         |  1954  |   1  |   3  | A    |
|    1 | Rear Window         |  1954  |   1  |   6  | A    |
|    2 | To Catch A Thief    |  1955  |   2  |   1  | D    |
|    2 | To Catch A Thief    |  1955  |   2  |   2  | A    |
|    2 | To Catch A Thief    |  1955  |   2  |   3  | A    |
|    3 | Maltese Falcon, The |  1941  |   3  |   4  | A    |
|    3 | Maltese Falcon, The |  1941  |   3  |   5  | A    |
|    4 | The Birds           |  1963  |   4  |   1  | D    |
|    5 | North By Northwest  |  1959  |   5  |   1  | D    |
|    5 | North By Northwest  |  1959  |   5  |   2  | A    |
|    6 | Casablanca          |  1942  |   6  |   4  | A    |
+------+---------------------+--------+------+------+------+
12 rows in set (0.00 sec)
```

In this case, the `movies` and `roles` tables have been joined together through the common field `mid`. Such a join is referred to as an *inner join,* because its result set contains only those records that match in all the tables in the join. Records that do not match are excluded from the final result set.

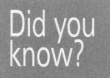

The Inner Circle

Inner joins are the most common type of join you'll see in this book (and in your PHP-MySQL development). Specifically, the previous join is known as an *equijoin,* because it attempts to equate records in one table with records in another. You can also create inner joins using inequalities between fields in different tables. In this case, the final result set will only include those rows from the joined tables that have matches in the specified fields.

10

You can also use INNER JOIN syntax to make things clearer. This next example, which is equivalent to the previous one, illustrates.

```
mysql> SELECT * FROM movies INNER JOIN roles USING (mid);
+-----+---------------------+--------+-----+-----+------+
| mid | mtitle              | myear  | mid | pid | role |
+-----+---------------------+--------+-----+-----+------+
|   1 | Rear Window         | 1954   |   1 |   1 | D    |
|   1 | Rear Window         | 1954   |   1 |   3 | A    |
|   1 | Rear Window         | 1954   |   1 |   6 | A    |
|   2 | To Catch A Thief    | 1955   |   2 |   1 | D    |
|   2 | To Catch A Thief    | 1955   |   2 |   2 | A    |
|   2 | To Catch A Thief    | 1955   |   2 |   3 | A    |
|   3 | Maltese Falcon, The | 1941   |   3 |   4 | A    |
|   3 | Maltese Falcon, The | 1941   |   3 |   5 | A    |
|   4 | The Birds           | 1963   |   4 |   1 | D    |
|   5 | North By Northwest  | 1959   |   5 |   1 | D    |
|   5 | North By Northwest  | 1959   |   5 |   2 | A    |
|   6 | Casablanca          | 1942   |   6 |   4 | A    |
+-----+---------------------+--------+-----+-----+------+
12 rows in set (0.00 sec)
```

You can join as many tables as you like in this manner. This next example adds the persons table to the previous join, and it also selects the rows and columns to be displayed in the output of the join by specifying them in the SELECT statement:

```
mysql> SELECT movies.mtitle, persons.pname, roles.role ⏎
FROM movies, persons, roles WHERE movies.mid = roles.mid ⏎
AND persons.pid = roles.pid;
+---------------------+---------------------+------+
| mtitle              | pname               | role |
+---------------------+---------------------+------+
| Rear Window         | Alfred Hitchcock    | D    |
| Rear Window         | Grace Kelly         | A    |
| Rear Window         | James Stewart       | A    |
| To Catch A Thief    | Alfred Hitchcock    | D    |
| To Catch A Thief    | Cary Grant          | A    |
| To Catch A Thief    | Grace Kelly         | A    |
| Maltese Falcon, The | Humphrey Bogart     | A    |
| Maltese Falcon, The | Sydney Greenstreet  | A    |
```

```
| The Birds          | Alfred Hitchcock   | D    |
| North By Northwest | Alfred Hitchcock   | D    |
| North By Northwest | Cary Grant         | A    |
| Casablanca         | Humphrey Bogart    | A    |
+--------------------+--------------------+------+
12 rows in set (0.00 sec)
```

Obviously, you can add more WHERE clauses to this join to further filter the result set. For example, this next query prints a list of all those movies directed by Alfred Hitchcock:

```
mysql> SELECT movies.mtitle, persons.pname, roles.role ⏎
FROM movies, persons, roles WHERE movies.mid = roles.mid ⏎
AND persons.pid = roles.pid AND roles.role = 'D' ⏎
AND persons.pname = 'Alfred Hitchcock';
+--------------------+------------------+------+
| mtitle             | pname            | role |
+--------------------+------------------+------+
| Rear Window        | Alfred Hitchcock | D    |
| To Catch A Thief   | Alfred Hitchcock | D    |
| The Birds          | Alfred Hitchcock | D    |
| North By Northwest | Alfred Hitchcock | D    |
+--------------------+------------------+------+
4 rows in set (0.06 sec)
```

Outer Joins

MySQL also supports *outer joins,* which are asymmetrical-all records from one side of the join are included in the final result set, regardless of whether they match

Joining Up

Inner and outer joins are not the only types of joins supported in MySQL. You can also use a *cross join* to multiply the contents of both tables together; a *self join* to join a table to a new, virtual copy of itself; and a *union* to join together the results of two SELECT queries. To read more about these types of joins and view examples, look in the online MySQL manual, at **http://dev.mysql .com/doc/mysql/en/JOIN.html**.

records on the other side of the join. Consider the following example, which illustrates by using a *left outer join* to connect the movies table to the roles table:

```
mysql> SELECT * FROM movies LEFT JOIN roles ⏎
ON movies.mid = roles.mid;
+-----+--------------------+-------+------+------+------+
| mid | mtitle             | myear | mid  | pid  | role |
+-----+--------------------+-------+------+------+------+
|   1 | Rear Window        | 1954  |    1 |    1 | D    |
|   1 | Rear Window        | 1954  |    1 |    3 | A    |
|   1 | Rear Window        | 1954  |    1 |    6 | A    |
|   2 | To Catch A Thief   | 1955  |    2 |    1 | D    |
|   2 | To Catch A Thief   | 1955  |    2 |    2 | A    |
|   2 | To Catch A Thief   | 1955  |    2 |    3 | A    |
|   3 | Maltese Falcon, The| 1941  |    3 |    4 | A    |
|   3 | Maltese Falcon, The| 1941  |    3 |    5 | A    |
|   4 | The Birds          | 1963  |    4 |    1 | D    |
|   5 | North By Northwest | 1959  |    5 |    1 | D    |
|   5 | North By Northwest | 1959  |    5 |    2 | A    |
|   6 | Casablanca         | 1942  |    6 |    4 | A    |
|   7 | Vertigo            | 1958  | NULL | NULL | NULL |
+-----+--------------------+-------+------+------+------+
13 rows in set (0.06 sec)
```

As you can see, all the rows from the table on the left side of the join appear in the final result set. Those that have a corresponding value in the table on the right side as per the match condition have that value displayed; the rest have a NULL value displayed.

This kind of join comes in handy when you need to see which values from one table are missing in another table-all you need to do is look for the NULL rows. From a quick glance at the previous example, you can see that entries for all the movies in the movies table exist in the roles table, except for the movie *Vertigo*. Thus, outer joins come in handy when you're looking for corrupted, or "dirty," data in interrelated tables.

> **TIP**   *Use the IS NULL operator to automatically isolate NULL rows in a left or right join.*

Just as there is a left outer join, there also exists a *right outer join,* which works in reverse. A right outer join displays all the records from the table on the right side of the join, and then tries to match them with records from the table on the left side of the join.

Using Subqueries

Subqueries, as the name suggests, are queries nested inside other queries. They make it possible to use the results of one query directly in the conditional tests or FROM clauses of other queries. Subqueries can substantially simplify the task of writing SQL-based applications, by reducing the number of application-level query statements to be executed in a given program.

Subqueries come in many shapes, sizes, and forms. The most common is a SELECT within a SELECT, such that the results of the inner SELECT serve as values for the WHERE clause of the outer SELECT. However, while this is certainly one of the most common uses of subqueries, it's not the only one. You can use subqueries in a number of other places, including within grouped result sets, with comparison and logical operators, with membership tests, in UPDATE and DELETE operations, and within a query's FROM clause.

 Subqueries are new to MySQL, so they are only available in MySQL 4.1 and above.

10

To see how a subquery works, try out the following example, which prints a list of all those movie IDs starring Cary Grant:

```
mysql> SELECT mid FROM roles WHERE role = 'A' ↵
AND pid = (SELECT pid FROM persons WHERE pname = 'Cary Grant');
+-----+
| mid |
+-----+
|   2 |
|   5 |
+-----+
2 rows in set (0.00 sec)
```

Here, the inner query is executed first, and returns the ID of the record for "Cary Grant" from the persons table. This ID (#1) is then substituted in the outer query's WHERE clause, and the query is executed on the roles table to list all those movies in which he performed.

However, this is still incomplete-the previous double query only returns a list of movie IDs, not titles. For this to be truly valuable, you need the movie titles. So, wrap the previous combination in yet another query, which takes the list of IDs generated and matches them against the `movies` table to return the corresponding titles:

```
mysql> SELECT mtitle FROM movies WHERE mid IN ↵
(SELECT mid FROM roles WHERE role = 'A' AND pid = ↵
(SELECT pid FROM persons WHERE pname = 'Cary Grant'));
+--------------------+
| mtitle             |
+--------------------+
| To Catch A Thief   |
| North By Northwest |
+--------------------+
2 rows in set (0.06 sec)
```

Thus, a subquery makes it possible to combine two or more queries into a single statement, and to use the results of one query in the conditional clause of the other. Subqueries are usually regular `SELECT` statements, separated from their parent query by parentheses. As the previous example illustrates, you can nest subqueries to any depth, as long as the basic rules are followed.

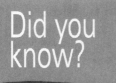

You Say Tom-Ah-To, I Say Tom-Ay-To...

Most of the time, subqueries can be rewritten as joins, and vice versa. For example, the queries `SELECT x FROM a WHERE y = (SELECT y FROM b WHERE condition)` and `SELECT x FROM a, b WHERE a.y = b.y AND condition` are equivalent. However, because subquery support in MySQL is still experimental, joins currently offer better performance than subqueries. Read more at **http://dev.mysql.com/doc/mysql/en/Subqueries.html**.

Using Table and Column Aliases

For table and field names that are either too long to comfortably use or too complex to read, use the AS keyword to alias the name to a different value. The following example demonstrates, by aliasing the name of the persons table to p and the psex, pname, and pdob fields to Sex, realName, and DateOfBirth:

```
mysql> SELECT p.psex AS Sex, p.pname AS RealName, ⏎
p.pdob AS DateOfBirth FROM persons AS p;
+-----+--------------------+-------------+
| Sex | RealName           | DateOfBirth |
+-----+--------------------+-------------+
|  M  | Alfred Hitchcock   | 1899-08-13  |
|  M  | Cary Grant         | 1904-01-18  |
|  F  | Grace Kelly        | 1929-11-12  |
|  M  | Humphrey Bogart    | 1899-12-25  |
|  M  | Sydney Greenstreet | 1879-12-27  |
|  M  | James Stewart      | 1908-05-20  |
+-----+--------------------+-------------+
6 rows in set (0.00 sec)
```

This also works on fields that are the result of a calculation or function operation. The following examples demonstrate this:

```
mysql> SELECT COUNT(*) AS total FROM movies;
+-------+
| total |
+-------+
|     7 |
+-------+
1 row in set (0.00 sec)
mysql> SELECT pname AS name, YEAR(NOW()) - YEAR (pdob) AS age ⏎
FROM persons ORDER BY age;
+--------------------+------+
| name               | age  |
+--------------------+------+
| Grace Kelly        |   75 |
| James Stewart      |   96 |
| Cary Grant         |  100 |
| Alfred Hitchcock   |  105 |
```

10

```
| Humphrey Bogart    |  105 |
| Sydney Greenstreet |  125 |
+--------------------+------+
6 rows in set (0.05 sec)
```

For many more examples of building sophisticated SELECT queries, visit Chapter 12.

Summary

This chapter took a big step forward in your MySQL education, showing you how to add, update, and remove data from a MySQL table, so you can begin using MySQL to store information. It also showed you how to do something with all that data once you have it safely inserted into one or more tables, by giving you a crash course in the SELECT statement and its numerous variants. The SELECT statement is one of the most versatile and useful commands in the SQL lexicon. You'll be using it frequently when you build PHP-MySQL applications.

While this chapter covered a fair bit of ground, it still barely scratched the surface of what you can do with MySQL. For more in-depth information about the topics in this chapter, you should visit the following links:

- The INSERT statement, at **http://dev.mysql.com/doc/mysql/en/ INSERT.html**

- The UPDATE statement, at **http://dev.mysql.com/doc/mysql/en/ UPDATE.html**

- The DELETE statement, at **http://dev.mysql.com/doc/mysql/en/ DELETE.html**

- More examples of using the SELECT statement in the MySQL manual, at **http://dev.mysql.com/doc/mysql/en/SELECT.html**

- MySQL operators, at **http://dev.mysql.com/doc/mysql/en/Non-typed_ Operators.html**

- Built-in MySQL functions, at **http://dev.mysql.com/doc/mysql/en/ Functions.html**

- Date and time functions in MySQL, at **http://www.melonfire.com/ community/columns/trog/article.php?id=241**

- String functions in MySQL, at **http://www.melonfire.com/community/ columns/trog/article.php?id=235**

- Group manipulation functions in MySQL, at **http://dev.mysql.com/doc/ mysql/en/Group_by_functions_and_modifiers.html**

- Joining tables, at **http://www.melonfire.com/community/columns/trog/ article.php?id=148**

- Using subqueries, at **http://www.melonfire.com/community/columns/ trog/article.php?id=204**

10

Chapter 11

Using the MySQL Security System

In previous chapters, you have been using the MySQL superuser account, `root`, to execute queries and run commands. While this is convenient, it goes contrary to one of the basic laws of multiuser system security: never use a privileged user account to perform tasks that can be performed as well with a nonprivileged account. Using a privileged account carelessly for your MySQL applications opens a security hole, and can also produce inconsistent results if your application is ever forced to run as a nonprivileged user (who has fewer capabilities and may, therefore, be unable to perform critical actions).

For this reason, it's important to understand the basics of the MySQL security subsystem, and to use it to enforce access control rules on your databases. A careful application of MySQL's privilege levels and authentication schemes can go a long way toward protecting the integrity of your data, and in ensuring that your applications work securely and consistently.

How to...

- Control access to MySQL on the basis of username and host
- Set (and reset) user passwords
- Grant and revoke user privileges to databases and tables
- Restrict the SQL commands a user is permitted to call on
- View the privileges assigned to a specific user
- Gain access to MySQL even if you lose or forget the root account password

Understanding the Need for Access Control

As you saw in previous chapters, you can only connect to the MySQL server through the MySQL client after sending the server a valid username and password. This username-password combination is used by MySQL to check which databases and tables you have access to, and which types of operations you are permitted to perform on them.

For convenience, previous chapters have directed you to use the MySQL superuser account, `root`, to execute queries and run commands. While this is acceptable for testing purposes, it cannot continue in production applications, for two reasons:

■ Allowing different applications superuser access to MySQL opens a serious security hole in your RDBMS, as it makes the sensitive data of one application visible to other applications and users. This lets an application or user concerned with one database make changes to other databases on the system, and thereby interfere with the security and reliability of other applications. In the worst-case scenario, a single badly written application could destroy the databases and tables of other applications sharing the same RDBMS.

■ Because all commands are routed through a single user account, it's extremely difficult to audit and log the applications of individual users or applications, because MySQL has no way of knowing which "real" person performed which command. For obvious reasons, this is a security no-no.

Given these reasons, it is preferable for every MySQL application you create to have a database of its own, to which it has complete access and that other applications cannot enter. By creating such database "bubbles" for each application, you can rest confident in the knowledge that applications are solely responsible for their own database and cannot interfere with each other. This improves security and database integrity, reduces the risk of a single application running amok, and—because each application now corresponds to a MySQL user—also makes it possible to create an audit trail for each application.

A good rule of thumb in this context is, "Grant no more permissions than are necessary for the requirements of each application." By being parsimonious with application permissions and giving each application only the minimum necessary privileges, you reduce the risk of a security breach in a single application affecting your entire MySQL installation. Spend some time thinking about exactly what actions your application needs to perform and assign privileges appropriately. The investment in time and thought will pay rich dividends in terms of a more robust and hack-proof MySQL server.

Understanding How MySQL Access Control Works

MySQL comes with a sophisticated access control and privilege system to prevent unauthorized users from accessing the system. This system, implemented as a five-tiered privilege hierarchy, enables MySQL administrators to protect access to sensitive data using a combination of user- and host-based authentication schemes. Users can be restricted to performing operations only on specified databases or fields, and MySQL even makes it possible to control which types of queries a user can run, at database, table, or field level.

All these privileges are controlled through MySQL's security subsystem which consists of five tables. These tables, known as *grant tables,* offer database administrators a great deal of power and flexibility in deciding the rules that govern access to the system. Each table has a different role to play in deciding whether a user has access to a specific database, table, or table column. Access rules may be set up on the basis of username, connecting host, or database requested.

In MySQL, access control takes place in two stages:

1. When a user requests a connection to the database server from a specific host, MySQL will first check whether there is an entry for the user in the grant tables, if the user's password is correct, and if the user is allowed to connect from that specific host. If the check is successful, a connection will be allowed to the server.

2. Once a connection is allowed, every subsequent request to the server—SELECT, DELETE, UPDATE, and other queries—will first be vetted to ensure that the user has the security privileges necessary to perform the corresponding action. A number of different levels of access are possible—some users may only have the ability to SELECT from the tables, while others may have INSERT and UPDATE capabilities, but not DELETE capabilities.

Normally, the MySQL superuser assigns rights and privileges to other users with the GRANT and REVOKE commands. These commands are the primary interface to the grant tables, and they should be used instead of manually modifying the tables through INSERT or UPDATE commands.

Assigning, Revoking, and Viewing User Privileges

MySQL users can be assigned any of almost 25 different privileges. Table 11-1 lists the important ones.

For a complete list of privilege levels and examples of how they may be assigned, visit the MySQL manual, at **http://dev.mysql.com/doc/mysql/en/ Privileges_provided.html**.

These privilege levels can be assigned to users with the special GRANT command. To see how the GRANT command works, use the following command to assign SELECT, INSERT, UPDATE, and DELETE privileges on the table db2.movies to the user joe connecting from localhost with password rosebud:

Privilege	What It Permits
ALTER	Altering tables after they have been created
DELETE	Deleting records from tables
INSERT	Inserting records into tables
SELECT	Retrieving records from tables
UPDATE	Updating records in tables
CREATE	Creating new tables and databases
DROP	Deleting tables and databases
GRANT	Granting other users privileges
PROCESS	Viewing MySQL process information
SHUTDOWN	Shutting down the MySQL server
USAGE	Using the MySQL server

TABLE 11-1   Important MySQL Privilege Levels

```
mysql> GRANT SELECT, INSERT, UPDATE, DELETE ON db2.movies ↵
TO joe@localhost IDENTIFIED BY 'rosebud';
Query OK, 0 rows affected (1.32 sec)
```

Now, once the user logs in, only the commands specified in the GRANT command are permitted to the user. All other commands are denied. Every time the user requests a specific command, MySQL refers to its grant tables and only permits the command to be executed if the privilege rules allow it.

To see how this works, try logging in to the server with the username joe and password rosebud, and performing different commands:

```
$ mysql -u joe -p
Password: *******
mysql> SELECT * FROM db2.movies;
+-----+---------------------+-------+
| mid | mtitle              | myear |
+-----+---------------------+-------+
|   1 | Rear Window         |  1954 |
|   2 | To Catch A Thief    |  1955 |
|   3 | Maltese Falcon, The |  1941 |
|   4 | The Birds           |  1963 |
|   5 | North By Northwest  |  1959 |
|   6 | Casablanca          |  1942 |
|   7 | Vertigo             |  1958 |
+-----+---------------------+-------+
```

```
7 rows in set (0.11 sec)
mysql> ALTER TABLE db2.movies DROP PRIMARY KEY;
ERROR 1142: alter command denied to user: 'joe@127.0.0.1' ↵
for table 'movies'
```

Thus, only commands specified in the GRANT statement are permitted to the user.

The following command enables the user admin connecting from localhost to perform SELECT queries on the db table in the mysql database.

```
mysql> GRANT SELECT ON mysql.db TO admin@localhost IDENTIFIED BY 'secret';
Query OK, 0 rows affected (0.1 sec)
```

If you like, you can even specify which fields the user is allowed to manipulate, by naming them in the GRANT command. Here's an example:

```
mysql> GRANT SELECT (mid, mtitle) ON db2.movies ↵
TO joe@localhost IDENTIFIED BY 'rosebud';
Query OK, 0 rows affected (0.1 sec)
```

You can use the * wildcard to mean "all databases" or "all tables" in the GRANT and REVOKE commands. As an example, consider the following command:

```
mysql> GRANT SELECT ON db2.* TO guest@localhost;
Query OK, 0 rows affected (0.3 sec)
```

This lets the user guest perform SELECT operations on all tables in the db2 database.

To permit access to a user from any machine within a domain, use the % wildcard in the hostname. Consider the following command:

```
mysql> GRANT USAGE ON *.* to 'guest'@'%.goodguys.com'
Query OK, 0 rows affected (0.3 sec)
```

This enables the user guest to access the server from any system in the goodguys.com domain.

The REVOKE command does the reverse of the GRANT command, making it possible to revoke privileges assigned to a user. Consider the following example, which rescinds joe's DELETE and UPDATE rights on the db2.movies table:

```
mysql> REVOKE DELETE, UPDATE ON db2.movies FROM joe@localhost;
Query OK, 0 rows affected (0.05 sec)
```

Now, try logging in as `joe` again and performing a `DELETE`:

```
$ mysql -u joe -p
Password: *******
mysql> DELETE FROM db2.movies WHERE id = 5;
ERROR 1142: delete command denied to user: 'joe@127.0.0.1' ↵
for table 'movies'
```

MySQL also lets you assign all privileges to a user with the shortcut keyword `ALL`. This is illustrated in the next example, which grants all privileges on database `employees` to user `hr` connecting from the `company.com` domain:

```
mysql> GRANT ALL ON employees.* TO hr@'%.company.com' ↵
IDENTIFIED BY 'secret';
Query OK, 0 rows affected (0.06 sec)
```

You can also use the `ALL` keyword in a `REVOKE` command to revoke all of a user's privileges to a database, as in the following example:

```
mysql> REVOKE ALL ON employees.* FROM hr@'%.company.com';
Query OK, 0 rows affected (0.05 sec)
```

To view the privileges assigned to a user, use the `SHOW GRANTS` command with the username and hostname as argument. Here's an example:

```
mysql> SHOW GRANTS FOR joe@localhost;
+------------------------------------------------------------+
| Grants for joe@localhost                                   |
+------------------------------------------------------------+
| GRANT USAGE ON *.* TO 'joe'@'localhost'                  | ↵
IDENTIFIED BY PASSWORD  '2469c1e2080e09ef'                   |
| GRANT SELECT, INSERT ON db2.movies TO 'joe'@'localhost' |
+------------------------------------------------------------+
2 rows in set (0.05 sec)
```

Working with User Accounts and Password

As you already know, a valid MySQL user account is required to connect to the MySQL server. This account may or may not be protected with a password, although using a password is recommended for the security of your MySQL installation. These user accounts and passwords are also controlled through the grant tables, and the following sections discuss how to create and use them.

Lockdown

MySQL 4.1 uses a new, encrypted, and highly secure protocol to handle client-server communication, which makes it harder for hackers to break your password.

Creating and Removing User Accounts

Normally, whenever you issue a GRANT command, MySQL automatically creates an account for the user in its grant tables (if one does not already exist, that is). If the GRANT command includes an IDENTIFIED BY clause, MySQL also encrypts the user password in that clause and stores it in the grant tables. If the IDENTIFIED BY clause is not present, MySQL assigns the account an empty password. Here is an example:

```
mysql> GRANT USAGE ON *.* to john@localhost;
Query OK, 0 rows affected (0.06 sec)
```

However, when a user's privileges are stripped with the REVOKE command, MySQL does not automatically delete the user account. To explicitly remove a user account, it is necessary to manually modify the grant tables with the DELETE command. For example, to remove joe's user account, you would need to run the following commands:

```
mysql> DELETE FROM mysql.user WHERE User = 'john' ↵
AND Host = 'localhost';
Query OK, 1 row affected (0.06 sec)
mysql> FLUSH PRIVILEGES;
Query OK, 0 rows affected (0.28 sec)
```

If you're using MySQL 4.1.1, you can also remove a user with the new DROP USER command. The next command is equivalent to the previous two:

```
mysql> DROP USER john@localhost;
Query OK, 1 row affected (0.06 sec)
```

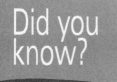

Starting from Zero

The FLUSH PRIVILEGES command forces MySQL to reread the privilege tables.

Altering User Passwords

Users with write access to the MySQL grant tables, such as root, can alter the passwords of other users by using the SET PASSWORD command. The following example sets the password for user joe to guessme:

```
mysql> SET PASSWORD FOR joe@localhost = PASSWORD('guessme');
Query OK, 1 row affected (0.06 sec)
```

Passwords can also be set in the IDENTIFIED BY clause of a GRANT command. Here is an example, which creates an account for user guest connecting from localhost with account password guest:

```
mysql> GRANT USAGE ON *.* to guest@localhost IDENTIFIED BY 'guest';
Query OK, 0 rows affected (0.06 sec)
```

11

Manual Labor

There is a difference between setting a password in the IDENTIFIED BY clause of the GRANT command and with the SET PASSWORD command. In the former case, the password is automatically encrypted by MySQL. In the latter, it must be manually encrypted with the built-in MySQL PASSWORD() function.

When a user logs in to the MySQL server and provides a password string, MySQL first encrypts the provided password string using the PASSWORD() function, and then compares the resulting value with the stored value. If the two values match (and other access rules permit it), the user is granted access. If the values do not match, access is denied.

How to ... Reset the MySQL root Password

If you forget the MySQL root password and are locked out of the system, don't panic—there's still hope! All you need to do is follow the simple steps outlined in the following:

1. Shut down MySQL, and then restart it, using the procedures outlined in Chapter 2 of this book. When restarting MySQL, add the following two options to the mysqld_safe command line:

   ```
   $ /usr/local/mysql/bin/mysqld_safe --skip-grant-tables ↵
   --skip-networking &
   ```

2. Log in to the MySQL server as root using the MySQL client. Because MySQL was started without the grant tables, you can use an empty password to gain access.

   ```
   $ /usr/local/bin/mysql -u root
   ```

3. Once logged in, set a new password for the root account, by directly modifying the grant tables as follows:

   ```
   mysql> UPDATE mysql.user SET ↵
   Password=PASSWORD('new-password') WHERE User='root';
   Query OK, 1 row affected (0.06 sec)
   ```

4. Log out of MySQL, and then shut down and restart the server in the normal manner. You should now be able to log in as the root user, with the new password you set in step 3.

Summary

This chapter focused on MySQL's implementation of the Data Control Language (DCL) component of SQL, teaching you how (and why) to use MySQL's security system to prevent unauthorized access to the server. The examples and commands in this chapter showed you how to create user accounts, set passwords, assign privileges, and create access rules to clearly define what each user can—and cannot—do after logging in to the MySQL server. The chapter also provided a solution to a common MySQL problem: gaining access to the server after forgetting the superuser password.

MySQL's security system is powerful and flexible, but it's only as good as the administrators who implement it. To improve your understanding of the MySQL security system and to learn more about how to secure your system against attacks, consider visiting the following links:

- A detailed discussion of the MySQL grant tables, at **http://www.melonfire .com/community/columns/trog/article.php?id=62**

- Information on MySQL privilege levels, at **http://dev.mysql.com/doc/ mysql/en/Privilege_system.html**

- Information on securing MySQL against network attacks, at **http://dev .mysql.com/doc/mysql/en/Security_against_attack.html**

- General MySQL security guidelines, at **http://dev.mysql.com/doc/mysql/ en/Security_guidelines.html**

- Using encrypted server connections with SSL, at **http://dev.mysql.com/ doc/mysql/en/Secure_connections.html**

- Tips on password security, at **http://dev.mysql.com/doc/mysql/en/ Password_security.html**

11

Chapter 12

Sample Application: Order Tracking System

The examples you've seen thus far have been fairly simple. However, in the real world (and in the rest of this book), you'll see MySQL being used for all manner of sophisticated applications and queries. To prepare you for these more complex uses, the next (and final) example in this chapter uses the techniques and commands taught in previous sections to design and use a slightly larger and more challenging database.

How to...

- Analyze the requirements for a simple order tracking system

- Design and normalize a set of relational tables

- Gain a better understanding of the SELECT statement through a range of sophisticated queries

Understanding Requirements

The application here is an order tracking system for a small business that has multiple customers for its products. It's not hard to think of such a business: the tools and hardware store down the road, the agency that delivers your newspaper, the web-hosting company that hosts your web site, and the stationery store that keeps your office stocked with supplies all fall into this broad category.

Every such business must do a number of basic things:

- It must maintain a list of its customers, with addresses and phone numbers. Some customers may have offices in multiple locations. In this case, branch locations and contact information must also be maintained.

- It must maintain a list of its currently available products, as well as its prices for each. For some products, local and state taxes may be applicable. These must be noted and added to the sale price of each item.

- It must maintain a list of the orders placed by a customer for its products, the date of the order, and the number of items ordered. This order list is used to generate invoices, either on a per transaction basis or, if the customer is a credit customer, at the end of a predefined billing cycle.

- As customers come and go, and as new products are added and older products discontinued, it must be easy to update the system to reflect these changes.

With these requirements in mind, it's time to design a database.

Creating an Optimized Database Design

When designing such a database, it's important to check it for minimal redundancies and repetitions, and for clear and logical relationships between its various entities. This is part of the process called normalization, and to illustrate how it is accomplished, each of the following subsections discuss two competing designs. The first one is an inefficient, nonnormalized design, while the second is an optimized, more compact and more scalable alternative.

Designing the Customer Tables

Let's begin with the customer list. As noted previously, this list must include the customer's name, address, and phone number. For customers with multiple branches, branch details must be included as well.

Here's what a nonnormalized database table might look like:

customerId	customerName	customerAddress	customerTel
1	ABC Inc. - Head Office	24 Wildgreen Street, Los Angeles, CA 84828	(234) 567 0890
2	ABC Inc. - Texas Accounting Branch	17 Boingo Towers, Houston, TX 34738	(567) 891 2345
3	ABC Inc. - HR Section	25A Underten Street, Houston, TX 34768	(567) 892 3456
4	Zee Corp.	76 Dreed Street, Miami, FL 36279	(246) 802 4680

This isn't a very satisfactory design, for two reasons:

- With this table structure, branch offices and customers are treated as though they were synonymous. Because there's no real differentiation between a customer and a customer's facilities, it is not possible to obtain an exact count of the business's customers. Thus, even though the previous table contains four records, in reality there are only two customers: ABC Inc. and Zee Corp. Further, if ABC Inc. alters its name, each record for ABC Inc.'s branches will have to be updated, as the name is repeated in each.

- A single field for addresses means that state and PIN code data is intermingled with street and building names. If the business plans to query on the basis of geographical region—say, to evaluate how many customers it has in each

12

state or to find out which locations should be targeted in advertising—the business will find both extracting state names and pin codes from the previous table, and sorting and comparing the records by region extremely hard.

To rectify these flaws, it is necessary to redesign the previous table to remove redundancies, establish a clear relationship between customers and branch offices, and make it possible to extract location-specific information easily. Here's the revised structure:

customerId	customerName
1	ABC Inc.
2	Zee Corp.

facilityId	FK_cust omerID	facilityName	facilityAddress	facilityCity	facilityState	facilityPinCode	facilityTel
1	1	Head Office	24 Wildgreen Street	Los Angeles	CA	84828	(234) 567 0890
2	1	Texas Accounting Branch	17 Boingo Towers	Houston	TX	34738	(567) 891 2345
3	1	HR Section	25A Underten Street	Houston	TX	34768	(567) 892 3456
4	2	Head Office	76 Dreed Street	Miami	FL	36279	(246) 802 4680

This structure is better, because it is now clear exactly how many customers exist (simply count the records in the `customers` table) and also how many branch offices each customer has. Because customer names appear only once, making a change involves updating only a single record instead of multiple records. Finally, the decomposition of the address into different fields makes it easier to sort and compare data by location.

Designing the Product Tables

Next up is the table that lists available products and services, and their prices. Here's what a nonnormalized table might look like:

productId	productDesc	productUnitPrice	taxType	taxPercent	productPostTaxPrice
1	Power drill	59.99	Sales Tax	10.00	65.98
2	Electric kettle	13.50	Sales Tax	10.00	14.85
3	Lawn mower	45.00	Sales Tax + Excise	15.00	51.75
4	Electronic tape measure	20.00	Sales Tax + Excise + Customs	40.00	28.00

Again, this nonnormalized table throws up several inconsistencies:

■ The numerous repetitions and illogical display of both product prices and tax information in the same table is not recommended. Notice that each record in the previous table contains a VARCHAR field stating either "Sales Tax" (9 characters) or "Sales Tax + Excise" (18 characters), and a field containing the tax percentage (4 bytes). Because these values are frequently repeated, between 13 and 22 bytes of storage are wasted per record. This might not seem like a lot, but imagine a table containing thousands of records, and it adds up to quite a large amount of disk space that's being unnecessarily wasted.

■ Notice also that the table contains hard-wired values for the pre-tax and post-tax prices. This is unwise, because if tax rates change, each value in the post-tax column will need to be recomputed and reentered. Because MySQL supports most arithmetic operations, it makes more sense to have MySQL calculate the post-tax price at run time, by adding the tax percentage to the pre-tax sale price.

■ Finally, the previous table makes no accommodation for the fact that more than one type of tax may be applicable to a particular product. However, in the real world, it's quite possible, for example, for state and local taxes both to be applied to a product, or for both local taxes and cross-border duties to be levied on products transported across borders.

Here is an optimized version of the previous table that rectifies these flaws:

productId	productDesc	productUnitPrice
1	Power drill	59.99
2	Electric kettle	13.50
3	Lawn mower	45.00
4	Electronic tape measure	20.00

taxId	taxType	taxPercent
1	Sales tax	10.00
2	Service tax	8.00
3	Excise	5.00
4	Customs	25.00

FK_productId	FK_taxId
1	1
2	1
3	1
3	3
4	1
4	3
4	4

12

This structure is far superior to the previous one, because it separates tax information from product information. Because the repeated tax values are now represented through foreign key relationships (which use integers instead of text strings), the previous tables save space, and are also more compact and easier to understand. Finally, the establishment of a many-to-many relationship between products and taxes through a third link table makes it possible to apply multiple taxes to a single product, or to have the same tax levied on multiple products.

Designing the Order Table

Now, we finally come to the table that handles customer orders. This table needs to store information on who placed the order, what was ordered, when the order was placed, and how many units were ordered. All this information will be used when generating the customer's invoice. The following table accomplishes all this:

orderId	customerName	productName	orderDate	orderQuantity
1	Zee Corp.	Lawn mower	2003-01-02	10
2	Zee Corp.	Electric kettle	2003-07-06	25
3	ABC Inc. - Texas Accounting Branch	Electric kettle	2003-07-10	5
4	ABC Inc. - HR Section	Lawn mower	2003-08-15	3
5	ABC Inc. - HR Section	Power drill	2003-08-15	5
6	ABC Inc. - Head Office	Lawn mower	2004-03-12	7
7	Zee Corp.	Lawn mower	2003-01-02	12
8	ABC Inc. - HR Section	Power drill	2004-04-22	1
9	ABC Inc. - Texas Accounting Branch	Electric kettle	2004-06-29	20

By now, the flaws should be visible to you. By repeating the customer name and the product name in each record, the table will reduce in value the moment a customer or product name changes, because it will become impossible to reconcile the new customer (or product) name in the customer (or product) tables with the old data in this table. Further, because this table also treats customers and branches as synonymous, it is impossible to calculate the total sales or total outstanding amount per branch or per customer.

What makes more sense is to adopt the normalized approach and create a table that stores only order data, and that links each order to products and customers through foreign keys. This illustration indicates what such a table might look like:

orderId	FK_facilityID	FK_productID	orderDate	orderQuantity
1	4	3	2003-01-02	10
2	4	2	2003-07-06	25
3	2	2	2003-07-10	5
4	3	3	2003-08-15	3
5	3	1	2003-08-15	5
6	1	3	2004-03-12	7
7	4	3	2003-01-02	12
8	3	1	2004-04-22	1
9	2	2	2004-06-29	20

With the tables now optimized, the next step is to assign appropriate data types to each field. If you paid attention to Chapter 9, this should be fairly simple to do, as the tables in this system mostly use the SMALLINT, DECIMAL, and VARCHAR data types.

With the table relationships defined and the data types set, let's look at the final product:

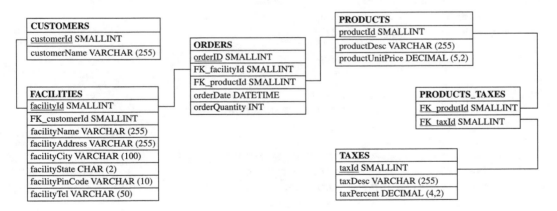

12

Creating and Populating the Tables

Once the database is designed on paper, the next step is to implement it in MySQL. If you have a diagram like the one just shown, this is largely a mechanical process

involving the CREATE TABLE and INSERT statements. The following shows
some sample commands:

```
mysql> CREATE TABLE taxes (
    -> taxId SMALLINT AUTO_INCREMENT NOT NULL,
    -> taxDesc VARCHAR(255) NOT NULL,
    -> taxPercent DECIMAL (4,2) NOT NULL,
    -> PRIMARY KEY (taxId)
    -> );
Query OK, 0 rows affected (0.28 sec)

mysql> CREATE TABLE customers (
    -> customerId SMALLINT AUTO_INCREMENT NOT NULL,
    -> customerName VARCHAR(255) NOT NULL,
    -> PRIMARY KEY (customerId)
    -> );
Query OK, 0 rows affected (0.00 sec)

mysql> CREATE TABLE products (
    -> productId SMALLINT AUTO_INCREMENT NOT NULL,
    -> productDesc VARCHAR(255) NOT NULL,
    -> productUnitPrice DECIMAL (5,2) NOT NULL,
    -> PRIMARY KEY (productId)
    -> );
Query OK, 0 rows affected (0.06 sec)

mysql> CREATE TABLE facilities (
    -> facilityId SMALLINT AUTO_INCREMENT NOT NULL,
    -> FK_customerId SMALLINT NOT NULL,
    -> facilityName VARCHAR(255) NOT NULL,
    -> facilityAddress VARCHAR(255) NOT NULL,
    -> facilityCity VARCHAR(100) NOT NULL,
    -> facilityState CHAR(2) NOT NULL,
    -> facilityPinCode VARCHAR(10) NOT NULL,
    -> facilityTel VARCHAR(50) NOT NULL,
    -> PRIMARY KEY (facilityId),
    -> INDEX (FK_customerId),
    -> INDEX (facilityState)
    -> );
Query OK, 0 rows affected (0.00 sec)

mysql> CREATE TABLE products_taxes (
    -> FK_productId SMALLINT NOT NULL,
```

```
    -> FK_taxId SMALLINT NOT NULL,
    -> PRIMARY KEY (FK_productId, FK_taxId)
    -> );
Query OK, 0 rows affected (0.05 sec)

mysql> CREATE TABLE orders (
    -> orderId SMALLINT AUTO_INCREMENT NOT NULL,
    -> FK_facilityId SMALLINT NOT NULL,
    -> FK_productId SMALLINT NOT NULL,
    -> orderDate DATETIME NOT NULL,
    -> orderQuantity INT NOT NULL,
    -> PRIMARY KEY (orderId),
    -> INDEX (FK_facilityId),
    -> INDEX (FK_productId)
    -> );
Query OK, 0 rows affected (0.05 sec)

mysql> INSERT INTO customers (customerName) ⏎
VALUES ('ABC Inc.'), ('Zee Corp.'), ('PQW Consulting Group'), ⏎
('Big Company plc');
Query OK, 4 rows affected (0.05 sec)

mysql> INSERT INTO facilities (facilityId, FK_customerId, ⏎
facilityName, facilityAddress, facilityCity, facilityState, ⏎
facilityPinCode, facilityTel, facilityStatus) ⏎
VALUES ⏎
(1, 1, 'Head Office', '24 Wildgreen Street', 'Los Angeles', ⏎
'CA', '84828', '234-567-0890', 1), ⏎
(2, 1, 'Texas Accounting Branch', '17 Boingo Towers', 'Houston', ⏎
'TX', '34738', '567-891-2345', 0), ⏎
(3, 1, 'HR Section', '25A Underten Street', 'Houston', 'TX', ⏎
'34768', '567-892-3456', 1), ⏎
(4, 2, 'Head Office', '76 Dreed Street', 'Miami', 'FL', ⏎
'36279', '246-802-4680', 1), ⏎
(5, 4, 'Operations', '45, Ingerstrasse Street', 'Boston', ⏎
'MA', '12389', '658-436-6362', 1), ⏎
(6, 4, 'Accounting', '9 Tigley Court', 'New York', 'NY', ⏎
'84932', '623-234-7299', 1), ⏎
(7, 3, 'Main Office', '12C Empryton Road', 'New York', 'NY', ⏎
'35653', '123-098-7654', 1);
Query OK, 7 rows affected (1.05 sec)
```

12

```
mysql> INSERT INTO taxes (taxDesc, taxPercent) ↵
VALUES ('Sales Tax', 10), ('Service Tax', 8), ↵
('Excise', 5), ('Customs', 25);
Query OK, 4 rows affected (0.06 sec)

mysql> INSERT INTO products (productDesc, productUnitPrice, ↵
productStatus) VALUES ('Power drill', 59.99, 1), ↵
('Electric kettle', 13.50, 1), ('Lawn mower', 45.00, 1), ↵
('Electronic tape measure', 20.00, 1), ('Alarm clock', 9.99, 1), ↵
('Toaster', 29.99, 1);
Query OK, 6 rows affected (0.06 sec)

mysql> INSERT INTO products_taxes (FK_productId, FK_taxId) ↵
VALUES (1,1), (2,1), (3,1), (3,3), (4,1), (4,3), (4,4), (6,1);
Query OK, 8 rows affected (0.06 sec)

mysql> INSERT INTO orders (orderId, FK_facilityId, FK_productId, ↵
orderDate, orderQuantity) VALUES ↵
(1, 4, 3, '2003-01-02 11:17:07', 10), ↵
(2, 4, 2, '2003-07-06 12:18:09', 25), ↵
(3, 2, 2, '2003-07-10 18:45:59', 5), ↵
(4, 3, 3, '2003-08-15 06:30:09', 3), ↵
(5, 3, 1, '2003-08-15 16:17:18', 5), ↵
(6, 1, 3, '2004-03-12 11:23:56', 7), ↵
(7, 4, 3, '2003-01-02 00:00:00', 12), ↵
(8, 3, 1, '2004-04-22 22:13:46', 1), ↵
(9, 2, 2, '2004-06-29 15:27:08', 20), ↵
(10, 5, 4, '2004-06-19 19:10:00', 20), ↵
(11, 7, 4, '2004-06-11 17:39:04', 35), ↵
(12, 7, 3, '2004-05-13 13:12:11', 2), ↵
(13, 1, 2, '2004-02-14 15:32:26', 4);
Query OK, 13 rows affected (0.06 sec)
```

You can download the complete set of queries needed to create this database from this book's web site at **http://www.everythingphpmysql.com/**.

Querying the Database

Once the database and tables are created and populated, it's time to begin doing something with them. This section runs different types of SELECT queries on the tables in an attempt to answer some basic questions.

Begin by finding out which branch offices belong to which customers. Because the `facilities` and `customers` tables are linked by the `customerID` field, a simple join accomplishes this:

```
mysql> SELECT c.customerName, f.facilityName, f.facilityState
    -> FROM customers AS c, facilities AS f
    -> WHERE c.customerId = f.FK_customerId;
+---------------------+-------------------------+----------------+
| customerName        | facilityName            | facilityState  |
+---------------------+-------------------------+----------------+
| ABC Inc.            | Head Office             | CA             |
| ABC Inc.            | Texas Accounting Branch | TX             |
| ABC Inc.            | HR Section              | TX             |
| Zee Corp.           | Head Office             | FL             |
| Big Company plc     | Operations              | MA             |
| Big Company plc     | Accounting              | NY             |
| PQW Consulting Group| Main Office             | NY             |
+---------------------+-------------------------+----------------+
7 rows in set (0.22 sec)
```

What about finding out how many branch offices each customer has? It's simple if you group the records in the `facilities` table together by the customer ID, and then count the total number of records in each group.

```
mysql> SELECT c.customerName, COUNT( c.customerId )  AS totalFacilities
    -> FROM customers AS c, facilities AS f
    -> WHERE c.customerId = f.FK_customerId
    -> GROUP  BY f.FK_customerID;
+---------------------+-----------------+
| customerName        | totalFacilities |
+---------------------+-----------------+
| ABC Inc.            |               3 |
| Zee Corp.           |               1 |
| PQW Consulting Group|               1 |
| Big Company plc     |               2 |
+---------------------+-----------------+
4 rows in set (0.00 sec)
```

Add a `HAVING` clause to get a list of all those customers that have no branches:

```
mysql> SELECT c.customerName
    -> FROM customers AS c, facilities AS f
    -> WHERE c.customerId = f.FK_customerId
```

12

```
    -> GROUP  BY f.FK_customerID
    -> HAVING count(c.customerId) = 1;
+----------------------+
| customerName         |
+----------------------+
| Zee Corp.            |
| PQW Consulting Group |
+----------------------+
2 rows in set (0.00 sec)
```

Take another tack now, and find out which taxes apply to which products, by joining the `products` and `taxes` tables:

```
mysql> SELECT p.productDesc, t.taxDesc
    -> FROM taxes AS t, products AS p, products_taxes AS pt
    -> WHERE t.taxId = pt.FK_taxId AND p.productId = pt.FK_productId;
+------------------------+-----------+
| productDesc            | taxDesc   |
+------------------------+-----------+
| Power drill            | Sales Tax |
| Electric kettle        | Sales Tax |
| Lawn mower             | Sales Tax |
| Lawn mower             | Excise    |
| Electronic tape measure | Sales Tax |
| Electronic tape measure | Excise    |
| Electronic tape measure | Customs   |
| Toaster                | Sales Tax |
+------------------------+-----------+
8 rows in set (0.00 sec)
```

To calculate the price of each item after applying all relevant taxes, run the following query:

```
mysql> SELECT p.productDesc, p.productUnitPrice,
    -> SUM(t.taxPercent) as totalTaxPercent,
    -> p.productUnitPrice + (p.productUnitPrice * SUM(t.taxPercent)/100)
    -> as productPostTaxPrice
    -> FROM taxes AS t, products AS p, products_taxes AS pt
    -> WHERE t.taxId = pt.FK_taxId AND p.productId = pt.FK_productId
    -> GROUP BY p.productId;
+--------------+------------------+-----------------+---------------------+
| productDesc  | productUnitPrice | totalTaxPercent | productPostTaxPrice |
```

```
+---------------+-------------------+-----------------+----------------------+
| Power drill   |           59.99 |           10.00 |              65.9890 |
| Electric      |                 |                 |                      |
  kettle        |           13.50 |           10.00 |              14.8500 |
| Lawn mower    |           45.00 |           15.00 |              51.7500 |
| Electronic    |                 |                 |                      |
  tape measure  |           20.00 |           40.00 |              28.0000 |
| Toaster       |           29.99 |           10.00 |              32.9890 |
+---------------+-------------------+-----------------+----------------------+
5 rows in set (0.11 sec)
```

This might appear complex, but it isn't. The `taxes`, `products`, and `products_taxes` tables are all joined together, and the total tax (in percentage terms) on each product is calculated by first grouping the records together by product, and then calculating the sum of all the tax values. Once the total tax percent on each product is known, calculating the post-tax price of each item is a simple matter.

 This assumes, however, that all taxes are levied on the base price of the product. If taxes are levied in a progressive manner—for example, customs duties are calculated on the price after sales and service taxes have been added—then the previous query will not return the correct result.

To calculate the total sales of a particular item—say, electric kettles—link the `orders` table with the `products` table (and toss in a subquery, to boot):

```
mysql> SELECT SUM(o.orderQuantity) FROM products AS p, orders AS o
    -> WHERE p.productId = o.FK_productId AND o.FK_productID =
    -> (SELECT productId from products
    -> WHERE productDesc = 'Electric kettle');
+----------------------+
| SUM(o.orderQuantity) |
+----------------------+
|                   54 |
+----------------------+
1 row in set (0.00 sec)
```

To find the total sales of each product, revise the previous query to group the records by product, and then calculate the sum of orders for each product:

```
mysql> SELECT p.productDesc, SUM(o.orderQuantity) as totalSales
    -> FROM products AS p, orders AS o
    -> WHERE p.productId = o.FK_productId GROUP BY o.FK_productID;
```

12

```
+--------------------------+------------+
| productDesc              | totalSales |
+--------------------------+------------+
| Power drill              |          6 |
| Electric kettle          |         54 |
| Lawn mower               |         34 |
| Electronic tape measure  |         55 |
+--------------------------+------------+
4 rows in set (0.05 sec)
```

To find the total sales by facility, join the `facilities` and `orders` tables together, and then use the `SUM()` function to obtain the total purchases by each branch office:

```
mysql> SELECT f.facilityId, f.facilityName, SUM( o.orderQuantity )
    -> AS totalSales FROM facilities AS f, orders AS o
    -> WHERE f.facilityId = o.FK_facilityId  GROUP  BY o.FK_facilityId;
+------------+------------------------+------------+
| facilityId | facilityName           | totalSales |
+------------+------------------------+------------+
|          1 | Head Office            |         11 |
|          2 | Texas Accounting Branch |        25 |
|          3 | HR Section             |          9 |
|          4 | Head Office            |         47 |
|          5 | Operations             |         20 |
|          7 | Main Office            |         37 |
+------------+------------------------+------------+
6 rows in set (0.05 sec)
```

This isn't useful by itself because it doesn't tell you which customer each branch belongs to. To display that information as well, pop in another join to the `customers` table:

```
mysql> SELECT c.customerName, f.facilityName, SUM( o.orderQuantity )
    -> AS totalSales FROM facilities AS f, orders AS o, customers AS c
    -> WHERE f.facilityId = o.FK_facilityId
    -> AND c.customerId = f.FK_customerId
    -> GROUP  BY o.FK_facilityId;
+----------------------+------------------------+------------+
| customerName         | facilityName           | totalSales |
+----------------------+------------------------+------------+
| ABC Inc.             | Head Office            |         11 |
```

```
| ABC Inc.              | Texas Accounting Branch |     25 |
| ABC Inc.              | HR Section              |      9 |
| Zee Corp.             | Head Office             |     47 |
| Big Company plc       | Operations              |     20 |
| PQW Consulting Group  | Main Office             |     37 |
+----------------------+-------------------------+--------+
6 rows in set (0.00 sec)
```

An alternative view of this same data would be to analyze the total sales of each item by state. To do this, group the orders by state code instead of branch code:

```
mysql> SELECT f.facilityState, SUM( o.orderQuantity )  AS totalSales
    -> FROM facilities AS f, orders AS o
    -> WHERE f.facilityId = o.FK_facilityId
    -> GROUP  BY f.facilityState;
+---------------+------------+
| facilityState | totalSales |
+---------------+------------+
| CA            |         11 |
| FL            |         47 |
| MA            |         20 |
| NY            |         37 |
| TX            |         34 |
+---------------+------------+
5 rows in set (0.00 sec)
```

To see all orders placed within the last month, join the orders and products tables, and use the DATE_SUB() function to filter results through the correct time window:

```
mysql> SELECT p.productDesc, o.orderQuantity, o.orderDate
    -> FROM products AS p, orders AS o
    -> WHERE p.productId = o.FK_productId AND o.orderDate >
    -> DATE_SUB(NOW(), INTERVAL 1 MONTH);
+------------------------+---------------+---------------------+
| productDesc            | orderQuantity | orderDate           |
+------------------------+---------------+---------------------+
| Electric kettle        |            20 | 2004-06-29 15:27:08 |
| Electronic tape measure |           20 | 2004-06-19 19:10:00 |
| Electronic tape measure |           35 | 2004-06-11 17:39:04 |
+------------------------+---------------+---------------------+
3 rows in set (0.06 sec)
```

12

To find the most popular product (the product with the maximum sales) over the last year, use the following query, which groups and sums the orders by product type, and then returns the product with the maximum number of orders:

```
mysql> SELECT p.productDesc, SUM( o.orderQuantity ) AS totalSales
    -> FROM products AS p, orders AS o
    -> WHERE p.productId = o.FK_productId
    -> AND o.orderDate > DATE_SUB(NOW(), INTERVAL 1 YEAR)
    -> GROUP BY o.FK_productID
    -> ORDER BY totalSales DESC
    -> LIMIT 0 , 1;
+----------------------------+------------+
| productDesc                | totalSales |
+----------------------------+------------+
| Electronic tape measure    |         55 |
+----------------------------+------------+
1 row in set (0.05 sec)
```

To see which products were never purchased in 2004, use a left join between the `products` and `orders` tables:

```
mysql> SELECT products.productDesc
    -> FROM products
    -> LEFT  JOIN orders ON products.productId = orders.FK_productId
    -> AND YEAR( orders.orderDate )  = 2004
    -> WHERE orders.FK_productId IS  NULL ;
+-------------+
| productDesc |
+-------------+
| Alarm clock |
| Toaster     |
+-------------+
2 rows in set (0.00 sec)
```

And now for the big kahuna: Figure 12-1 shows the total purchases made by each facility of each product within the current month, together with the pre-tax and post-tax price, and a subtotal.

```
mysql> SELECT f.facilityName, p.productDesc, o.orderQuantity, p.productUnitPrice as preTaxPrice, SUM(t.taxPercent) as tax-
Percent, (p.productUnitPrice*(1+SUM(t.taxPercent)/100)) as postTaxPrice, (p.productUnitPrice*(1+SUM(t.taxPercent)/100)*o.
orderQuantity) as subTotal FROM facilities as f, products as o, products_taxes as pt, taxes as t WHERE
f.facilityId=o.FK_facilityId AND o.FK_productId=p.productId AND p.productId=pt.FK_productId AND pt.FK_taxId=t.taxId GROUP
BY f.facilityId, p.productId, o.orderId;
```

facilityName	productDesc	orderQuantity	preTaxPrice	taxPercent	postTaxPrice	subTotal
Head Office	Electric kettle	4	13.50	10.00	14.8500	59.4000
Head Office	Lawn mower	7	45.00	15.00	51.7500	362.2500
Texas Accounting Branch	Electric kettle	5	13.50	10.00	14.8500	74.2500
Texas Accounting Branch	Electric kettle	20	13.50	10.00	14.8500	297.0000
HR Section	Power drill	5	59.99	10.00	65.9890	329.9450
HR Section	Power drill	1	59.99	10.00	65.9890	65.9890
HR Section	Lawn mower	3	45.00	15.00	51.7500	155.2500
Head Office	Electric kettle	25	13.50	10.00	14.8500	371.2500
Head Office	Lawn mower	10	45.00	15.00	51.7500	517.5000
Head Office	Lawn mower	12	45.00	15.00	51.7500	621.0000
Operations	Electronic tape measure	20	20.00	40.00	28.0000	560.0000
Main Office	Lawn mower	2	45.00	15.00	51.7500	103.5000
Main Office	Electronic tape measure	35	20.00	40.00	28.0000	980.0000

13 rows in set (0.05 sec)

FIGURE 12-1   Post-tax prices and totals, sorted by product and location

12

Summary

This chapter was designed to demonstrate a practical application of MySQL: creating a simple order tracking system, and then using SQL to obtain answers to common questions from the raw data stored inside it. This application used many of the structures and techniques—normalization, data types, operators, groups, joins, and built-in functions—taught in earlier chapters, and if you were able to follow it all the way through, you now know enough to begin using MySQL on your own.

To improve your knowledge of MySQL's capabilities and also to learn how to design more sophisticated queries, consider visiting the following links:

- Database normalization, at **http://support.microsoft.com/default .aspx?kbid=283878**

- Examples of common queries, at **http://dev.mysql.com/doc/mysql/en/ Examples.html**

- Devshed's MySQL section, at **http://www.devshed.com/c/a/MySQL/**

- Building sophisticated MySQL subqueries, at **http://www.melonfire.com/ community/columns/trog/article.php?id=204**

- Using different types of joins, at **http://www.melonfire.com/community/ columns/trog/article.php?id=148**

- Using the MySQL query cache, at **http://dev.mysql.com/doc/mysql/en/ Query_Cache.html**

- Optimizing MySQL queries, at **http://dev.mysql.com/doc/mysql/en/ Query_Speed.html**

- MySQL replication, at **http://dev.mysql.com/doc/mysql/en/Replication.html**

- More articles and tutorials on MySQL, at **http://www.melonfire.com/ community/columns/trog/archives.php?category=MySQL** and **http:// www.mysql-tcr.com/**

Part IV

Using PHP with MySQL

Chapter 13

Querying a MySQL Database with PHP

B y now, you've seen PHP and MySQL in action, and you should have a fair appreciation of what they can do individually. But why stop there? It's also possible to use them together. Because PHP comes with built-in support for MySQL, developers can access and query MySQL databases through a PHP script, and then use the results of the query to dynamically generate web pages. This close integration makes it possible to significantly simplify the task of creating database-driven web applications, and it has made the PHP-MySQL combination extremely popular with open-source developers.

This chapter examines the MySQL API in PHP, explaining how it can be used to perform MySQL queries and process the results of those queries.

How to...

- Connect to (and disconnect from) a MySQL database server

- Execute an SQL query and process the results

- Dynamically populate an HTML page with the results of an SQL query

- Catch errors in MySQL query execution

- Obtain information on the current state of the MySQL server

Using MySQL and PHP Together

PHP has included support for MySQL since version 3.x, although the procedure to activate this support has varied widely between versions. PHP 4.x included a set of MySQL client libraries, which were activated by default. PHP 5.x no longer bundles these libraries, however, due to licensing issues, so you need to obtain and install them separately. Then, you need to explicitly activate the MySQL extension—ext/mysql—by adding the --with-mysql option to PHP's configure script. The procedure to accomplish this is outlined in Chapter 2.

The MySQL API built into PHP is designed to accomplish four primary goals:

- Manage database connections

- Execute queries

- Process query results

- Provide debugging and diagnostic information

To illustrate these functions, let's create a simple MySQL database table, and then use PHP to connect to the server, retrieve a set of results, and format them for display on a web page. The sample table used here consists of a single table named items, which holds a list of products and their prices. Here are the SQL queries needed to create and initialize this table:

```
CREATE TABLE items (
itemID int(11) NOT NULL auto_increment,
itemName varchar(255) NOT NULL default '',
itemPrice float NOT NULL default '0',
PRIMARY KEY  (itemID) ) TYPE=MyISAM;

INSERT INTO items VALUES (1, 'Paperweight', '3.99');
INSERT INTO items VALUES (2, 'Key ring', '2.99');
INSERT INTO items VALUES (3, 'Commemorative plate', '14.99');
INSERT INTO items VALUES (4, 'Pencils (set of 4)', '1.99');
INSERT INTO items VALUES (5, 'Coasters (set of 3)', '4.99');
```

You can enter these commands either interactively or noninteractively through the MySQL client program. Once entered, run a SELECT query to ensure that the data has been successfully imported.

```
mysql> SELECT * FROM items;
+---------+----------------------+-----------+
| itemID | itemName             | itemPrice |
+---------+----------------------+-----------+
|       1 | Paperweight          |      3.99 |
|       2 | Key ring             |      2.99 |
|       3 | Commemorative plate  |     14.99 |
|       4 | Pencils (set of 4)   |      1.99 |
|       5 | Coasters (set of 3)  |      4.99 |
+---------+----------------------+-----------+
5 rows in set (0.00 sec)
```

Now, to do the same thing using PHP, create the following PHP script:

```
<html>
<head></head>
<body>

<?php
// open connection to MySQL server
$connection = mysql_connect('localhost', 'guest', 'pass') ↵
or die ('Unable to connect!');
```

13

```php
// select database for use
mysql_select_db('db2') or die ('Unable to select database!');

// create and execute query
$query = 'SELECT * FROM items';
$result = mysql_query($query) ↵
or die ('Error in query: $query. ' . mysql_error());

// check if records were returned
if (mysql_num_rows($result) > 0)
{
    // print HTML table
    echo '<table width=100% cellpadding=10 cellspacing=0 border=1>';
    echo
'<tr><td><b>ID</b></td><td><b>Name</b></td><td><b>Price</b></td></tr>';

     // iterate over record set
     // print each field
    while($row = mysql_fetch_row($result))
    {
        echo '<tr>';
        echo '<td>' . $row[0] . '</td>';
        echo '<td>' . $row[1] . '</td>';
        echo '<td>' . $row[2] . '</td>';
        echo '</tr>';
    }
    echo '</table>';
}
else
{
    // print error message
    echo 'No rows found!';
}

// once processing is complete
// free result set
mysql_free_result($result);

// close connection to MySQL server
mysql_close($connection);
?>

</body>
</html>
```

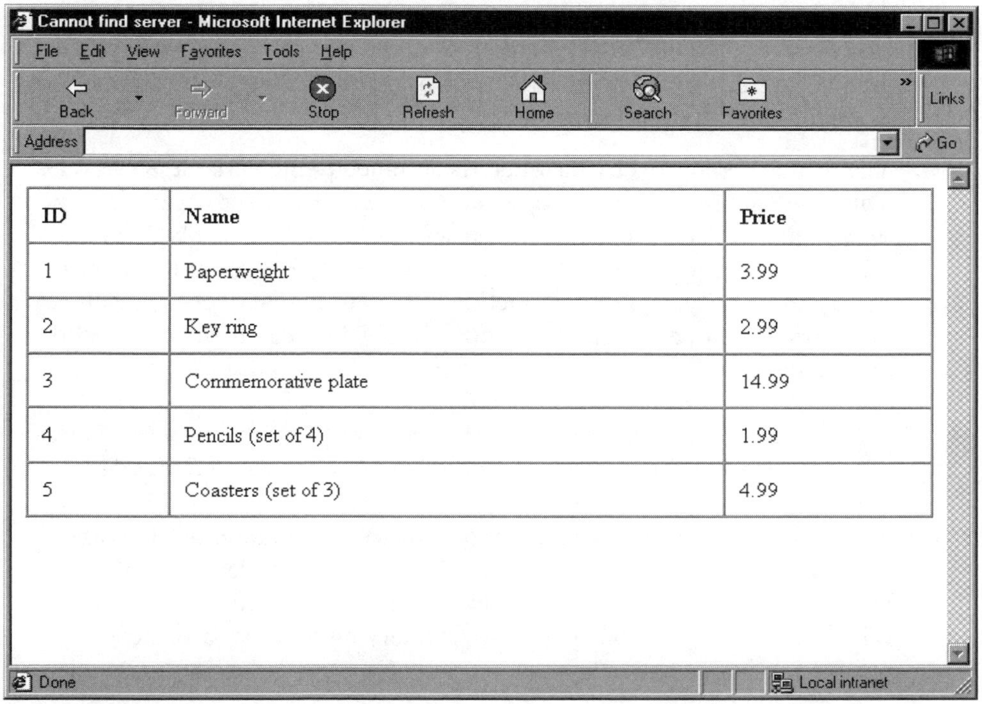

ID	Name	Price
1	Paperweight	3.99
2	Key ring	2.99
3	Commemorative plate	14.99
4	Pencils (set of 4)	1.99
5	Coasters (set of 3)	4.99

FIGURE 13-1   Querying a MySQL database through PHP

When you view this through your browser, you will see something that looks like Figure 13-1.

An examination of the previous script will reveal that using PHP to perform and process a MySQL query involves several steps, which the following explains.

1. To begin communication with the MySQL database server, you first need to open a connection to the server. All communication between PHP and the database server takes place through this connection, which is initialized by the mysql_connect() function.

   The mysql_connect() function requires three parameters: the host name of the MySQL server, and the MySQL username and password required to gain access to it. If the function is able to successfully initialize a connection, it returns a link identifier, which is stored in the variable $connection. This identifier is used throughout the script when communicating with the database.

13

2. Once a connection has been initialized, the next step is to select a database for use (this is equivalent to the SQL USE command) with the `mysql_select_db()` command, and then send the server a query through the `mysql_query()` function. Both functions use the last opened connection as their default for all operations.

3. The result set returned by the query is assigned to the variable `$result`. This result set may contain, depending on your query, zero or more rows or columns of data. The number of rows in the result set is obtained from the `mysql_num_rows()` function. Assuming one or more rows exist, the `mysql_fetch_row()` function is used to iterate over the result set and retrieve rows as arrays. Individual field values can then be accessed as array elements.

> **TIP** *There are several other alternatives to `mysql_fetch_row()`. These are discussed in detail in the section entitled "Processing Result Sets."*

4. Each result set returned by a query occupies some amount of memory. Once you're done processing it, therefore, it's a good idea to use the `mysql_free_result()` function to free up the used memory for other purposes. And, once you're done querying the database, close the connection with a call to `mysql_close()`.

The previous steps outlined the standard process for using data from a MySQL database in PHP. The following sections examine each of these steps in greater detail.

Managing Database Connections

In PHP, connections to the MySQL server are opened via the `mysql_connect()` function, which accepts a number of different arguments: the hostname (and, optionally, the port number) of the MySQL server, the MySQL username to gain access, and the corresponding password. Here are some examples:

```php
<?php
// open connection to MySQL server
$connection = mysql_connect('mydbserver', 'guest', 'pass');
```

```
// print status message
if ($connection)
{
    echo 'Connected!';
}
else
{
    echo 'Could not connect!';
}
?>

<?php
// open connection to MySQL server on custom port
$connection = mysql_connect('localhost:3316', 'root', 'secret') ⏎
or die ('Unable to connect');
?>
```

If a connection can be established, the `mysql_connect()` function returns a *link identifier*, which is used by other functions to communicate with the server. If a connection cannot be established, the function returns false and, depending on the default error level of the PHP script, an error message indicating the cause of failure will be printed to the output device (usually the browser).

To avoid this automatically generated error message, it is necessary to prefix the call to `mysql_connect()` with PHP's special error-suppression operator: @. Here is an example:

```
<?php
// open connection to MySQL server
$connection = @mysql_connect('mydbserver', 'guest', 'pass');

// print status message
echo $connection ? 'Connected!' : 'Could not connect!';
?>
```

Normally, the link to the server remains open for the lifetime of the script, and is automatically closed by PHP once the script completes executing. That said, just as it's good manners to close the doors you open, it's good programming practice to explicitly close the MySQL connection once you finish using it.

13

This is accomplished by calling the `mysql_close()` function, which closes the link and returns the used memory to the system. Here is an example:

```php
<?php
// open connection to MySQL server
$connection = @mysql_connect('mydbserver', 'guest', 'pass');

if ($connection)
{
    // close connection
    mysql_close($connection);
}
?>
```

Using Persistent Connections

When dealing with high-traffic sites, the constant opening and closing of MySQL server connections can often prove a drain on resources. In such situations, it is possible to obtain a reduction in overhead, as well as some performance gain, by replacing the call to `mysql_connect()` with a call to `mysql_pconnect()`.

The `mysql_pconnect()` function opens a "persistent" connection to the server. Such a persistent connection does not automatically end when the script creating it ends; rather, it remains available for use by other scripts requesting an equivalent connection to the MySQL server. Because such "persistent" connections reduce the need for scripts to open a different connection for every request, they are considered more efficient and can produce performance gains in certain situations.

The arguments passed to the `mysql_pconnect()` function are identical to those passed to the `mysql_connect()` function. Here is an example:

```php
<?php
// open connection to MySQL server on custom port
$connection = mysql_pconnect('mydbserver', 'myuser', 'mypass') ↵
or die ('Unable to connect!');

// print status message
echo $connection ? 'Persistent connection open!' : ↵
'Could not open persistent connection!';
?>
```

TIP	*If your web server and MySQL server are on the same physical machine, you can obtain a performance boost by passing a UNIX socket to mysql_ connect(), instead of a hostname. See **http://www.php.net/manual/en/ function.mysql-connect.php** for examples and syntax.*

Performing Queries

Once a connection has been opened, the next step is to select a database for use. This is done with the mysql_select_db() function, which accepts a database name as argument. It can optionally also accept a link identifier; if this is not specified, the function defaults to using the last opened connection. Here's an example of how it may be used:

```php
<?php
// select the database "mydb"
mysql_select_db('mydb'),
?>
```

Once the database has been selected, it becomes possible to execute queries on it. In PHP, MySQL queries are handled via the mysql_query() function, which accepts a query string and a link identifier and sends it to the server represented by the link identifier. If no link identifier is specified, the last opened link is used as the default. Here is an example:

```php
<?php
// execute query
$result = mysql_query('SELECT * FROM items WHERE price < 10.00');
?>
```

 *Don't use a semicolon to terminate the query string passed to* mysql_ *query().*

Depending on the type of query, the return value of mysql_query() differs:

- If the query is a data-retrieval query—for example, a SELECT or SHOW query—then mysql_query() returns a resource identifier pointing to the query's result set, or false on failure. The resource identifier can then be used to process the records in the result set.

- If the query is a data manipulation query—for example, an INSERT or UPDATE query—then mysql_query() returns true if the query succeeds, or false on failure.

The result-set processing functions outlined in the next section can now be used to extract data from the return value of mysql_query().

13

Out with the Old...

PHP 5.0 includes a brand-spanking-new MySQL extension called MySQLi (MySQL Improved). This extension, intended for use only with MySQL 4.1.3 or better, boasts improved security, an object-oriented interface, and support for upcoming MySQL features. If you need the new features in MySQL 4.1.3 or better, or if you're using an older version of MySQL, but you still want to benefit from the speed/security improvements in the new extension, you may want to consider using it. MySQLi works almost exactly like the "old" MySQL extension described in this chapter, except that function names begin with mysqli_*() instead of mysql_*(). Read more about it at **www .php.net/manual/en/ref.mysqli.php**.

Processing Result Sets

The return value of a successful mysql_query() invocation can be processed in a number of different ways, depending on the type of query executed.

Queries Which Return Data

For SELECT-type queries, a number of techniques exist to process the returned data. The simplest is the mysql_fetch_row() function, which returns each record as a numerically indexed PHP array. Individual fields within the record can then be accessed using standard PHP-array notation. The following example illustrates this:

```php
<?php
// open connection to MySQL server
$connection = mysql_connect('localhost', 'guest', 'pass') ↵
or die ('Unable to connect!');

// select database for use
mysql_select_db('db2') or die ('Unable to select database!');
```

```php
// create and execute query
$query = 'SELECT itemName, itemPrice FROM items';
$result = mysql_query($query) ↵
or die ('Error in query: $query. ' . mysql_error());

// check if records were returned
if (mysql_num_rows($result) > 0)
{
     // iterate over record set
     // print each field
    while($row = mysql_fetch_row($result))
    {
         echo $row[0] . " - " . $row[1] . "\n";
    }
}
else
{
    // print error message
    echo 'No rows found!';
}

// once processing is complete
// free result set
mysql_free_result($result);

// close connection to MySQL server
mysql_close($connection);
?>
```

Notice, in the previous listing, how the call to `mysql_fetch_row()` is wrapped in a `mysql_num_rows()` conditional test. The `mysql_num_rows()` function returns the number of records in the result set and comes in handy to check whether the query returned any records at all.

Did you know?   **A Clean Field**

There's also a `mysql_num_fields()` function, which returns the number of fields in each record of the result set.

You can use PHP's `mysql_fetch_assoc()` function to represent each row as an associative array of field-value pairs, a minor variation of the previously used technique. Take a look:

```php
<?php
// open connection to MySQL server
$connection = mysql_connect('localhost', 'guest', 'pass') ↵
or die ('Unable to connect!');

// select database for use
mysql_select_db('db2') or die ('Unable to select database!');

// create and execute query
$query = 'SELECT itemName, itemPrice FROM items';
$result = mysql_query($query) ↵
or die ('Error in query: $query. ' . mysql_error());

// check if records were returned
if (mysql_num_rows($result) > 0)
{
    // iterate over record set
    // print each field
    while($row = mysql_fetch_assoc($result))
    {
        echo $row['itemName'] . " - " . $row['itemPrice'] . "\n";
    }
}
else
{
    // print error message
    echo 'No rows found!';
}

// once processing is complete
// free result set
mysql_free_result($result);

// close connection to MySQL server
mysql_close($connection);
?>
```

In this case, field values are accessed using the field name instead of the index.

There's also the `mysql_fetch_object()` function, which returns each row as an object, with properties corresponding to the field names. Here is an example:

```php
<?php
// open connection to MySQL server
$connection = mysql_connect('localhost', 'guest', 'pass') ↵
or die ('Unable to connect!');

// select database for use
mysql_select_db('db2') or die ('Unable to select database!');

// create and execute query
$query = 'SELECT itemName, itemPrice FROM items';
$result = mysql_query($query) ↵
or die ('Error in query: $query. ' . mysql_error());

// check if records were returned
if (mysql_num_rows($result) > 0)
{
    // iterate over record set
    // print each field
    while($row = mysql_fetch_object($result))
    {
        echo $row->itemName . " - " . $row->itemPrice . "\n";
    }
}
else
{
    // print error message
    echo 'No rows found!';
}

// once processing is complete
// free result set
mysql_free_result($result);

// close connection to MySQL server
mysql_close($connection);
?>
```

In this case, each `$row` object is created with properties corresponding to the field names in that row. Row values can be accessed using standard `$object->property` notation.

If you like having your cake and eating it too, you will probably enjoy the `mysql_fetch_array()` *function, which returns both an associative array and a numerically indexed array, a combination of the* `mysql_fetch_row()` *and* `mysql_fetch_assoc()` *functions. Read about it at* **http://www.php.net/manual/en/function.mysql-fetch-array.php**.

Queries That Alter Data

You can also use PHP's MySQL API for queries that don't return a result set, for example, INSERT or UPDATE queries. Consider the following example, which demonstrates by asking for user input through a form, and then INSERT-ing that data into the database:

```
<html>
<head>
<basefont face="Arial">
</head>
<body>
<?php
if (!$_POST['submit'])
{
     // form not submitted
?>
     <form action="<?=$_SERVER['PHP_SELF']?>" method="post">
     Item name: <input type="text" name="name">
     Item price: <input type="text" name="price">
     <input type="submit" name="submit">
     </form>
<?php
}
else
{
    // get form input
    // escape input values for greater safety
    $name = (trim($_POST['name']) == '') ? ↵
die ('ERROR: Enter a name') : mysql_escape_string($_POST['name']);
    $price = (trim($_POST['price'] == '') || !is_numeric($_POST['price'])) ↵
? die ('ERROR: Enter a price') : $_POST['price'];
    // open connection
    $connection = mysql_connect('localhost', 'guest', 'pass') ↵
or die ('Unable to connect!');

    // select database
    mysql_select_db('db2') or die ('Unable to select database!');
```

```
    // create query
    $query = "INSERT INTO items (itemName, itemPrice) ⏎
VALUES ('$name', '$price')";

    // execute query
    $result = mysql_query($query) ⏎
or die ("Error in query: $query. " . mysql_error());

    // print ID of inserted record
    echo 'New record inserted with ID ' . mysql_insert_id() . '<br \>';

    // print number of rows affected
    echo mysql_affected_rows() . ' record(s) affected';

    // close connection
    mysql_close($connection);
}
?>
</body>
</html>
```

Here, the user is first presented with a form asking for an item and its associated price. Once the form is submitted, the form input is used inside to create an INSERT query, which is then sent to the database with the `mysql_query()` method. Because `mysql_query()` returns a Boolean indicating whether the query was successful, it is possible to check whether the INSERT took place and return an appropriate message.

The previous example has three new functions:

- The `mysql_escape_string()` function escapes special characters (like quotes) in the user input, so it can be safely entered into the database. If the `magic_quotes_gpc` setting in your PHP configuration file is enabled, you might need to first call `stripslashes()` on the user input before calling `mysql_escape_string()`, to avoid characters getting escaped twice.

- The `mysql_insert_id()` function returns the ID generated by the previous INSERT query (useful only if the table into which the INSERT occurs contains an AUTO_INCREMENT field).

- The `mysql_affected_rows()` function returns the total number of rows affected by the last operation.

All these functions come in handy when dealing with queries that alter the database.

13

Handling Errors

Before you go out there and start building data-driven web sites, you should be aware that PHP's MySQL API also comes with some powerful error-tracking functions that can reduce debugging time. Take a look at the following example, which contains a deliberate error in the SELECT query string:

```php
<?php
// open connection to MySQL server
$connection = mysql_connect('localhost', 'guest', 'pass') ↵
or die ('Unable to connect!');

// select database for use
mysql_select_db('db2') or die ('Unable to select database!');

// create and execute query
$query = 'SELECT FROM items';
$result = mysql_query($query);

// if no result
// print MySQL error message
if(!$result)
{
    echo 'MySQL error ' . mysql_errno() . ': ' . mysql_error();
    mysql_close($connection);
}
?>
```

The mysql_errno() function displays the error code returned by MySQL if there's an error in your SQL statement, while the mysql_error() function returns the actual error message. Turn these both on, and you'll find they can significantly reduce the time you spend fixing bugs.

Using Ancillary Functions

In addition to the functions discussed in previous sections, PHP's MySQL API comes with a number of ancillary functions that may be used to find out more about the databases and tables on the MySQL server or to obtain server status information. Table 13-1 lists the important functions in this category.

Function	What It Does
mysql_get_server_info()	Returns the version number of the MySQL server
mysql_get_proto_info()	Returns the version number of the MySQL protocol
mysql_get_client_info()	Returns the version number of the MySQL client
mysql_get_host_info()	Returns information on the MySQL host
mysql_thread_id()	Returns the thread ID for the current MySQL connection
mysql_list_dbs()	Returns a list of databases available on the MySQL server
mysql_list_tables()	Returns a list of tables available in a specified MySQL database
mysql_list_fields()	Returns information about the fields of a specified MySQL table
mysql_stat()	Returns status information about the MySQL server
mysql_info()	Returns information about the last executed query
mysql_db_name()	Returns a name of a database from the list generated by mysql_list_dbs()
mysql_tablename()	Returns a name of a table from the list generated by mysql_list_tables()
mysql_ping()	Tests the server connection

TABLE 13-1   Useful Debugging and Diagnostic Functions

And here's an example that demonstrates some of these functions in action:

```
<html>
<head>
<basefont face="Arial">
</head>
<body>

<?php
// open connection
$connection = mysql_connect('localhost', 'guest', 'pass') ⏎
or die ('Unable to connect!');

// get list of available databases and tables
$dbs = mysql_list_dbs($connection);
echo 'Available databases and tables:';
echo '<ul>';
for ($x=0; $x<mysql_num_rows($dbs); $x++)
```

13

```
{
        // print database name
        $db = mysql_db_name($dbs, $x);
        echo '<li>' . $db . '</li>';
        // for each database, get list of tables within it
        $tables = mysql_list_tables($db, $connection);
        echo '<ul>';
        // iterate over table list
        for ($y=0; $y<mysql_num_rows($tables); $y++)
        {
                // print table name
                echo '<li>' . mysql_tablename($tables, $y) . '</li>';
        }
        echo '</ul>';
}

// get version and host information
echo "Client version: " . mysql_get_client_info() . "<br />";
echo "Server version: " . mysql_get_server_info() . "<br />";
echo "Protocol version: " . mysql_get_proto_info() . "<br />";
echo "Host: " . mysql_get_host_info() . "<br />";
echo "Thread ID: " . mysql_thread_id() . "<br />";

// get server status
$status = mysql_stat();
echo $status;

// close connection
mysql_close($connection);
?>

</body>
</html>
```

Figure 13-2 illustrates what the output might look like.

The first part of this script is fairly simple: it runs the mysql_list_dbs() function to get a list of databases, and then it iterates over the list and runs the mysql_list_tables() function to retrieve the list of tables inside each. Next, the mysql_get_*_info() functions provide the client version number, the MySQL version number, the version number of the special MySQL client-server protocol used for communication between the two, the current hostname,

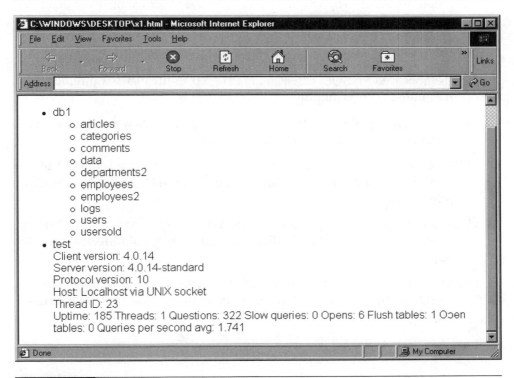

FIGURE 13-2   Viewing MySQL databases and tables through PHP

how it is connected to the MySQL server, and the connection thread ID. Finally, new in PHP 4.3.0, is the `mysql_stat()` function, which returns a string containing status information on the MySQL server (including information on server uptime, open tables, queries per second, and other statistical information).

Summary

The whole is frequently greater than the sum of its parts . . . and so it is with PHP and MySQL. The combined capabilities of the two technologies make it possible to integrate the results of database queries into web pages quickly and efficiently, and thereby speed the development of database-driven web sites and applications.

This chapter examined the PHP-MySQL API in detail, showing you how to use PHP to manage MySQL server connections, perform queries, and process query results. It also demonstrated many of the ancillary functions built into the PHP-MySQL API, including functions to retrieve error messages, obtain server status at run time, and list database, table, and field information.

To learn more about PHP's MySQL functions and to see examples of them in action, consider visiting the following links:

- PHP's MySQL extension, at **http://www.php.net/manual/en/ref.mysql.php**

- The improved MySQLi extension in PHP 5.0, at **http://www.php.net/ manual/en/ref.mysqli.php**

- More examples of using PHP with MySQL, at **http://www.melonfire.com/ community/columns/trog/article.php?id=18**

- A case study of building an online recruitment application with PHP and MySQL, at **http://www.melonfire.com/community/columns/trog/article .php?id=74**

- A case study of building a time-and-material tracking system with PHP and MySQL, at **http://www.melonfire.com/community/columns/trog/article .php?id=92**

- A case study of building a document management system with PHP and MySQL, at **http://www.melonfire.com/community/columns/trog/article .php?id=64**

Chapter 14

Validating User Input

Y ou may have heard the acronym GIGO before. It stands for "Garbage In, Garbage Out" and, very simply, it means that bad input produces bad output. Or, in PHP-MySQL terms, if the raw data inserted into a MySQL database is flawed, any subsequent analysis or report based on that data is sure to be misleading or incorrect.

That's where input validation comes in. By sanitizing and validating user input before it reaches the database, a developer guarantees the integrity of the database and creates a sound foundation for future calculations and operations. Such input validation is a critical part of your PHP-MySQL application development.

How to...

- Use database constraints to reduce the incidence of empty or duplicate records

- Set field data types to make input data more consistent

- Ensure that required form fields are filled

- Validate the length and data type of user input

- Use regular expressions for more complex pattern matching

- Capture validation errors in a single list, instead of one by one

NOTE   *This chapter makes frequent reference to the terms "application layer" and "database layer." For the uninitiated, the* database *layer in this context refers to the MySQL server, and the built-in functions and features it provides. The* application *layer here is the PHP script, or application, that interacts with the MySQL server to perform calculations or read/write data.*

Setting Input Constraints at the Database Layer

When it comes to maintaining the integrity of your database, a powerful tool is provided by the database system itself: the capability to restrict the type of data entered into a field or make certain fields mandatory, using field definitions or constraints.

Using the NULL Modifier

As you've seen in Chapter 9, MySQL enables you to specify whether a field is allowed to be empty or if it must necessarily be filled with data, by placing the NULL and NOT NULL modifiers after each field definition. This is a good way to ensure that required fields of a record are never left empty, because MySQL will simply reject entries that do not have all the necessary fields filled in. Here's an example of this in action:

```
mysql> CREATE TABLE products (
    -> id int(4),
    -> name varchar(50)
    -> );
Query OK, 0 rows affected (0.06 sec)
```

Here, the name field can hold NULL values, which means the following INSERT will go unchallenged,

```
mysql> INSERT INTO products VALUES (NULL, NULL);
Query OK, 1 row affected (0.06 sec)
```

and create the following nonsense entry in the table:

```
mysql> SELECT * FROM products;
+------+------+
| id   | name |
+------+------+
| NULL | NULL |
+------+------+
1 row in set (0.11 sec)
```

Now, look what happens if you make the name field mandatory:

```
mysql> CREATE TABLE products (
    -> id int(4),
    -> name varchar(50) NOT NULL
    -> );
Query OK, 0 rows affected (0.05 sec)
mysql> INSERT INTO products VALUES (NULL, NULL);
ERROR 1048: Column 'name' cannot be null
```

Of course, because MySQL makes a distinction between a NULL value and an empty string (' '), the following record—which is also meaningless—would be accepted.

```
mysql> INSERT INTO products VALUES ('', '');
Query OK, 1 row affected (0.05 sec)
```

14

```
mysql> SELECT * FROM products;
+------+------+
| id   | name |
+------+------+
|    0 |      |
+------+------+
1 row in set (0.00 sec)
```

Thus, while the NOT NULL modifier can help reduce the incidence of empty or incomplete records in a database, it is not a comprehensive solution. It needs to be supplemented by application-level verification to ensure that empty strings are caught before they get to the database.

Using the UNIQUE Modifier

Using MySQL's built-in validation mechanisms has an important advantage: it makes it easy to perform certain types of validation that would be lengthy and time-consuming to write code for. Consider, for example, the situation of ensuring that a particular field contains only unique values. MySQL makes it possible to do this, simply by attaching a UNIQUE modifier to the field, as in the following example:

```
mysql> CREATE TABLE users (
    -> username VARCHAR(50) NOT NULL UNIQUE
    -> );
Query OK, 0 rows affected (0.06 sec)
mysql> INSERT INTO users (username) VALUES ('tim');
Query OK, 1 row affected (0.06 sec)
mysql> INSERT INTO users (username) VALUES ('jon');
Query OK, 1 row affected (0.00 sec)
```

Now, if you attempt to enter another record with the value *tim* in the username field, MySQL will reject your entry with an error:

```
mysql> INSERT INTO users (username) VALUES ('tim');
ERROR 1062: Duplicate entry 'tim' for key 1
```

If you had to perform this type of validation at the application layer, the only way to do it would be to select all the records in the table, scan the username field to obtain a list of all values present in it, and check the user's input against each to eliminate duplication. Needless to say, this is expensive, both in terms of CPU cycles and time. Fortunately, the UNIQUE modifier renders it unnecessary.

Using Field Data Types

Of course, checking for mandatory and unique values are just small pieces of a much bigger picture. It's also necessary to make sure that the data being entered is of the correct type—after all, you don't want string values in a numeric field or decimal values in a timestamp field. To this end, MySQL also requires you to specify the type of data a particular field can hold at the time of defining a table. Input that does not match the named data type is automatically converted into a more acceptable, though incorrect, value.

Here's an example of this:

```
mysql> CREATE TABLE items (
    -> id INT(2) NOT NULL,
    -> price INT(4) NOT NULL
    -> );
Query OK, 0 rows affected (0.05 sec)
mysql> INSERT INTO items (id, price) VALUES (1, 'five');
Query OK, 1 row affected (0.00 sec)
mysql> SELECT * FROM items;
+----+-------+
| id | price |
+----+-------+
|  1 |     0 |
+----+-------+
1 row in set (0.05 sec)
```

In this case, because the price field has been constrained to only store integers, the string *five* has been converted into a *0* and saved.

Of course, this isn't perfect. Sure, you were able to avoid storing a string instead of a number, but you also simply replaced one problem with another: the field now contains a 0 instead of a valid price. This is a good example of how database constraints can help restrict input errors, yet not solve them completely. To close the gap between what should happen and what actually happens, it's necessary to also validate input at the application layer, before it even reaches the database. The next section discusses this in some detail.

Validating Input at the Application Layer

When it comes to catching errors in user input, the best place to do this is at the point of entry—the application itself. That's why a good part of this chapter is devoted to showing you techniques you can use to catch common input errors and ensure that they don't get into your database.

Checking for Required Values

One of the most common mistakes a novice programmer makes is forgetting to check for required field values. This can result in a database with numerous empty records, and these empty records can, in turn, affect the accuracy of your queries.

To see what I mean by this, consider the following `users` table:

```
mysql> CREATE TABLE users (
    -> username varchar(8) NOT NULL DEFAULT '',
    -> password varchar(8) NOT NULL DEFAULT ''
    -> ) TYPE=MyISAM;
Query OK, 0 rows affected (0.05 sec)
```

When inserting a record into this table, values must be specified for both username and password fields (this is reinforced by the use of NOT NULL constraints on these fields). Here's a script that enforces these constraints at the application level:

```
<html>
<head>
<basefont face="Arial">
</head>
<body>
<?php
if (!$_POST['submit'])
{
     // form not submitted
?>
     <form action="<?=$_SERVER['PHP_SELF']?>" method="post">
     Username: <input type="text" name="username">
     <br />
     Password: <input type="password" name="password">
     <br /><br />
     <input type="submit" name="submit" value="Sign Up">
     </form>
```

```php
<?php
}
else
{
    // form submitted

    // check the username field
    $username = ↵
(!isset($_POST['username']) || trim($_POST['username']) == "") ↵
? die ('ERROR: Enter a username') : ↵
mysql_escape_string(trim($_POST['username']));

    // check the password field
    $password = ↵
(!isset($_POST['password']) || trim($_POST['password'] == "")) ↵
? die ('ERROR: Enter a password') : ↵
mysql_escape_string(trim($_POST['password']));

    // connect to database

    // open connection
    $connection = mysql_connect('localhost', 'guest', 'pass') ↵
or die ('Unable to connect!');

    // select database
    mysql_select_db('db2') or die ('Unable to select database!');

    // create query
    $query = "INSERT INTO users (username, password) ↵
VALUES ('$username', '$password')";

    // execute query
    $result = mysql_query($query) ↵
or die ("Error in query: $query. " . mysql_error());

    // close connection
    mysql_close($connection);
}
?>
</body>
</html>
```

14

To see this in action, attempt to submit the previous form with either of the two fields empty. The script will simply die() with an error message. This is because of the additional lines of input validation code in the script.

In the previous listing, the validation test consists of checking for data in the username and password field, by using a combination of PHP's isset() and trim() functions. The isset() function checks whether the named variable is set or not, and returns false if the variable has either not been set or assigned a NULL value. The trim() function removes the white space around the ends of the string, and then compares it with an empty string (" ") to ensure that it contains at least one character.

If both tests return true, then the script proceeds to connect to the database and insert the record into the table (this process is explained in detail in Chapter 13). If either one returns false, the user clearly has not entered the corresponding form value, and the script terminates immediately, without even attempting to open a connection to the database.

This listing makes it clear that a simple conditional test is all you need to ensure that required fields in your forms are never left empty. In the absence of these lines of validation code, the script would save a record to the database without first checking it for validity. In the context of the previous example, this means a user could successfully sign up without providing a username or a password—a clear error that also has serious ramifications for the security of your application (because an empty record exists, a user could gain access to the application, even without a username and password). This can be easily avoided by testing the user's input before it is saved to the database, in the manner described previously.

Notice my use of the ternary operator ? in the previous listing. This operator, akin to an if-else() conditional statement, is discussed in detail in Chapter 4.

Restricting the Size of Input Data

As you've seen in Chapter 9, MySQL enables you to control the length of a particular field by adding a size modifier to the field data type. Now, the way MySQL works, values greater than the specified length are automatically truncated, with no notification or exception generated to let the user know about the change.

This is disturbing, because it means that user data can easily get corrupted without the user's awareness. As an example, go back a couple of pages and read the definition of the users table created in the previous section. You'll see that the two fields of the table are restricted to eight characters each. Now, if a user enters the user name *jamesscott,* MySQL will automatically (and silently) truncate it to eight characters and save it as *jamessco*. Obviously, any subsequent attempt by the user to log in as *jamesscott* will fail, as MySQL will have no record of that particular username.

One way around this is, of course, to set sensible length restrictions for your database fields. However, this must be coupled with application-level input validation of entered data, to alert users if their input goes above the prescribed limit and to allow them to modify it. To see an example of this in action, consider the following database table, which constrains data entered into the title field to 50 characters:

```
mysql> CREATE TABLE news (
    -> id INT (10) NOT NULL,
    -> title VARCHAR(50) NOT NULL
    -> );
Query OK, 0 rows affected (0.05 sec)
```

And here's the PHP script that replicates this constraint in a form:

```
<html>
<head>
<basefont face="Arial">
</head>
<body>

<?php
if (!$_POST['submit'])
{
      // form not submitted
?>
      <form action="<?=$_SERVER['PHP_SELF']?>" method="post">
      Title: <input type="text" name="title">
      <br />
      <input type="submit" name="submit" value="Save">
      </form>
<?php
}
else
{
      // form submitted

      // trim the title field
      $title = trim ($_POST['title']);
```

14

```
            // check its length
            if (strlen($title) > 50)
            {
                die ('ERROR: Title contains more than 50 characters');
            }

            // connect to database
            // save record
    }
    ?>
    </body>
    </html>
```

To see this in action, try entering a string greater than 50 characters in the title field. When you submit the form, you'll see an error message, and the data will not be saved to the database until you correct the error.

The code behind this is straightforward—just pass the user input to PHP's strlen() function, which returns the length of the string. You can then wrap this in an if () test to ensure that only strings under the specified limit pass muster.

TIP   *Another simple way to implement a field length restriction is to use the MAXLENGTH attribute of the INPUT form tag. This attribute enables you to specify the maximum number of characters that can be entered in a form text input field. This is a quick way to restrict the length of user input. Note, this assumes the device you're displaying the form on supports this attribute. The major browsers all support it, but PDAs or cell phones running a reduced HTML implementation might not. For this reason, an application-level check should be performed, regardless of browser features like MAXLENGTH support.*

Checking the Type of Input Data

You've already seen how MySQL automatically "corrects" values that don't match the data type specified in the table definition. Often, the assumptions MySQL makes when performing these corrections aren't true, and the corrected (but incorrect) values subsequently affect the integrity of your database. Therefore, an important test of user input involves checking the data type of input values against the database's expectations, and raising an error in the event of a mismatch.

To see an example of this, consider the following table definition:

```
mysql> CREATE TABLE items (
    -> itemID INT(11) NOT NULL AUTO_INCREMENT,
    -> itemName VARCHAR(255) NOT NULL DEFAULT '',
    -> itemSPrice FLOAT NOT NULL DEFAULT '0',
    -> itemCPrice FLOAT NOT NULL DEFAULT '0',
    -> itemQuantity INT(11) NOT NULL DEFAULT '0',
    -> PRIMARY KEY  (itemID)
    -> ) TYPE=MyISAM;
Query OK, 0 rows affected (0.07 sec)
```

Now, if you attempt to enter a string into any of the INT or FLOAT fields, MySQL will simply convert that string to a 0. At first glance, this might seem like an intelligent thing to do, because it avoids having to deal with error messages. However, it isn't, because the database now contains incorrect data.

What is needed, then, is a way to verify the data type of a value before allowing it to be entered into the database. A useful PHP function to accomplish this is the is_numeric() function, demonstrated in the next example:

```html
<html>
<head>
<basefont face="Arial">
</head>
<body>
<?php
if (!$_POST['submit'])
{
     // form not submitted
?>
     <form action="<?=$_SERVER['PHP_SELF']?>" method="post">
     Item name:
     <br />
     <input type="text" name="itemName">
     <br />
     Item sale price:
     <br />
     <input type="text" name="itemSPrice">
     <br />
     Item cost price:
     <br />
     <input type="text" name="itemCPrice">
     <br />
```

```
      Item quantity:
      <br />
      <input type="text" name="itemQuantity">
      <br/><br />
      <input type="submit" name="submit" value="Enter Data">
      </form>
<?php
}
else
{

      // form submitted

      // check the itemName field
      $itemName = ↵
(!isset($_POST['itemName']) || trim($_POST['itemName']) == "") ↵
? die ('ERROR: Enter the item name') : ↵
mysql_escape_string(trim($_POST['itemName']));

      // check the itemSPrice field
      if(!isset($_POST['itemSPrice']) || ↵
trim($_POST['itemSPrice']) == "")
      {
         die ('ERROR: Enter the item\'s selling price');
      }
      elseif(!is_numeric(trim($_POST['itemSPrice'])))
      {
         die ('ERROR: Enter numeric value for the item\'s selling price');
      }
      else
      {
         $itemPrice = floatval(trim($_POST['itemSPrice']));
      }

      // check the itemCPrice field
      if(!isset($_POST['itemCPrice']) || ↵
trim($_POST['itemCPrice']) == "")
      {
         die ('ERROR: Enter the item\'s cost price');
      }
      elseif (!is_numeric(trim($_POST['itemCPrice'])))
      {
         die ('ERROR: Enter numeric value for the item\'s cost price');
      }
      else
      {
         $itemCost = floatval(trim($_POST['itemCPrice']));
      }
```

```
        // check the itemQuantity field
        if(!isset($_POST['itemQuantity']) || ↵
trim($_POST['itemQuantity']) == "")
        {
                die ('ERROR: Enter the quantity');
        }
        elseif (!is_numeric(trim($_POST['itemQuantity'])))
        {
                die ('ERROR: Enter numeric value for quantity');
        }
        else
        {
                $itemQuantity = intval(trim($_POST['itemQuantity']));
        }


        // connect to database
        // save record
}
?>
</body>
</html>
```

Load this script, and try entering a nonnumeric value for the `itemSPrice`, `itemCPrice`, and `itemQuantity` fields. Each attempt will be rejected with the display of an error message.

In this example, the first test is to ensure that the field is not empty. If this is true, the second test involves checking whether the value entered is a numeric string, with the `is_numeric()` function. Only if the user input passes both tests is it allowed to proceed into the database.

*You cannot use the `is_int()` or the `is_float()` functions to test if a value submitted through a web form is an integer or a floating-point value. This is because data submitted through a form is always stored as a string within the special $_POST array. All you can do is use the `is_numeric()` function to check if a value is a numeric string. Read more about this at **http://www.php.net/manual/en/function.is-int.php**.*

14

In addition to the `is_numeric()` function, you may also use PHP's character type extension to further test input before saving them to your database. The important functions supported by this extension are listed in Table 14-1.

Function	What It Does
ctype_alnum()	Check if a value contains only alphanumeric characters.
ctype_alpha()	Check if a value contains only alphabetic characters.
ctype_digit()	Check if a value contains only numeric characters.
ctype_print()	Check if a value contains only printable characters.
ctype_space()	Check if a value contains only white space characters.

TABLE 14-1   Character Type Functions

Here's an example that illustrates some of these functions in action:

```
<html>
<head>
<basefont face="Arial">
</head>
<body>
<?php
if (!$_POST['submit'])
{
      // form not submitted
?>
      <form action="<?php echo $SERVER['PHP_SELF']; ?>" ↵
method="post">
      First Name:
      <br />
      <input type="text" name="firstName">
      <br />
      Last Name:
      <br />
      <input type="text" name="lastName">
      <br />
      Age:
      <br />
      <input type="text" name="age">
      <br /><br />
      <input type="submit" name="submit" value="Enter Data">
      </form>
<?php
}
else
{
      // form submitted

      // check the firstName field
      if (!isset($_POST['firstName']) || ↵
trim($_POST['firstName']) == "")
```

```php
      {
          die ('ERROR: Enter first name');
      }
      elseif(!ctype_alpha(trim($_POST['firstName'])))
      {
          die ('ERROR: Enter alphabetic value for first name');
      }
      else
      {
          $firstName = mysql_escape_string(trim($_POST['firstName']));
      }

      // check the lastName field
      if(!isset($_POST['lastName']) || ↵
trim($_POST['lastName']) == "")
      {
          die ('ERROR: Enter last name');
      }
      elseif(!ctype_alpha(trim($_POST['lastName'])))
      {
          die ('ERROR: Enter alphabetic value for last name');
      }
      else
      {
          $lastName = mysql_escape_string(trim($_POST['lastName']));
      }


      // check the age field
      if(!isset($_POST['age']) || trim($_POST['age']) == "")
      {
              die ('ERROR: Enter age');
      }
      elseif (!ctype_digit(trim($_POST['age'])))
      {
              die ('ERROR: Enter numeric value for age');
      }
      else
      {
              $age = floatval(trim($_POST['age']));
      }

      // connect to database
      // save record
}
?>
```

14

In this script, after performing the basic tests, the `ctype_alpha()` function tests the input string for alphabetic characters, while the `ctype_digit()` function tests for digits from 0 to 9.

Note, for values containing more than one character, every character is tested and a positive result is returned only if all *the characters satisfy the data type requirements. While this rigidity is useful at times, it can also be a double-edged sword, for example, the number 20.50 would not pass a* ctype_digit() *test, because it contains a decimal point (which is not a digit).*

Checking for Illegal Input Values

In addition to the tests listed in previous sections, an application's particular business logic often demands custom validation routines of its own. To illustrate this, consider the example of a form that asks the user to enter a positive two-digit number. Here, it is necessary to write a validation test to check if the user's input falls between 10 and 99 (both inclusive) and to display an error if it doesn't. Take a look at the next script, which demonstrates what the code for such a validation test would look like:

```
<html>
<head>
<basefont face="Arial">
</head>
<body>
<?php
if (!$_POST['submit'])
{
     // form not submitted
?>
     <form action="<?=$_SERVER['PHP_SELF']?>" method="post">
     Enter any positive two-digit number:
     <input type="text" name="num" size="2">
     <br />
     <input type="submit" name="submit" value="Check">
     </form>
<?php
}
```

```
else
{
    // form submitted

    // check for presence of number
    $num = ⏎
(!isset($_POST['num']) || trim($_POST['num']) == "" || ⏎
!is_numeric($_POST['num'])) ⏎
? die ('ERROR: Enter a number') : trim($_POST['num']);

    // check for number range
    if ($num < 10 || $num > 99)
    {
        die ('ERROR: Enter a number between 10 and 99');
    }
}
?>
</body>
</html>
```

This type of custom validation can play an important role in avoiding common errors, such as the dreaded division-by-zero error. Harking back to the example in the previous section, assume you have a table containing the following data,

```
mysql> SELECT * FROM items;
+--------+----------+------------+------------+--------------+
| itemID | itemName | itemSPrice | itemCPrice | itemQuantity |
+--------+----------+------------+------------+--------------+
|      1 | Syringe  |         10 |          5 |          200 |
|      2 | Swab     |          1 |       0.25 |         1000 |
|      3 | Pump     |         95 |          0 |            5 |
+--------+----------+------------+------------+--------------+
3 rows in set (0.00 sec)
```

and you'd like to calculate the percentage profit on each item using the formula `Percentage Profit = (Profit/Cost Price) * 100`. You'd probably need to run a SELECT query like this:

```
mysql> SELECT itemName, (((itemSPrice - itemCPrice)/itemCPrice) * 100) ⏎
AS percentProfit FROM items;
```

```
+----------+----------------+
| itemName | percentProfit  |
+----------+----------------+
| Syringe  |            100 |
| Swab     |            300 |
| Pump     |           NULL |
+----------+----------------+
3 rows in set (0.00 sec)
```

Notice how one of the records in the output displays a NULL value. This is because the cost price for that item was stored as 0, causing a division-by-zero error and forcing MySQL to display a NULL as the result of the calculation.

This error might have been avoided if the application developer had thought to include a custom check to avoid zero values entering the database. Here's an example of what that test might have looked like:

```php
<html>
<head>
<basefont face="Arial">
</head>
<body>
<?php
if (!$_POST['submit'])
{
      // form not submitted
?>
      <form action="<?=$_SERVER['PHP_SELF']?>" method="post">
      Item name:
      <br />
      <input type="text" name="itemName">
      <br />
      Item sale price:
      <br />
      <input type="text" name="itemSPrice">
      <br />
      Item cost price:
      <br />
      <input type="text" name="itemCPrice">
      <br />
      Item quantity:
      <br />
      <input type="text" name="itemQuantity">
      <br/><br />
      <input type="submit" name="submit" value="Enter Data">
      </form>
<?php
}
```

```
else
{
     // form submitted

     // check the itemCPrice field
     $itemCost = ( ↵
!isset($_POST['itemCPrice']) || trim($_POST['itemCPrice']) == "") ↵
? die ('ERROR: Enter the item\'s cost price') : ↵
 (!is_numeric(trim($_POST['itemCPrice']))) ↵
? die ('ERROR: Enter numeric value for the item\'s cost price') : ↵
floatval(trim($_POST['itemCPrice']));

     // check if itemCPrice field is equal to zero
     if($itemCost == 0)
     {
          die ('ERROR: Please enter an item cost price greater ↵
than zero');
     }

     // connect to database
     // save record
}
?>
```

Validating Dates

Dates often play an important role in an application's business logic, and users are prone to errors when entering these values. Luckily, PHP comes with a `checkdate()` function that provides an easy way to validate user-provided date values.

To see how this works, consider the following simple script, which asks the user to enter a date, and then tests it for validity:

```
<html>
<head>
<basefont face="Arial">
</head>
<body>
<?php
if (!$_POST['submit'])
{
     // form not submitted
?>
     <form action="<?=$_SERVER['PHP_SELF']?>" method="post">
     Day <input type="text" name="day" size="2">
```

```
        Month <input type="text" name="month" size="2">
        Year <input type="text" name="year" size="2">
        <br />
        <input type="submit" name="submit" value="Check">
        </form>
<?php
}
else
{
    // form submitted

    // check date
    if (!checkdate($_POST['month'], $_POST['day'], $_POST['year'])) ↵
    {
      die ('ERROR: Enter a valid date');
    }
}
?>
</body>
</html>
```

To see this in action, enter an incorrect date—for example, 31 February 2005—and submit the form. Your date will be rejected with an error message.

Most of the magic here happens with the `checkdate()` function. This function accepts three numeric arguments, representing the month, day, and year, respectively, and returns true if the combination is a valid Gregorian date. A good idea is to always check user-supplied date values in this manner before using them.

(Un)Intelligent Automation

MySQL expects application developers to enforce date checking within their application. If you enter an invalid date, MySQL will either store it as is, or convert it to a series of zeroes. From the usability point of view, both alternatives are equally bad. Read more about this at **http://dev.mysql.com/doc/mysql/en/Using_DATE.html**.

Validating Multiple-Choice Input

Checkboxes and drop-down lists are an important component of web forms, and it's often necessary to include validation for these controls in your PHP applications. Normally, the user's selections from these controls are submitted to the form processor in the form of an array, and it's necessary to use PHP's array functions to validate them.

To see this in action, consider the following script, which requires the user to fill out a brief user profile and select at least three hobbies and two subscriptions from the multiple-choice controls presented.

```
<html>
<head>
<basefont face="Arial">
</head>
<body>
<?php
if (!$_POST['submit'])
{
    // form not submitted
?>
<form action="<?=$_SERVER['PHP_SELF']?>" method="post">
Username:
<br />
<input type="text" name="username">
<p />
Password:
<br />
<input type="password" name="password">
<p />
Date of Birth:
<br />
Month <input type="text" name="month" size="2">
Day <input type="text" name="day" size="2">
Year <input type="text" name="year" size="4">
<p />
Hobbies (select at least <b>three</b>):
<br />
<input type="checkbox" name="hobbies[]" value="Sports">Sports
<input type="checkbox" name="hobbies[]" value="Reading">Reading
<input type="checkbox" name="hobbies[]" value="Travel">Travel
<input type="checkbox" name="hobbies[]" value="Television">Television
<input type="checkbox" name="hobbies[]" value="Cooking">Cooking
<p />
Subscriptions (Select at least <b>two</b>):
```

```html
<br />
<select name="subscriptions[]" multiple>
<option value="General">General Newsletter</option>
<option value="Members">Members Newsletter</option>
<option value="Premium">Premium Newsletter</option>
</select>
<p />
<input type="submit" name="submit" value="Sign Up">
</form>
<?php
}
else
{
 // form submitted

 // validate "username", "password" and "date of birth" fields
 $username = (!isset($_POST['username']) || ↵
trim($_POST['username']) == "") ↵
? die ('ERROR: Enter a username') : trim($_POST['username']);

 $password = (!isset($_POST['password']) ↵
|| trim($_POST['password'] == "")) ↵
? die ('ERROR: Enter a password') : trim($_POST['password']);

 if (!checkdate($_POST['month'], $_POST['day'], $_POST['year']))
 {
    die ('ERROR: Enter a valid date');
 }

 // check the "hobbies" field for valid values
 $hobbies = ((sizeof($_POST['hobbies']) < 3) ? ↵
die ('ERROR: Please select at least 3 hobbies') : ↵
implode(',', $_POST['hobbies']));

 // check the "subscriptions" field for valid values
 $subscriptions = ((sizeof($_POST['subscriptions']) < 2) ? ↵
die ('ERROR: Please select at least 2 subscriptions') : ↵
implode(',', $_POST['subscriptions']));

 // connect to database
 // save record
}
?>
</body>
</html>
```

Now, try submitting the form without first selecting the required number of items from each multiple-choice control, and you will be presented with an error message.

The options selected by a user from each multiple-choice control are submitted in the form of a PHP array. Thus, it is convenient to use PHP's array functions—namely, the `sizeof()` function, which returns the number of elements in an array—to check whether the required number of options was selected.

Matching Patterns

Often, input validation requires more sophisticated tools than the primitive checks and tests shown in previous sections of this chapter. Fortunately, PHP comes with these tools built in, with its support for regular expressions.

Regular expressions (regex) are a powerful tool used in pattern-matching and substitution. Commonly associated with almost all *NIX-based tools, scripting languages, and shell programs, a regular expression lets you build patterns using a set of special characters. These patterns can then be compared with text in a file, data entered into an application, or input from a form filled up by users on a web site. Depending on whether or not there's a match, appropriate action can be taken and appropriate program code executed. Regular expressions play an important role in the decision-making routines of web applications, and in complex find-and-replace operations.

To see how regular expressions work, consider a form that requires the user to enter a name, password, and e-mail address. The application needs to enforce the following constraints:

- The name may contain only uppercase (A–Z) or lowercase characters (a–z), with a minimum of three and a maximum of eight.

- The password may contain only lowercase characters (a–z) or integers (0–9), with a minimum of five and a maximum of eight.

- The e-mail address must conform to the standard *user@domain* format.

As you can see in the code listing that follows, these restrictions can be implemented using regular expressions without adding too many extra lines of code:

```
<html>
<head>
<basefont face="Arial">
</head>
<body>
```

14

```php
<?php
if (!$_POST['submit'])
{
      // form not submitted
?>
      <form action="<?=$_SERVER['PHP_SELF']?>" method="post">
      Username:
      <br />
      <input type="text" name="username">
      <p />
      Password:
      <br />
      <input type="password" name="password">
      <p />
      Email address:
      <br />
      <input type="text" name="email">
      <p />
      <input type="submit" name="submit" value="Sign Up">
      </form>
<?php
}
else
{
      // form submitted

      // validate "username", "password" and "email" fields
      // using regular expressions
      $username = (!isset($_POST['username']) || ↵
!ereg('^([a-zA-Z]){3,8}$', $_POST['username'])) ? ↵
die ('ERROR: Enter valid username') : ↵
mysql_escape_string(trim($_POST['username']));

      $password = (!isset($_POST['password']) || ↵
!ereg('^([a-z0-9]){5,8}$', $_POST['password'])) ? ↵
die ('ERROR: Enter valid password') : ↵
mysql_escape_string(trim($_POST['password']));

      $email = (!isset($_POST['email']) || ↵
!ereg('^([a-zA-Z0-9_-]+)([\.a-zA-Z0-9_-]+)@([a-zA-Z0-9_-]+) ↵
(\.[a-zA-Z0-9_-]+)+$', $_POST['email'])) ? ↵
die ('ERROR: Enter valid email address') : ↵
mysql_escape_string(trim($_POST['email']));
```

```
        // connect to database
        // save record
}
?>
</body>
</html>
```

This listing uses PHP's `ereg()` function to ensure that the user's input conforms to the constraints listed previously. This `ereg()` function requires two compulsory arguments: the pattern to be matched, and the string to match it against.

Coming to the regular expressions themselves, the first two are self-explanatory, especially if you some familiarity with the syntax. Both of them list the allowed characters and also test the length of the string. The third and final pattern is a little more complex, because it uses numerous modifiers and special characters. To understand it better, consider reading the article on regular expressions, or visit the PHP manual page for the `ereg()` function, at **http://www.php.net/manual/ en/function.ereg.php**.

> TIP
>
> *Migrating from Perl to PHP? No problem—PHP comes equipped with a* `preg_match()` *function that lets you use Perl Compatible Regular Expressions (PCRE) in your code. This enables you to easily reuse patterns from your Perl scripts in your PHP scripts. Read more at http://www.php.net/manual/en/ref.pcre.php.*

Listing Multiple Validation Errors at Once

In all the examples demonstrated so far, I have used the `die()` function to terminate script processing and display an error message if input validation fails. Now, while this is fine for forms with just a few fields, it doesn't make sense for forms that contain a large number of fields. For such forms, it is often more efficient to display a comprehensive list of errors at once, instead of displaying them one at a time, so that the user immediately has clear visibility of what (s)he did wrong. For some applications, you might even want to save the errors to a log file or database for future reference.

These varied requirements mean that it isn't enough for you only to catch errors in user input, but also present them in a manner that is efficient, extensible, and easy to understand. This next listing shows you how to validate all the data submitted by a user, prepare a list of errors encountered, and display them all at once.

```
<html>
<head>
<basefont face="Arial">
</head>
```

```php
<body>
<?php
if (!$_POST['submit'])
{
      // form not submitted
?>
 <form action="<?=$_SERVER['PHP_SELF']?>" method="post">
 Username (3-8 char):
 <br />
 <input type="text" name="username">
 <p />
 Password (5-8 char):
 <br />
 <input type="password" name="password">
 <p />
 Email address:
 <br />
 <input type="text" name="email">
 <p />
 Date of Birth:
 <br />
 Month <input type="text" name="month" size="2">
 Day <input type="text" name="day" size="2">
 Year <input type="text" name="year" size="4">
 <p />
 Hobbies (select at least <b>three</b>):
 <br />
 <input type="checkbox" name="hobbies[]" value="Sports">Sports
 <input type="checkbox" name="hobbies[]" value="Reading">Reading
 <input type="checkbox" name="hobbies[]" value="Travel">Travel
 <input type="checkbox" name="hobbies[]" value="Television">Television
 <input type="checkbox" name="hobbies[]" value="Cooking">Cooking
 <p />
 Subscriptions (Select at least <b>two</b>):
 <br />
 <select name="subscriptions[]" multiple>
 <option value="General">General Newsletter</option>
 <option value="Members">Members Newsletter</option>
 <option value="Premium">Premium Newsletter</option>
 </select>
 <p />
 <input type="submit" name="submit" value="Sign Up">
 </form>
<?php
}
else
{
 // array to store the error messages
 $ERRORS = array();
```

```
 // validate "username" field
 $username = !ereg('^([a-zA-Z]){3,8}$', $_POST['username']) ? ↵
$ERRORS[] = 'Enter valid username' : ↵
mysql_escape_string(trim($_POST['username']));

 // validate "password" field
 $password = !ereg('^([a-z0-9]){5,8}$', $_POST['password']) ? ↵
$ERRORS[] = 'Enter valid password' : trim($_POST['password']);

 // validate "email" field
 $email = !ereg('^([a-zA-Z0-9_-]+)([\.a-zA-Z0-9_-]+)@([a-zA-Z0-9_-]+)(\ ↵
[a-zA-Z0-9_-]+)+$', $_POST['email']) ? ↵
$ERRORS[] ='Enter valid email address' : trim($_POST['email']);

 // validate "date of birth" field
 $dob = (!checkdate($_POST['month'], $_POST['day'], $_POST['year']) ? ↵
$ERRORS[] = 'Enter valid date of birth' : ↵
date("Y-m-d", mktime(0, 0, 0, $_POST['month'], $_POST['day'], ↵
$_POST['year'])));

 // validate "hobbies" field
 $hobbies = (sizeof($_POST['hobbies']) < 3) ? ↵
$ERRORS[] = 'Please select at least three hobbies' : ↵
implode(',', $_POST['hobbies']);

 // validate "subscriptions" field
 $subscriptions = (sizeof($_POST['subscriptions']) < 2) ?  $ERRORS[] = ↵
'Please select at least two subscriptions' : ↵
implode(',', $_POST['subscriptions']);

 // verify if there were any errors by checking
 // the number of elements in the $ERRORS array
 if(sizeof($ERRORS) > 0)
 {
     // format and display error list
     echo "<ul>";
     foreach ($ERRORS as $e)
     {
        echo "<li>$e</li>";
     }
     echo "</ul>";
     die();
 }

 // no errors?
 // connect to database
 // save record
}
?>
</body>
</html>
```

14

Here, for every input test that fails, a new element is added to the global $ERRORS array. At the end of the tests, before connecting to the database, this array is checked. If it contains one or more elements, script processing stops and the errors are displayed to the user as a bulleted list.

 *If you prefer, you can also log the errors, by using the* file_put_ contents() *function to dump the array elements to a file. Look at Chapter 6 for more information on this function.*

Summary

Input validation is a critical part of any web application, and this chapter focused on showing you how to use it to reduce the incidence of errors and illegal values in your MySQL tables. Techniques covered included checking for required values, testing the type and length of user input, using regular expressions and pattern-matching techniques to ensure input conforms to predefined rules, and validating multiple-choice input and date values.

Of course, input validation is simply too vast a topic to be covered in a single chapter. To this end, you should read more about it at the following places:

- The basics of regular expressions, at **http://www.melonfire.com/ community/columns/trog/article.php?id=2**

- More tutorials on regular expressions, at **http://gnosis.cx/publish/ programming/regular_expressions.html**, **http://www.pcre.org/man.txt**, and **http://sitescooper.org/tao_regexps.html**

- The PHP character type extension, at **http://www.php.net/ref.ctype**

- A discussion of SQL Injection attacks, at **http://www.php.net/manual/en/ security.database.sql-injection.php**

- Securing user-submitted data, at **http://www.php.net/manual/en/security .variables.php**

- Input validation on the client using JavaScript, at **http://www.sitepoint .com/article/client-side-form-validation** and **http://home.cogeco .ca/~ve3ll/jstutor5.htm**

- Building an extensible form validator, at **http://www.melonfire.com/ community/columns/trog/article.php?id=119**

Chapter 15

Formatting Query Output

A s a developer, it's easy to fall in love with your code and to spend hours tuning
it for performance. Remember, though, no matter how engrossing the loops
and swirls of your PHP code are to you, it's unlikely that the person for whom
you're developing the application will care about them (or even see them). To the
application end user, all that matters is how user friendly your product is, and how
it will help him or her get things done better. The elegance of your SQL queries
or the impeccable logic of your PHP conditionals will be completely lost on the
end user.

That's where this chapter comes in. The focus of this chapter is massaging the
output of your MySQL queries so it conforms to the expectations of your users,
and, thereby, becomes more readable and useful. Both PHP and the MySQL RDBMS
come with a number of built-in functions to perform such output formatting. This
chapter describes most of the important ones.

How to...

- Join multiple fields into a single string, using custom separators

- Make string or numeric data a uniform size with left/right padding

- Translate line breaks and special characters in text fields to their HTML equivalents

- Format numbers according to local or international currency conventions

- Use commas or other user-defined characters to make large numeric values more readable

- Truncate or round large floating-point values to one or two decimal places

- Display English-equivalent day and month names for UNIX timestamps or numeric date/time values

- Perform simple date arithmetic

- Break the results of a SELECT query into multiple "pages," and dynamically present links to move between pages

Formatting Character Data

A lot of your MySQL data is going to be stored as strings or text blocks, in CHAR,
VARCHAR, or TEXT fields. It's essential that you know how to manipulate this string
data and adjust it to fit the requirements of your application user interface. Both PHP

and MySQL come equipped with numerous string manipulation functions (in fact, they overlap in functionality in many places), and the following sections discuss the important ones.

Concatenating String Values

You learned about string concatenation in PHP in Chapter 3. It's pretty simple—just string together the variables you want to concatenate using the PHP concatenation operation, a period (.). Concatenating fields from a MySQL result set is equally simple—just assign the field values to PHP variables and concatenate the variables together in the normal manner.

To see how this works, consider the following table:

```
mysql> SELECT * FROM users;
+------------+----------+----------+
| username   | fname    | lname    |
+------------+----------+----------+
| matt       | Matthew  | Johnson  |
| har56      | Harry    | Thompson |
| kellynoor  | Kelly    | Noor     |
| jimbo2003  | Jim      | Doe      |
| x          | Xavier   | Belgudui |
+------------+----------+----------+
5 rows in set (0.00 sec)
```

Now, assume you need to concatenate the first- and last-name fields into a single value (a common requirement). Here's how:

```
<html>
<head></head>
<body>

<?php
// open connection to MySQL server
$connection = mysql_connect('localhost', 'guest', 'pass') ↵
or die ('Unable to connect!');

// select database for use
mysql_select_db('db2') or die ('Unable to select database!');
```

15

```
// create and execute query
$query = 'SELECT fname, lname FROM users';
$result = mysql_query($query) ↵
or die ('Error in query: $query. ' . mysql_error());

// check if records were returned
if (mysql_num_rows($result) > 0)
{
    // print HTML table
    echo '<ul>';

    // iterate over record set
    // print each field
    while($row = mysql_fetch_object($result))
    {
        // prints in format "last-name, first-name"
        echo '<li>' . $row->lname . ', ' . $row->fname;
    }
    echo '</ul>';
}
else
{
    // print error message
    echo 'No rows found!';
}

// once processing is complete
// free result set
mysql_free_result($result);

// close connection to MySQL server
mysql_close($connection);
?>

</body>
</html>
```

Figure 15-1 illustrates what the output looks like.

There's another way to do this as well, though. MySQL comes with two built-in functions—CONCAT() and CONCAT_WS()—which can be used to glue fields together within the SQL query itself. Take a look at this next snippet from the MySQL interactive client, which shows these functions in action:

```
mysql> SELECT CONCAT(fname, lname) FROM users ↵
WHERE username = 'matt';
+----------------------+
| CONCAT(fname, lname) |
+----------------------+
| MatthewJohnson       |
+----------------------+
1 row in set (0.02 sec)

mysql> SELECT CONCAT_WS(', ', lname, fname) FROM users ↵
WHERE username = 'matt';
+------------------------------+
| CONCAT_WS(', ', lname, fname) |
+------------------------------+
| Johnson, Matthew             |
+------------------------------+
1 row in set (0.00 sec)
```

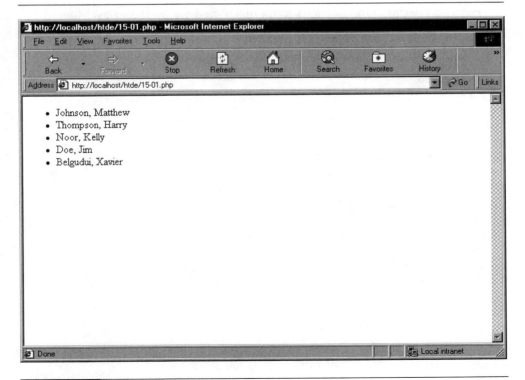

FIGURE 15-1   Concatenating string values

15

Note the difference between the two functions: the CONCAT() function concatenates two or more fields, while the CONCAT_WS() function lets you specify a string separator between the concatenated field values. Obviously, the CONCAT_WS() function is used more often; it's also more forgiving of NULLs in your table (see the following Caution for more information).

CAUTION   *Ensure that none of the fields you're trying to join with CONCAT() contain NULLs. This is because the function returns a NULL value if any of its input arguments are NULL. This quirk can produce unexpected results, damaging the carefully cultivated look of your output screens. To avoid this, check for NULL values prior to using the function, and ensure that your database and validation rules are rigid enough to prevent the entry of empty/NULL values into fields that aren't supposed to contain them (Chapter 14 has more information on how to do this).*
The CONCAT_WS() function is more forgiving, simply ignoring NULL values if it encounters them.

Here's a rewrite of the previous script that uses these database-level functions to perform the concatenation and achieve the same result:

```php
<html>
<head></head>
<body>

<?php
// open connection to MySQL server
$connection = mysql_connect('localhost', 'guest', 'pass') ↵
or die ('Unable to connect!');

// select database for use
mysql_select_db('db2') or die ('Unable to select database!');

// create and execute query
$query = "SELECT CONCAT_WS(', ', lname, fname) AS name ↵
FROM users";

$result = mysql_query($query) ↵
or die ('Error in query: $query. ' . mysql_error());
```

```
// check if records were returned
if (mysql_num_rows($result) > 0)
{
    // print HTML table
    echo '<ul>';

    // iterate over record set
    // print each field
    while($row = mysql_fetch_object($result))
    {
        // prints in format "last-name, first-name"
        echo '<li>' . $row->name;
    }
    echo '</ul>';
}
else
{
    // print error message
    echo 'No rows found!';
}

// once processing is complete
// free result set
mysql_free_result($result);

// close connection to MySQL server
mysql_close($connection);
?>

</body>
</html>
```

Padding String Values

In Chapter 14, you read about the PHP trim() function, used to strip leading and trailing white space from string values prior to testing them for validity or inserting them into a database. However, PHP also comes with the str_pad() function, which does just the reverse: it pads strings to a specified length using either white space or a user-specified character sequence. This can come in handy if you need to artificially elongate string values for display or layout purposes.

15

Here's a table containing string values of differing lengths:

```
mysql> SELECT * FROM ingredients;
+----------------+
| name           |
+----------------+
| cinnamon       |
| ginger         |
| red pepper     |
| cloves         |
| peas           |
| tender coconut |
+----------------+
6 rows in set (0.00 sec)
```

And here's some PHP code that demonstrates padding them:

```php
<html>
<head></head>
<body>

<pre>
<?php
// open connection to MySQL server
$connection = mysql_connect('localhost', 'guest', 'pass') ↵
or die ('Unable to connect!');

// select database for use
mysql_select_db('db2') or die ('Unable to select database!');

// create and execute query
$query = "SELECT name FROM ingredients";
$result = mysql_query($query) ↵
or die ('Error in query: $query. ' . mysql_error());

// check if records were returned
if (mysql_num_rows($result) > 0)
{
```

```
      // iterate over record set
      // print each field
      while($row = mysql_fetch_object($result))
      {
        // prints "              name"
        echo str_pad($row->name, 30, ' ', STR_PAD_LEFT) . '<br />';
      }
}
else
{
      // print error message
      echo 'No rows found!';
}

// once processing is complete
// free result set
mysql_free_result($result);

// close connection to MySQL server
mysql_close($connection);
?>
</pre>

</body>
</html>
```

Figure 15-2 illustrates what the output looks like.

The str_pad() function takes three parameters: the variable to be padded, the size it should be padded to, and the character to use for padding. By default, the function pads the string on the right side. You can alter this default, however, by passing one of the constants STR_PAD_LEFT or STR_PAD_BOTH to the function as an optional fourth parameter.

The PHP str_pad() function is functionally equivalent to MySQL's RPAD() and LPAD() functions, which pad a string from the right and left, respectively. The following snippets demonstrate how these functions work:

```
mysql> SELECT RPAD(name, 20,'_'), LPAD(name, 20, '_') ⏎
FROM ingredients LIMIT 0,2;
+----------------------+----------------------+
| RPAD(name, 20,'_')   | LPAD(name, 20, '_')  |
+----------------------+----------------------+
| cinnamon_____ | _____cinnamon |
```

```
+------------------------+------------------------+
| ginger_____  | _____ginger  |
+------------------------+------------------------+
2 rows in set (0.00 sec)
```

A word of caution: if the total length specified in the RPAD() and LPAD() function call is less than the length of the field value, the value will be truncated. The next snippet illustrates this:

```
mysql> SELECT RPAD(name, 5, '_') FROM ingredients ↵
WHERE name = 'cinnamon';
+------------------------+
| RPAD(name, 5, '_')     |
+------------------------+
| cinna                  |
+------------------------+
1 row in set (0.00 sec)
```

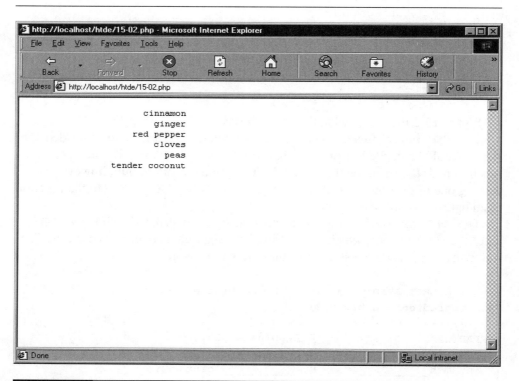

FIGURE 15-2   Padding string values

PHP's `str_pad()` function, however, does not truncate strings in equivalent situations.

Altering String Case

If you need case manipulation, just reach for PHP's string manipulation API again. Four useful functions are here: `strtolower()`, which converts all characters in a string to lowercase; `strtoupper()`, which converts all characters to uppercase; `ucfirst()`, which converts the first character of a string to uppercase, and the useful `ucwords()`, which converts the first character of all the words in a string to uppercase.

The following example demonstrates these functions, using them on the different fields of the following table:

```
mysql> SELECT * FROM customers;
+-------+--------+-----------------+----------+----------------------------+
| fname | lname  | addr            | city     | email                      |
+-------+--------+-----------------+----------+----------------------------+
| David | Johnson | 18 mcgoo place,            |          |                            |
|       |        |   ray road       | boston   | David_Johnson@CORPMAIL.DOM |
| Flora | Bharti | 239/a harkrishna bldg,      |          |                            |
|       |        |   j b marg       | hyderabad| bharti@MyOwnCompany.in     |
| joe   | cool   | 15 hill view,              |          |                            |
|       |        |   east end road  | yorktown | joecool@guess.it           |
+-------+--------+-----------------+----------+----------------------------+
3 rows in set (0.00 sec)
```

Here's the code that reformats all this data to a more consistent casing style:

```php
<html>
<head></head>
<body>

<?php
// open connection to MySQL server
$connection = mysql_connect('localhost', 'guest', 'pass') ↵
or die ('Unable to connect!');

// select database for use
mysql_select_db('db2') or die ('Unable to select database!');
```

15

```php
// create and execute query
$query = "SELECT * FROM customers";
$result = mysql_query($query)
or die ('Error in query: $query. ' . mysql_error());

// check if records were returned
if (mysql_num_rows($result) > 0)
{

    // iterate over record set
    // print each field
    echo '<table border=1 cellpadding=10>';
    echo '<tr><td>Name</td><td>Mailing Address</td>
<td>Email Address</td></tr>';
    while($row = mysql_fetch_object($result))
    {
        echo '<tr>';
        echo '<td>' . ucfirst($row->fname) . ' ' .
ucfirst($row->lname) . '</td>';
        echo '<td>' . ucwords($row->addr) . '<br />' .
strtoupper($row->city) . '</td>';
        echo '<td>' . strtolower($row->email) . '</td>';
        echo '</tr>';
    }
    echo '</table>';
}
else
{
    // print error message
    echo 'No rows found!';
}

// once processing is complete
// free result set
mysql_free_result($result);

// close connection to MySQL server
mysql_close($connection);
?>

</body>
</html>
```

Figure 15-3 shows an output sample.

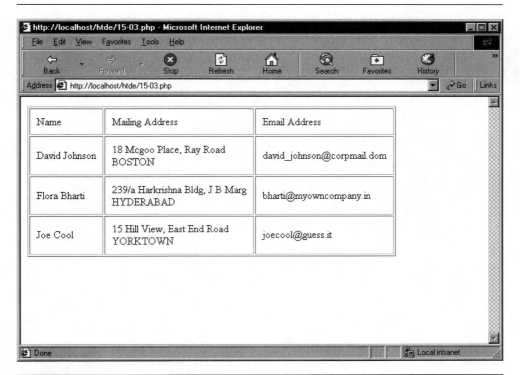

FIGURE 15-3 Changing string case

If you want to, you could also do some of this in the query string itself, by using MySQL's UCASE() and LCASE() functions. The following snippet illustrates this:

```
mysql> SELECT CONCAT_WS('\n', UCASE(addr), UCASE(city)) ↵
AS address, LCASE(email) AS email FROM customers;
+-------------------------------+------------------------------+
| address                       | email                        |
+-------------------------------+------------------------------+
| 18 MCGOO PLACE, RAY ROAD      |                              |
| BOSTON                        | david_johnson@corpmail.dom   |
| 239/A HARKRISHNA BLDG, J B MARG |                            |
| HYDERABAD                     | bharti@myowncompany.in       |
```

15

Repeat Business

MySQL also provides a REPEAT() function, which can be used to display a string field multiple times. Here's an example:

```
mysql> SELECT REPEAT('ho ', 5);
+------------------+
| REPEAT('ho ', 5) |
+------------------+
| ho ho ho ho ho   |
+------------------+
1 row in set (0.00 sec)
```

PHP's equivalent function is the str_repeat() function.

```
| 15 HILL VIEW, EAST END ROAD    |                         |
| YORKTOWN                       | joecool@guess.it        |
+--------------------------------+-------------------------+
3 rows in set (0.11 sec)
```

 *MySQL does not offer functions to capitalize the first character of a string value. If you need to do this, use the PHP functions described previously.*

Dealing with Special Characters

When it comes to displaying large text blocks on a web page, a PHP developer must grapple with a number of issues. Special characters need to be protected, white space and line breaks must be preserved, and potentially malicious HTML code must be defanged. PHP comes with a number of functions designed to perform just these tasks.

To illustrate, consider a table containing large blocks of text data, like the following one:

```
mysql> SELECT id, data FROM newsdata LIMIT 0,1;
+----+----------------------------------------------------------------+
| id | data                                                           |
+----+----------------------------------------------------------------+
|  1 | Recently, I put together a Web site and the public actually liked |
|      my <html> & <javascript>. People...                           |
+----+----------------------------------------------------------------+
1 row in set (0.00 sec)
```

Now, here's how you'd normally retrieve and display this information in a web page:

```php
<html>
<head></head>
<body>

<font face="Arial" size="-1">
<?php
// open connection to MySQL server
$connection = mysql_connect('localhost', 'guest', 'pass') ↵
or die ('Unable to connect!');

// select database for use
mysql_select_db('db2') or die ('Unable to select database!');

// create and execute query
$query = "SELECT title, data FROM newsdata";
$result = mysql_query($query) ↵
or die ('Error in query: $query. ' . mysql_error());

// check if records were returned
if (mysql_num_rows($result) > 0)
{
    // iterate over record set
    while($row = mysql_fetch_object($result))
    {
        echo '<b>' . $row->title . '</b>';
        echo '<p />';
```

15

```
            echo $row->data;
            echo '<p />';
        }
    }
    else
    {
        // print error message
        echo 'No rows found!';
    }

    // once processing is complete
    // free result set
    mysql_free_result($result);

    // close connection to MySQL server
    mysql_close($connection);
    ?>
    </font>

    </body>
    </html>
```

Figure 15-4 illustrates what this looks like.

If you compare the output of the previous script with the original table data, you'll see numerous discrepancies: line breaks and white space are not correctly rendered, and characters like <,>, and & are interpreted as HTML by the browser instead of being displayed as is. The integrity of the original text block has, therefore, been compromised.

To correct these discrepancies, alter the script so it looks like this:

```
<html>
<head></head>
<body>

<font face="Arial" size="-1">
<?php
// open connection to MySQL server
$connection = mysql_connect('localhost', 'guest', 'pass') ↵
or die ('Unable to connect!');

// select database for use
mysql_select_db('db2') or die ('Unable to select database!');
```

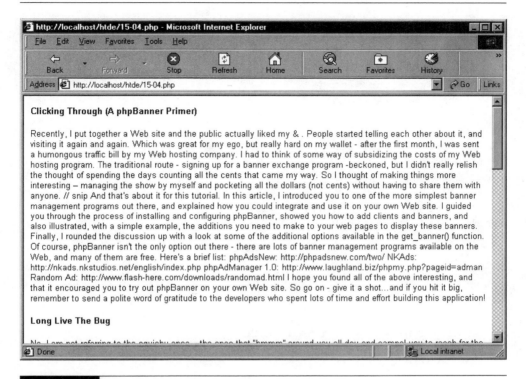

FIGURE 15-4 Printing a text block as is, resulting in display errors

```
// create and execute query
$query = "SELECT title, data FROM newsdata";
$result = mysql_query($query) ↵
or die ('Error in query: $query. ' . mysql_error());

// check if records were returned
if (mysql_num_rows($result) > 0)
{
    // iterate over record set
    while($row = mysql_fetch_object($result))
    {
        echo '<b>' . $row->title . '</b>';
        echo '<p />';
        echo nl2br(wordwrap(htmlentities($row->data), 70));
```

15

```
            echo '<p />';
        }
    }
else
{
    // print error message
    echo 'No rows found!';
}

// once processing is complete
// free result set
mysql_free_result($result);

// close connection to MySQL server
mysql_close($connection);
?>
</font>

</body>
</html>
```

Figure 15-5 illustrates the revised output.
The revised listing uses three new functions.

- The `htmlentities()` function takes care of replacing special characters like ", &, <, and > with their corresponding HTML entity values. This function is useful to defang user-supplied HTML text and render it incapable of effecting the display or functionality of your web page. This function also translates these special characters and prevents them from being interpreted as HTML code by the browser.

- Next, the `wordwrap()` function wraps text to the next line once it reaches a particular, user-defined size, by inserting the /n newline character at appropriate points in the text block (these are then converted into HTML line breaks by the next function). This can be used to set artificial boundaries on the width of your text display area, and to maintain the integrity of your page layout.

- Finally, the `nl2br()` function automatically preserves newlines in a text block, by converting them to HTML <br /> elements. This makes it possible to reproduce the original formatting of the text when it is displayed.

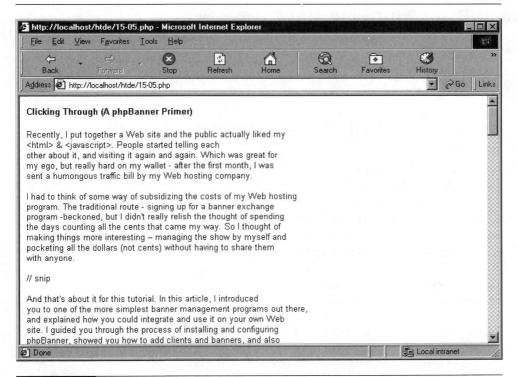

FIGURE 15-5   Printing a text block, after correcting for special characters and line breaks

CAUTION   *While* `wordwrap()` *is a useful way to restrict your text display areas to specific dimensions, it isn't the best. Using CSS width and height rules or constrained* `<div>`*s to control the size of your text display areas is usually more appropriate.*

15

TIP   *PHP also comes with a* `strip_tags()` *function, which enables you to strip all the HTML and PHP tags out of a string, returning only the ASCII output. This can be useful if your application has a rigid "no HTML input" policy.*

Formatting Numeric Data

Just as you can massage string values into a number of different shapes, so, too, can you format numeric data. Both PHP and MySQL come with a full set of functions to manipulate integer and floating-point numbers, and to format large numeric values for greater readability.

Using Decimal and Comma Separators

When it comes to formatting numeric values in PHP, there are only two functions: number_format() and sprintf(). Of these, the former is easier to understand and use, so let's begin with that function.

The number_format() function is used to display large numbers with comma and decimal separators. It can be used to control both the visibility and the appearance of the decimal digits, as well as the character used as the thousands separator.

To see how this works, consider the following table:

```
mysql> SELECT accountNumber, accountName, ↵
accountBalance FROM accounts;
+---------------+-------------+----------------+
| accountNumber | accountName | accountBalance |
+---------------+-------------+----------------+
|    1265489921 | James D     |     2346.00000 |
|    2147483647 | Timothy J   |    56347.50000 |
|    5739304575 | Harish K    |   996564.87500 |
|    2173467271 | Kingston X  |   634238.00000 |
|    2312934021 | Sue U       |       34.67000 |
|    1248954638 | Ila T       |     5373.81982 |
|    2384371001 | Anil V      |    72460.00000 |
|    9430125467 | Katrina P   |      100.00000 |
|    1890192554 | Pooja B     |    17337.11914 |
|    2388282010 | Sue U       |   388883.12500 |
|    2374845291 | Jacob N     |    18410.00000 |
+---------------+-------------+----------------+
11 rows in set (0.05 sec)
```

Here's a PHP script that displays this information on a web page, using number_format() to display account balances with two decimal places and commas as thousand separators:

```
<html>
<head></head>
<body>

<?php
// open connection to MySQL server
$connection = mysql_connect('localhost', 'guest', 'pass') ↵
or die ('Unable to connect!');

// select database for use
mysql_select_db('db2') or die ('Unable to select database!');

// create and execute query
$query = "SELECT accountNumber, accountName, accountBalance ↵
FROM accounts";
$result = mysql_query($query) ↵
or die ('Error in query: $query. ' . mysql_error());

// check if records were returned
if (mysql_num_rows($result) > 0)
{
    echo '<table border=1 cellpadding=10>';
    echo '<tr><td>Number</td><td>Name</td><td>Balance</td></tr>';
    // iterate over record set
    while($row = mysql_fetch_object($result))
    {
        echo '<tr>';
        echo '<td>' . $row->accountNumber . '</td>';
        echo '<td>' . $row->accountName . '</td>';
        echo '<td align=right>' . ↵
number_format($row->accountBalance, 2, '.', ',') . '</td>';
        echo '</tr>';
    }
    echo '</table>';
}
else
{
    // print error message
    echo 'No rows found!';
}
```

15

```
// once processing is complete
// free result set
mysql_free_result($result);

// close connection to MySQL server
mysql_close($connection);
?>

</body>
</html>
```

Figure 15-6 shows the output of this script. Notice how the use of a comma separator significantly increases the readability of the numbers.

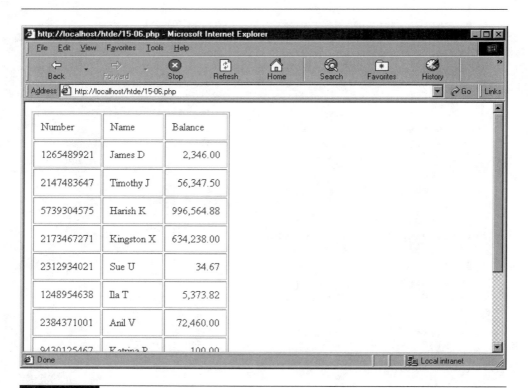

FIGURE 15-6   Formatting numbers with the `number_format()` function

You've already used the echo() function extensively to display output. However, echo() doesn't let you format output in any significant manner, for example, you can't write 1 as 00001.00. So, another common function used to perform this type of number formatting is the sprintf() function, which enables you to define the format in which data is output.

Consider the following example:

```php
<?php
// returns 1.6666666666667
print(5/3);
?>
```

As you might imagine, that's not very friendly. Ideally, you'd like to display just the significant digits of the result, so you'd use the sprintf() function, as in the following:

```php
<?php
// returns 1.67
echo sprintf("%1.2f", (5/3));
?>
```

The PHP sprintf() function is similar to the sprintf() function that C programmers are used to. To format the output, you need to use *field templates,* templates that represent the format you'd like to display. Common field templates are listed in Table 15-1.

You can also combine these field templates with numbers that indicate the number of digits to display—for example, %1.2f implies that PHP should only display two digits after the decimal point. If you'd like the formatted string to have a minimum length, you can tell PHP which character to use for padding by prefixing it with a single quote (').

15

Template	What It Represents
%s	string
%d	decimal number
%x	hexadecimal number
%o	octal number
%f	float number

TABLE 15-1   Common Field Templates Supported by the sprintf() Function

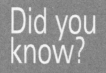

Target Selection

The `sprintf()` function returns the result of output formatting, while the `printf()` function prints the result directly to the standard output device.

Here are a few more examples of `sprintf()` in action:

```php
<?php
// returns 00003
echo sprintf("%05d", 3);

// returns $25.99
echo sprintf("$%2.2f", 25.99);

// returns ****56
printf("%'*6d", 56);
?>
```

To see a real-world example of `sprintf()` usage, consider the following number-heavy MySQL table:

```
mysql> SELECT * FROM stocks;
+--------+--------------+-------------+-------------+-------------+-------------+
| symbol | qty          | buy         | sell        | high        | low         |
+--------+--------------+-------------+-------------+-------------+-------------+
| HGTY   |    17000.0000 |    289.9786 |    195.7474 |    315.7643 |    187.9540|
| HDYS   |        5.8701 |  19000.2734 |  21759.6465 |  21759.6465 |  18639.2988|
| IWIK   |  2174733.0000 |    868.0000 |    870.0000 |    891.0000 |    800.0000|
+--------+--------------+-------------+-------------+-------------+-------------+
3 rows in set (0.00 sec)
```

Here's the PHP script that formats this mass of data into something more readable:

```html
<html>
<head></head>
<body>
```

```php
<?php
// open connection to MySQL server
$connection = mysql_connect('localhost', 'guest', 'pass') ↵
or die ('Unable to connect!');

// select database for use
mysql_select_db('db2') or die ('Unable to select database!');

// create and execute query
$query = "SELECT * FROM stocks";
$result = mysql_query($query) ↵
or die ('Error in query: $query. ' . mysql_error());

// check if records were returned
if (mysql_num_rows($result) > 0)
{
    echo '<table border=1 cellpadding=10>';
    echo '<tr><td>Stock</td> <td>Purchase value</td>';
    echo '<td>Sale value</td><td>Profit/Loss</td>';
    echo '<td>High/Low</td></tr>';

    // iterate over record set
    // format and print numeric data
    while($row = mysql_fetch_object($result))
    {
      echo '<tr>';
      echo '<td>' . $row->symbol . '</td>';
      printf('<td align=right>%s</td>', ↵
number_format($row->qty * $row->buy));
      printf('<td align=right>%s</td>', ↵
number_format($row->qty * $row->sell));
      printf('<td align=right>%s</td>', ↵
number_format($row->qty * ($row->sell - $row->buy)));
      printf('<td align=right>%s / %s</td>', ↵
number_format($row->high), number_format($row->low));
         echo '</tr>';
    }
    echo '</table>';
}
else
{
    // print error message
    echo 'No rows found!';
}
```

15

```
// once processing is complete
// free result set
mysql_free_result($result);

// close connection to MySQL server
mysql_close($connection);
?>

</body>
</html>
```

Figure 15-7 shows the output of this script.

Formatting Currency Values

At this point, it's appropriate to mention PHP's money_format() function, introduced in PHP 4.3.0. This function is designed specifically for use with currency

Rounding Off

If you have a decimal value that you need to round up or down, you can do it using either PHP or MySQL. MySQL offers the CEIL() and FLOOR() functions, while PHP offers the round(), ceil(), and floor() functions. Take a look at the following examples to see how these functions work:

```
mysql> SELECT CEIL(12.052),
FLOOR(12.052);
+--------------+--------------+
| ceil(12.052) | floor(12.052)|
+--------------+--------------+
|           13 |           12|
+--------------+--------------+
1 row in set (0.00 sec)
```

```
<?php
// returns 13
echo ceil(12.052);

// returns 12
echo floor(12.052);

// returns 12.1
// the second argument specifies ⏎
// the number of decimals to round to
echo round(12.052, 1);
?>
```

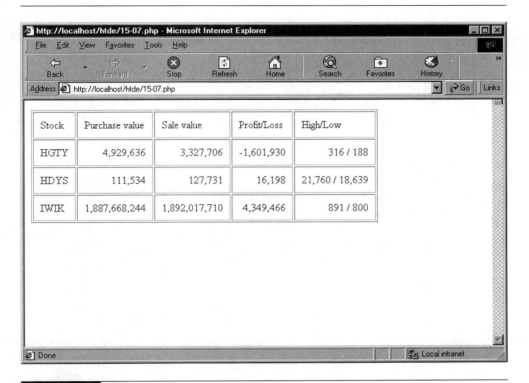

FIGURE 15-7   Formatting numbers with the `printf()` function

values, and it formats numbers in accordance with local or international conventions for currency display.

> NOTE
> *The* `money_format()` *function is not available in the Windows version of PHP.*

15

To see how this works, consider the following revision of a previous script, which formats account balances using American, Indian, and French conventions:

```
<html>
<head></head>
<body>

<?php
// open connection to MySQL server
$connection = mysql_connect('localhost', 'guest', 'pass') ↵
or die ('Unable to connect!');
```

```php
// select database for use
mysql_select_db('db2') or die ('Unable to select database!');

// create and execute query
$query = "SELECT accountNumber, accountName, accountBalance ↵
FROM accounts";
$result = mysql_query($query) ↵
or die ('Error in query: $query. ' . mysql_error());

// check if records were returned
if (mysql_num_rows($result) > 0)
{
    echo '<table border=1 cellpadding=10>';
    echo '<tr><td>Number</td><td>Name</td><td>Balance</td>
<td>Balance</td><td>Balance</td></tr>';
    // iterate over record set
    while($row = mysql_fetch_object($result))
    {
        echo '<tr>';
        echo '<td>' . $row->accountNumber . '</td>';
        echo '<td>' . $row->accountName . '</td>';

        // display in Indian rupees
        setlocale(LC_MONETARY, 'en_IN');
        echo '<td align=right>' . ↵
money_format('%i', $row->accountBalance) . '</td>';

        // display in US dollars (convert using 1 USD = 45 INR)
        setlocale(LC_MONETARY, 'en_US');
        echo '<td align=right>' . ↵
money_format('%i', $row->accountBalance/45) . '</td>';

        // display in euros (convert using 1 EUR = 52 INR)
        setlocale(LC_MONETARY, 'fr_FR');
        echo '<td align=right>' . ↵
money_format('%i', $row->accountBalance/52) . '</td>';

        echo '</tr>';
    }
    echo '</table>';
}
else
{
```

```
    // print error message
    echo 'No rows found!';
}

// once processing is complete
// free result set
mysql_free_result($result);

// close connection to MySQL server
mysql_close($connection);
?>

</body>
</html>
```

Figure 15-8 demonstrates what the output looks like.

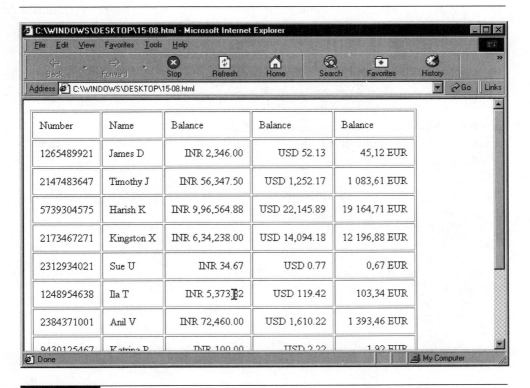

FIGURE 15-8   Formatting numbers with the `money_format()` function

Here, the `money_format()` function formats numeric values as per international currency conventions, using the appropriate separators. As the output illustrates, the French locale uses commas instead of decimals and spaces instead of commas, while the Indian locale differs from the American locale in its placement of thousand separators. Locale information is set with PHP's `setlocale()` function, and numerous adjustments can be made to the alignment and precision of the final currency value using `sprintf()`-type field templates (you can obtain a complete list of these from **http://www.php.net/manual/en/function.money-format.php**).

To display the national currency symbol instead of the three-letter international currency code, replace the `%i` symbol in the call to `money_ format()` with `%n`.

Formatting Dates and Times

As you saw in Chapter 6, you can use PHP's `mktime()` function to obtain a UNIX timestamp for any arbitrary date/time value. However, because the timestamp returned by `mktime()` does not resemble traditional date/time displays, it is usually necessary to format this timestamp, so it is understandable to humans. This is particularly true in web applications, where dates and times are frequently displayed in human-readable, rather than machine-readable, form. To this end, PHP offers the `date()` function, which accepts two arguments: one or more *format specifiers,* which indicates how the timestamp should be formatted, and the timestamp itself (optional; PHP assumes the current time if this second argument is not provided).

To see a few examples of the `date()` function in action, create and run the following script:

```php
<?php
// retrieve current date and time
// prints a date and time like "09:18 pm 19 Jun 2004"
echo date("h:i a d M Y", mktime());

// returns just the date "27 April 2003"
echo date("d F Y", mktime(0, 0, 0, 04, 27, 2003));

// returns the time in 24-hr format "21:18"
echo date("H:i", mktime());
?>
```

Specifier	What It Means
d	Day of the month; numeric
D	Day of the week; short string
F	Month of the year; long string
h	Hour; numeric 12-hour format
H	Hour; numeric 24-hour format
i	Minute; numeric
l	Day of the week; long string
L	Boolean indicating whether it is a leap year
m	Month of the year; numeric
M	Month of the year; short string
s	Seconds; numeric
T	Timezone
Y	Year; numeric
z	Day of the year; numeric

TABLE 15-2   Common Format Specifiers Supported by the `date()` Function

Table 15-2 lists some of the more useful format specifiers recognized by the `date()` function.

Let's see an example of this in action. Consider the following database table, which holds a list of users and their birth dates:

```
mysql> SELECT * FROM birthdays;
+-------+------------+
| name  | dob        |
+-------+------------+
| raoul | 1978-06-04 |
| luis  | 1970-11-17 |
| larry | 1971-08-19 |
| moe   | 1992-01-23 |
+-------+------------+
4 rows in set (0.00 sec)
```

15

Now, create and run a PHP script to retrieve these dates and format them into more readable values:

```
<html>
<head></head>
<body>

<?php
// open connection to MySQL server
$connection = mysql_connect('localhost', 'guest', 'pass') ↵
or die ('Unable to connect!');

// select database for use
mysql_select_db('db2') or die ('Unable to select database!');

// create and execute query
$query = 'SELECT name, UNIX_TIMESTAMP(dob) AS dob ↵
FROM birthdays';
$result = mysql_query($query) ↵
or die ('Error in query: $query. ' . mysql_error());

// check if records were returned
if (mysql_num_rows($result) > 0)
{
    // print HTML table
    echo '<table border=1 cellpadding=10>';

    // iterate over record set
    // print each field
    while($row = mysql_fetch_object($result))
    {
        echo '<tr>';
        echo "<td>$row->name</td><td>" . ↵
date("d M Y", $row->dob) . "</td>";
        echo '</tr>';
    }
    echo '</table>';
}
else
{
    // print error message
    echo 'No rows found!';
}
```

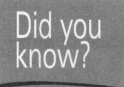

Just in Time

The MySQL UNIX_TIMESTAMP() function converts a MySQL-compliant date or time value into a UNIX timestamp suitable for use with the PHP date() function.

```
// once processing is complete
// free result set
mysql_free_result($result);

// close connection to MySQL server
mysql_close($connection);
?>

</body>
</html>
```

Figure 15-9 demonstrates the output.

MySQL isn't far behind either: the RDBMS comes with powerful DATE_FORMAT() and TIME_FORMAT() functions to manipulate the display of date and time values until they're exactly the way you want them. As with the PHP date() function, format specifiers are used to control the appearance of the output.

Table 15-3 demonstrates the specifiers supported by the DATE_FORMAT() and TIME_FORMAT() functions.

Here are some examples demonstrating these in action:

```
mysql> SELECT DATE_FORMAT(NOW(), '%W, %D %M %Y %r');
+-----------------------------------------+
| DATE_FORMAT(NOW(), '%W, %D %M %Y %r')   |
+-----------------------------------------+
| Thursday, 18th November 2004 12:07:55 PM |
+-----------------------------------------+
1 row in set (0.22 sec)
```

15

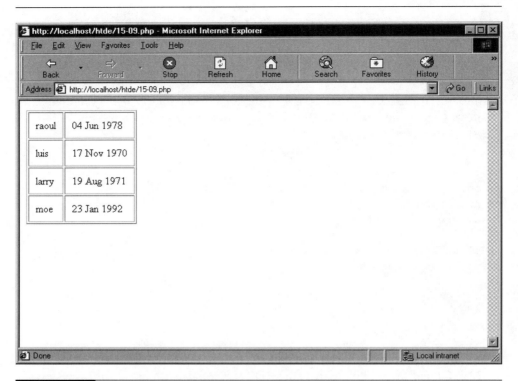

FIGURE 15-9 Formatting dates with the date() function

```
mysql> SELECT DATE_FORMAT(19980317, '%d/%m/%Y');
+-----------------------------------+
| DATE_FORMAT(19980317, '%d/%m/%Y') |
+-----------------------------------+
| 17/03/1998                        |
+-----------------------------------+
1 row in set (0.00 sec)
mysql> SELECT DATE_FORMAT("20011215101030", ↵
"%H%i hrs on %a %d %M %y");
+-----------------------------------------------------------+
| DATE_FORMAT("20011215101030", "%H%i hrs on %a %d %M %y") |
+-----------------------------------------------------------+
| 1010 hrs on Sat 15 December 01                            |
+-----------------------------------------------------------+
1 row in set (0.00 sec)
```

Symbol	What It Means
%a	Short weekday name (Sun, Mon . . .)
%b	Short month name (Jan, Feb . . .)
%d	Day of the month
%H	Hour (01, 02 . . .)
%I	Minute (00, 01 . . .)
%j	Day of the year (001, 002 . . .)
%m	2-digit month (00, 01 . . .)
%M	Long month name (January, February . . . .)
%p	AM/PM
%r	Time in 12-hour format
%S	Second (00, 01 . . .)
%T	Time in 24-hour format
%w	Day of the week (0,1 . . .)
%W	Long weekday name (Sunday, Monday . . .)
%Y	4-digit year

TABLE 15-3   MySQL Date/Time Formatting Codes

```
mysql> SELECT TIME_FORMAT(19690609140256, '%h:%i %p');
+-----------------------------------------+
| TIME_FORMAT(19690609140256, '%h:%i %p') |
+-----------------------------------------+
| 02:02 PM                                |
+-----------------------------------------+
1 row in set (0.00 sec)
```

Using the DATE_FORMAT() function, you can perform date formatting within your SQL query itself, without needing PHP's date() function. This next script revisits the previous PHP listing, moving the formatting task to the database layer:

```
<html>
<head></head>
<body>
```

15

```php
<?php
// open connection to MySQL server
$connection = mysql_connect('localhost', 'guest', 'pass') ↵
or die ('Unable to connect!');

// select database for use
mysql_select_db('db2') or die ('Unable to select database!');

// create and execute query
$query = "SELECT name, DATE_FORMAT(dob, '%d %b %Y') ↵
AS dob FROM birthdays";
$result = mysql_query($query) ↵
or die ('Error in query: $query. ' . mysql_error());

// check if records were returned
if (mysql_num_rows($result) > 0)
{
    // print HTML table
    echo '<table border=1 cellpadding=10>';

    // iterate over record set
    // print each field
    while($row = mysql_fetch_object($result))
    {
        echo '<tr>';
        echo "<td>$row->name</td><td>$row->dob</td>";
        echo '</tr>';
    }
    echo '</table>';
}
else
{
    // print error message
    echo 'No rows found!';
}

// once processing is complete
// free result set
mysql_free_result($result);

// close connection to MySQL server
mysql_close($connection);
?>

</body>
</html>
```

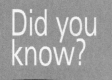

Calculating Your Age with MySQL

MySQL comes with a comprehensive date/time manipulation API that lets you perform complex date arithmetic and extraction. While the list of available functions is too large to list, two of the more interesting ones are the `PERIOD_DIFF()` and `TO_DAYS()` functions, which return the difference, in months and days, respectively, between two date values.

To see how this works, consider the following variant of the previous listing, which lists the current age of each user in the table, given their date of birth:

```
mysql> SELECT name, dob, ↵
ROUND(PERIOD_DIFF(DATE_FORMAT(NOW(), '%Y%m'), ↵
DATE_FORMAT(dob, '%Y%m')) / 12, 1) AS age ↵
FROM birthdays;
+-------+------------+------+
| name  | dob        | age  |
+-------+------------+------+
| raoul | 1978-06-04 | 26.4 |
| luis  | 1970-11-17 | 34.0 |
| larry | 1971-08-19 | 33.2 |
| moe   | 1992-01-23 | 12.8 |
+-------+------------+------+
4 rows in set (0.06 sec)
mysql> SELECT name, dob, ↵
(TO_DAYS(NOW()) - TO_DAYS(dob)) / 365 AS age ↵
FROM birthdays;
+-------+------------+-------+
| name  | dob        | age   |
+-------+------------+-------+
| raoul | 1978-06-04 | 26.48 |
| luis  | 1970-11-17 | 34.03 |
| larry | 1971-08-19 | 33.28 |
| moe   | 1992-01-23 | 12.83 |
+-------+------------+-------+
4 rows in set (0.00 sec)
```

15

Function	What It Does
DAYOFWEEK()	Returns a number (1 to 7) representing the day of the week for a date
DAYOFMONTH()	Returns the day component (1 to 31) of a date
DAYOFYEAR()	Returns a number (1 to 366) representing the day of the year for a date
DAYNAME()	Returns the weekday name for a date
HOUR()	Returns the hour component (0–23) of a time
MINUTE()	Returns the minute component (0–59) of a time
MONTH()	Returns the month component (1 to 12) for a date
MONTHNAME()	Returns the month name for a date
QUARTER()	Returns the quarter (1–2) in which a date falls
WEEK()	Returns the week number (0–53) for a date
YEAR()	Returns the year component (1000–9999) of a date

TABLE 15-4   More MySQL Date Functions

There's also an entire family of functions designed to extract each component of a timestamp separately. Take a look at Table 15-4, which has a list, and the examples following it to see how these work.

Here are some examples of these in action:

```
mysql> SELECT DAYOFMONTH(NOW()), DAYOFYEAR('1979-01-02');
+-------------------+-------------------------+
| DAYOFMONTH(NOW()) | DAYOFYEAR('1979-01-02') |
+-------------------+-------------------------+
|                23 |                       2 |
+-------------------+-------------------------+
1 row in set (0.00 sec)

mysql> SELECT DAYNAME(NOW()), MONTHNAME(NOW()), YEAR(NOW());
+----------------+------------------+-------------+
| DAYNAME(NOW()) | MONTHNAME(NOW()) | YEAR(NOW()) |
+----------------+------------------+-------------+
| Tuesday        | November         |        2004 |
+----------------+------------------+-------------+
1 row in set (0.00 sec)
```

```
mysql> SELECT HOUR(NOW()), MINUTE('14:36');
+-------------+-----------------+
| HOUR(NOW()) | MINUTE('14:36') |
+-------------+-----------------+
|          21 |              36 |
+-------------+-----------------+
1 row in set (0.05 sec)
```

Read more about these functions at **http://dev.mysql.com/doc/mysql/en/ Date_and_time_functions.html**.

Paginating Large Result Sets

In previous sections of this chapter, you've seen how to massage and reformat individual records so they meet your display requirements. In this concluding segment, it's time to step back and understand how to better present the entire set of records returned by an SQL query.

It's not uncommon for query result sets to contain hundreds or even thousands of records. In such cases, it's usually not user friendly to display the entire result set on a single HTML page, as doing so forces the user to scroll up and down endlessly to view the results. This is where *pagination*—the act of breaking up large record collections into smaller subsets and displaying them one page at a time—can help. By breaking the large mass of data into smaller, more easily navigable pages, you increase the usability of your application, and you also avoid overwhelming the user with mountains of data at once.

Writing PHP code to paginate a MySQL result set is fairly simple and grounded in common sense. First, you decide how many results you want to display at a time, say, ten. Next, you COUNT() how many records exist in the result set. Now you can extract the first ten records using a LIMIT clause, and provide a link to enable the user to select the next ten records. On each "page," the last record identifier serves as the starting point for the next page of records. This continues until all the records in the collection have been processed.

Once you understand the underlying principle, writing the code to implement it is simple. Take a look at the next listing, which illustrates this:

```
<html>
<head>
<basefont face="Arial">
</head>
<body>
```

15

```php
<?php
// number of records to be displayed per page
$records_per_page = 10;

// look for starting marker
// if not available, assume 0
(!$_GET['start']) ? $start = 0 : $start = $_GET['start'];

// open connection to MySQL server
$connection = mysql_connect('localhost', 'guest', 'pass') ↵
or die ('Unable to connect!');

// select database for use
mysql_select_db('db2') or die ('Unable to select database!');

// create and execute query to count records
$query = "SELECT COUNT(*) FROM books WHERE rating > 3";
$result = mysql_query($query) ↵
or die ('Error in query: $query. ' . mysql_error());

// get total number of records
$row = mysql_fetch_row($result);
$total_records = $row[0];

// if records exist
if (($total_records > 0) && ($start < $total_records))
{
    // create and execute query to get batch of records
    $query = "SELECT title, author, DATE_FORMAT(date, '%d %M %Y') ↵
AS date FROM books WHERE rating > 3 LIMIT $start, $records_per_page";
    $result = mysql_query($query) ↵
or die ('Error in query: $query. ' . mysql_error());

    // iterate over record set
    // print data
    echo '<table border=1 cellpadding=10>';
    while($row = mysql_fetch_object($result))
    {
        echo '<tr>';
        echo "<td>$row->title</td>";
        echo "<td>$row->author</td>";
        echo "<td>$row->date</td>";
```

```
        echo '</tr>';
    }
    echo '</table>';

    // set up the previous page link
    // this should appear on all pages except the first page
    // the start point for the previous page will be
    // the start point for this page
    // less the number of records per page
    if ($start >= $records_per_page)
    {
        echo "<a href=" . $_SERVER['PHP_SELF'] . ↵
"?start=" . ($start-$records_per_page) . ">Previous ↵
Page</a>      ";
    }

    // set up the "next page" link
    // this should appear on all pages except the last page
    // the start point for the next page
    // will be the end point for this page
    if ($start+$records_per_page < $total_records && $start >= 0)
    {
        echo "<a href=" . $_SERVER['PHP_SELF'] . ↵
"?start=" . ($start+$records_per_page) . ">Next Page</a>";
    }
}
?>
</body>
</html>
```

In this listing, the key variable is $records_per_page$, which controls
the number of records displayed at one time. This value is used as the upper
boundary in the SELECT query's LIMIT clause to restrict the number of records
returned by the query (the lower boundary is the number of the last record
displayed, received from the previous instance of the page through the URL
GET method).

For each batch of records, further calculations are performed to assess if
"next page" and "previous page" links should be displayed. The presence of
these links is heavily dependent on the interaction between the total number
of records in the result set, and the number of records to be displayed at any
one time.

Figure 15-10 illustrates what the output looks like.

15

Paginating a MySQL result set

Summary

Output formatting is an important aspect of application design. This chapter highlighted the important MySQL and PHP functions in this category. It taught you how to pad and concatenate string values, change case, and handle special characters and embedded HTML. Next, this chapter discussed formatting numeric data, with examples and information on breaking up large values with separators, rounding and truncating floating-point values, and attaching local and international currency symbols to numbers. Finally, it showed you the numerous date/time display options available, and demonstrated how to break a large result set into separate pages for greater readability.

As noted at the outset of this chapter, both PHP and MySQL come with numerous functions for data manipulation and display. To find out more, consider visiting the following links:

- PHP string functions, at **http://www.php.net/manual/en/ref.strings.php** and **http://www.melonfire.com/community/columns/trog/article.php?id=88**

- PHP date/time functions, at **http://www.php.net/manual/en/ref.datetime .php** and **http://www.melonfire.com/community/columns/trog/article .php?id=118**

- MySQL string functions, at **http://dev.mysql.com/doc/mysql/en/String_ functions.html** and **http://www.melonfire.com/community/columns/ trog/article.php?id=235**

- MySQL numeric functions, at **http://dev.mysql.com/doc/mysql/en/ Mathematical_functions.html**

- MySQL date/time functions, at **http://dev.mysql.com/doc/mysql/en/Date_ and_time_functions.html**

- A discussion of PHP's automatic quoting (aka "magic quotes") of special characters, at **http://www.php.net/manual/en/security.magicquotes.php**

- A discussion of MySQL's date/time field types, date manipulation, and date arithmetic, at **http://www.melonfire.com/community/columns/trog/ article.php?id=241**

- Ready-to-use code for result set pagination, at **http://pear.php.net/ package/Pager**

15

Chapter 16

Sample Application: News Publishing System

O ver the last three chapters, you learned a little bit about how PHP and MySQL can be used together. It's now time for you to put that knowledge to use, by building a real-world application that retrieves data from a MySQL database to create a dynamic PHP-based web site. This application is more challenging than the examples you've seen in previous chapters. Once you complete this exercise, however, you will have practical, hands-on knowledge of how to use PHP and MySQL together to build usable web applications.

Understanding Requirements

The application here is a news publishing system for a business web site, either on an intranet or the public Internet. It's intended to provide the organization's administrative and press personnel with a way to post news items, press releases, and articles on the web site, and to easily maintain (view, edit, and delete) this information. A MySQL database stores this information, with PHP taking care of retrieving and manipulating the information through a web browser.

This application has two pieces: the "public" piece, which consists of the code that displays the latest news and press releases to the site's visitors, and the "private" piece, which consists of the administration interface for individual editors within the PR department to publish new content to the web site. Both these pieces interact with the MySQL database (which contains the actual news stories and press releases) using the MySQL API built into PHP.

With this in mind, it should be clear that this application must support the following tasks:

- It must be able to display a list of all news items in the database (or the most recent ones), and enable users to view the complete contents of each.

- It must let administrators add new items and press releases to the database.

- It must enable administrators to edit existing releases, to make corrections or update them with new information.

- It must permit the removal of older, out-of-date releases, and news items from the database.

With these requirements in mind, it's time to design the database.

Designing the Database

Because the content for the application is stored in a MySQL table, it's important to define exactly what constitutes a press release. If you think about it, you'll see that a *press release* or article can typically be broken down into three subsections: a title, a main body containing the text of the press release or news item, and an information section with the publication date and name of the contact person.

To begin, create a database to store this information, and select it for use:

```
mysql> CREATE DATABASE news;
Query OK, 1 row affected (0.16 sec)
mysql> USE news;
Database changed
```

Next, create a table to hold press releases and news:

```
mysql> CREATE TABLE news (
    ->      id SMALLINT(5) unsigned NOT NULL auto_increment,
    ->      title TEXT NOT NULL,
    ->      content TEXT NOT NULL,
    ->      contact VARCHAR(255),
    ->      timestamp DATETIME DEFAULT '0000-00-00 00:00:00'
    ->      NOT NULL,
    ->      PRIMARY KEY (id)
    -> );
Query OK, 0 rows affected (0.05 sec)
```

As you can see, this maps right into the information provided previously. The table has one field for every element of a press release.

To get things rolling, populate this table with a couple of dummy records, like the following ones:

```
mysql> INSERT INTO news (id, title, content, contact, timestamp)
VALUES ( '1', 'Megalomaniacs Inc. Is Born', 'EARTH -- A new star was
born today on the planet third closest to the sun. Megalomaniacs
Inc., a venture of WeWantItAll Corp., today threw open its doors
for business in the ritzy Jefferson Square business district.
```

16

```
Created with the sole goal of colonizing every single planet in the
known Universe (and beyond), Megalomaniacs Inc. hopes to quickly
acquire a monopoly over the vast tracts of uncharted real estate
in space. Speaking at a press conference, Megalomaniacs Inc. CEO
warned reporters that Megalomaniacs Inc. would "take everything it
could, and then some". ', 'Peter Paul (peter@megalo.mania)', '2003-
12-11 17:29:25');

Query OK, 1 row affected (0.01 sec)

mysql> INSERT INTO news (id, title, content, contact, timestamp)
VALUES ( '2', 'Megalomaniacs Inc. Expands To Mars', 'MARS -- As part
of its business strategy of "expand and swallow", Megalomaniacs
Inc. today announced that it had successfully sent a team of corporate
raiders to Mars, in an effort to persuade the inhabitants of that
planet to surrender their planet for colonization.

Megalomaniacs Inc. COO today said that the move was a "friendly
overture", but that a failure to comply with the company\'s
colonization plans would result in a "swift and sure eviction of
those little green guys". ', 'Tim Jr. (tim@megalo.mania)', '2004-08-30
12:13:48');

Query OK, 1 row affected (0.07 sec)
```

If the previous commands are unfamiliar to you, page back to Chapters 9 and 10, which explain them in greater detail.

Listing and Displaying News Items

You'll remember from the requirements discussion a couple of pages back, that this development effort can broadly be split into two parts. One part consists of the scripts that retrieve the list of newest items from the database and display this list to the user. The other part consists of administrative tools that enable editors to manage this list, enter new information, and edit or delete existing information.

Because the first part is simpler, let's get that out of the way first. Two scripts are involved here: *list.php*, which retrieves a list of the five newest entries in the database; and *story.php*, which displays the full text for the selected story.

Listing News Items

Create *list.php* first:

```
<html>
<head>
<basefont face="Verdana">
</head>

<body>

<!-- standard page header begins -->
<p> <p>

<table width="100%" cellspacing="0" cellpadding="5">
<tr>
    <td></td>
</tr>
<tr>
    <td bgcolor="Navy"><font size="-1" color="White">
    <b>Megalomaniacs Inc : Press Releases</b></font>
    </td>
</tr>
</table>
<!-- standard page header ends -->

<ul>
<?php
// includes
include('../conf.php');
include('../functions.php');

// open database connection
$connection = mysql_connect($host, $user, $pass) ⤶
or die ('Unable to connect!');

// select database
mysql_select_db($db) or die ('Unable to select database!');

// generate and execute query
$query = "SELECT id, title, timestamp FROM news ⤶
ORDER BY timestamp DESC LIMIT 0, 5";

$result = mysql_query($query) ⤶
or die ("Error in query: $query. " . mysql_error());
```

16

```php
// if records present
if (mysql_num_rows($result) > 0)
{
    // iterate through resultset
    // print article titles
    while($row = mysql_fetch_object($result))
    {
    ?>
        <li><font size="-1"><b><a href="story.php?id= ↵
        <?php echo $row->id; ?>"><?php echo $row->title; ?></a></b></font>
        <br>
        <font size="-2"><?php echo formatDate($row->timestamp); ?>
        </font>
        <p>
    <?php
    }
}
// if no records present
// display message
else
{
?>
    <font size="-1">No press releases currently available</font>
<?php
}


// close database connection
mysql_close($connection);
?>
</ul>

<!-- standard page footer begins -->
<p>
<table width="100%" cellspacing="0" cellpadding="5">
<tr>
    <td align="center"><font size="-2">
    All rights reserved. Visit Melonfire
    <a href="http://www.melonfire.com/community/columns/trog/">
    here</a> for more.</td>
</tr>
</table>
<!-- standard page footer ends -->

</body>
</html>
```

This script connects to the database, retrieves a set of records, and formats them for display in a web browser. You've already seen this in Chapter 13, so none of it should be a surprise. Pay special attention to the SELECT query that retrieves the records from the MySQL table: it contains a DESC clause to order the items in the order of most recent first, and a LIMIT clause to restrict the result set to five items only.

The formatDate() function used in the previous code listing is a user-defined function that turns a MySQL timestamp into a human-friendly date string (Chapter 5 has more information on how to define such a function). The function is defined in the *functions.php* file and looks like this:

```php
<?php
// format MySQL DATETIME value into a more readable string
function formatDate($val)
{
  $arr = explode('-', $val);
  return date('d M Y', mktime(0,0,0, $arr[1], $arr[2], $arr[0]));
}
?>
```

Also necessary is to include some code that tells the script what to do if no records are returned by the query (this could happen when the application is installed for the first time, and no records are present in the database). Without this code, the generated page would be completely empty—not a nice thing to show to users, especially on a potentially high-traffic page. The solution is to use an if() loop to check if any records were returned by the query and display a neat little message if none were returned.

Here's a fragment that outlines how this would work:

```php
<?php
// if records present
if (mysql_num_rows($result) > 0)
{
    // iterate through resultset
    // print article titles
}
// if no records present
else
```

16

```
{
     // display error message
}
?>
```

Figure 16-1 shows what it looks like when you view this script through a browser.

As a developer, it's important to think through all possible situations and write code that handles each one intelligently. The possibility of an empty database doesn't even occur to many novice developers—and this can lead to embarrassing situations if you're demonstrating the application to your boss . . . or worse, the customer!

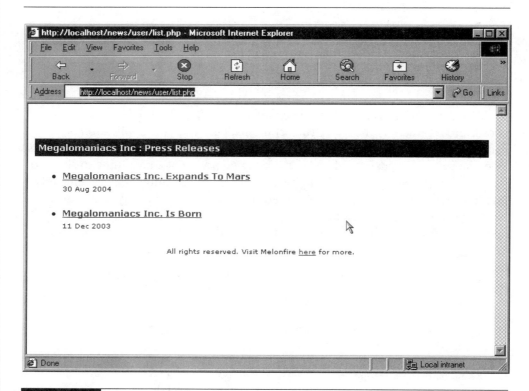

FIGURE 16-1   A list of available news items

The Configuration File

In case you're wondering, the MySQL hostname, the username, and the password used by the `mysql_connect()` function are all variables sourced from the configuration file *conf.php*. This file has been `include()`-d at the top of each script and it looks like this:

```php
<?php
// database configuration
$host = 'localhost';
$user = 'newuser';
$pass = 'newspass';
$db = 'news';

// default contact person
$def_contact = 'Johnny Doe (jd@megalo.mania)';
?>
```

Extracting this configuration information into a separate file makes it easier to update the application in case the database username or password changes. Updating a single file is far easier than updating multiple scripts, each with the values hard-wired into it.

Displaying Story Content

You'll notice, from the previous code listing, that every press release title is linked to *story.php* via its unique ID. The *story.php* script uses this ID to connect to the database and retrieve the full text of the release. Here is what it looks like:

```html
<html>
<head></head>
<body>

<!-- standard page header -->

<?php
// includes
include('../conf.php');
include('../functions.php');
```

16

```php
// check for record ID
if ((!isset($_GET['id']) || trim($_GET['id']) == ''))
{
  die('Missing record ID!');
}

// open database connection
$connection = mysql_connect($host, $user, $pass) ↵
or die ('Unable to connect!');

// select database
mysql_select_db($db) or die ('Unable to select database!');

// generate and execute query
$id = $_GET['id'];
$query = "SELECT title, content, contact, timestamp FROM news ↵
WHERE id = '$id'";

$result = mysql_query($query) ↵
or die ("Error in query: $query. " . mysql_error());

// get resultset as object
$row = mysql_fetch_object($result);

// print details
if ($row)
{
?>
    <p>
    <b><?php echo $row->title; ?></b>
    <p>
    <font size="-1"><?php echo nl2br($row->content); ?></font>
    <p>
    <font size="-2">This release was published on
    <?php echo formatDate($row->timestamp); ?>.
    For more information, please contact <?php echo $row->contact; ?>
    </font>
<?php
}
else
{
?>
    <p>
    <font size="-1">That release could not be located in
    our database.</font>
<?php
}
```

```
// close database connection
mysql_close($connection);
?>

<!-- standard page footer -->

</body>
</html>
```

Again, extremely simple—connect, use the ID to get the full text for the corresponding item, and display it. Figure 16-2 illustrates what it looks like.

At this point, you have a primitive publishing system that can be used to provide users of a web site with news, press releases, and other information. There's only one small hitch. . . .

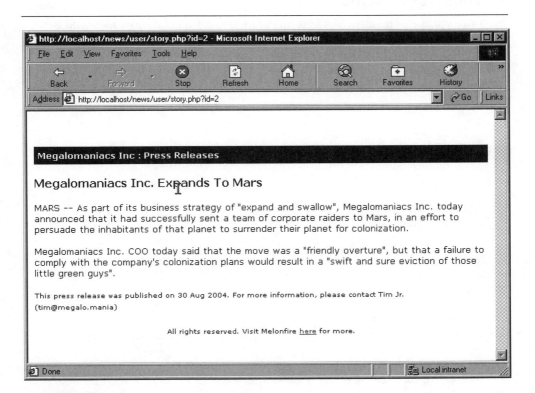

FIGURE 16-2   Displaying story content

Manipulating News Items

At this point in time, there is no simple way to update the database with new information. To insert or edit information, an administrator needs to know SQL and have access to a MySQL client. This may not always be possible, so it's necessary to also develop a simple, friendly interface for database updates.

Based on the requirements outlined previously, this administration module will consist of at least the following four scripts: *list.php,* which lists all press releases currently in the database and lets the administrator select an individual record for an edit or delete operation; *edit.php,* which enables the administrator to update a record; *delete.php,* which lets the administrator delete a record; and *add.php,* which enables the administrator to add a new record.

Let's look at each of these in turn.

Listing News Items

First up, the *list.php* script. As you might imagine, this is almost identical to the previous *list.php*—it displays a list of all press releases currently stored in the database, with additional links to edit or delete them. Here it is.

```
<html>
<head></head>
<body>

<!-- standard page header -->

<?php
// includes
include('../conf.php');
include('../functions.php');

// open database connection
$connection = mysql_connect($host, $user, $pass) ⏎
or die ('Unable to connect!');

// select database
mysql_select_db($db) or die ('Unable to select database!');

// generate and execute query
$query = "SELECT id, title, timestamp FROM news ORDER BY timestamp ⏎
DESC";
```

```php
$result = mysql_query($query) ↵
or die ("Error in query: $query. " . mysql_error());

// if records present
if (mysql_num_rows($result) > 0)
{
    // iterate through resultset
    // print title with links to edit and delete scripts
    while($row = mysql_fetch_object($result))
    {
    ?>
    <font size="-1"><b><?php echo $row->title; ?></b>
    [<?php echo formatDate($row->timestamp); ?>]</font>
    <br>
    <font size="-2"><a href="edit.php?id=<?php echo $row->id; ?>">
    edit</a> | <a href="delete.php?id=<?php echo $row->id; ?>">
    delete</a></font>
    <p>
    <?php
    }
}
// if no records present
// display message
else
{
?>
    <font size="-1">No releases currently available</font><p>
<?php
}

// close connection
mysql_close($connection);
?>
<font size="-2"><a href="add.php">add new</a></font>

<!-- standard page footer -->

</body>
</html>
```

Pay special attention to the links to *edit.php* and *delete.php* in the previous script. You'll see that each of these scripts is passed an additional $id variable, which contains the unique record identifier for that particular item. More on this shortly.

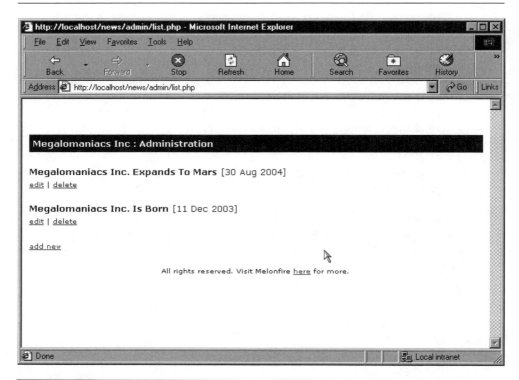

FIGURE 16-3   A list of available news items, with administrative functions

Figure 16-3 demonstrates what page generated by the previous script looks like. Notice the differences between Figure 16-3 and Figure 16-1—namely, the additional links next to each record, and the link to add new items at the end of the page.

Adding News Items

Next, *add.php*. If you think about it, you'll realize this script has two components: a form, which displays fields for the administrator to enter information, and a form processor, which validates the input and inserts it into the database.

This next listing compresses both these components into the same script, using a conditional test to decide which one gets used when (Chapter 4 has more information on this technique). Here is the listing:

```
<html>
<head></head>
<body>

<!-- standard page header -->

<?php
// form not yet submitted
// display initial form
if (!$_POST['submit'])
{
?>
<table cellspacing="5" cellpadding="5">
<form action="<?php echo $_SERVER['PHP_SELF']; ?>" method="POST">
<tr>
    <td valign="top"><b><font size="-1">Title</font></b></td>
    <td>
      <input size="50" maxlength="250" type="text" name="title">
    </td>
</tr>
<tr>
    <td valign="top"><b><font size="-1">Content</font></b></td>
    <td>
      <textarea name="content" cols="40" rows="10"></textarea>
    </td>
</tr>
<tr>
    <td valign="top"><font size="-1">Contact person</font></td>
    <td>
      <input size="50" maxlength="250" type="text" name="contact">
    </td>
</tr>
<tr>
    <td colspan=2>
      <input type="Submit" name="submit" value="Add">
    </td>
</tr>
</form>
</table>
<?php
}
```

```php
else
{
    // includes
    include('../conf.php');
    include('../functions.php');

    // set up error list array
    $errorList = array();

    $title = $_POST['title'];
    $content = $_POST['content'];
    $contact = $_POST['contact'];

    // validate text input fields
    if (trim($_POST['title']) == '')
    {
        $errorList[] = 'Invalid entry: Title';
    }

    if (trim($_POST['content']) == '')
    {
        $errorList[] = "Invalid entry: Content";
    }

    // set default value for contact person
    if (trim($_POST['contact']) == '')
    {
        $contact = $def_contact;
    }

    // check for errors
    // if none found...
    if (sizeof($errorList) == 0)
    {
        // open database connection
        $connection = mysql_connect($host, $user, $pass) ↵
or die ('Unable to connect!');

        // select database
        mysql_select_db($db) ↵
or die ('Unable to select database!');
```

```
        // generate and execute query
        $query = "INSERT INTO ↵
news(title, content, contact, timestamp) ↵
VALUES('$title', '$content', '$contact', NOW())";

        $result = mysql_query($query) ↵
or die ("Error in query: $query. " . mysql_error());

        // print result
        echo '<font size=-1>Update successful. ↵
<a href=list.php>Go back to the main menu</a>.</font>';

        // close database connection
        mysql_close($connection);
    }
    else
    {
        // errors found
        // print as list
        echo '<font size=-1>The following errors were encountered:';
        echo '<br>';
        echo '<ul>';
        for ($x=0; $x<sizeof($errorList); $x++)
        {
            echo "<li>$errorList[$x]";
        }
        echo '</ul></font>';
    }
}
?>

<!-- standard page footer -->

</body>
</html>
```

When this script is first executed, it will display a form like that shown in Figure 16-4.

Now, once the administrator enters data into this form and submits it, the same script is called again to process the data (note the presence of the special $_SERVER['PHP_SELF'] variable in the form's ACTION attribute). Because the $submit variable will now exist, control will transfer to the latter half of the script.

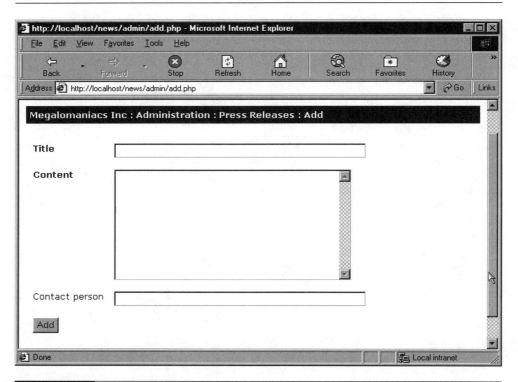

FIGURE 16-4   A form to add news items

As a prelude to any other activity, this branch of the script first ensures that all required values are present and generates errors if they are not. These errors are stored in the array $errorList. Once all the input validation is complete, the $errorList array is checked for elements. If entries are present in this array, a message is displayed listing the errors; if not, an INSERT query is generated to add the data to the database, and a success message is printed to the browser (Figure 16-5).

NOTE   *For less significant fields, where it doesn't matter as much if the user enters a value or not, you can always substitute a default value instead of generating an error. An example of this can be seen in the previous script where, in the event that the contact person field is left empty, a default value is used from the configuration file.*

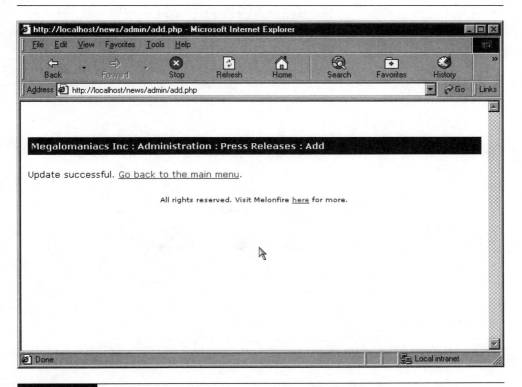

FIGURE 16-5 Successful addition of a news item to the database

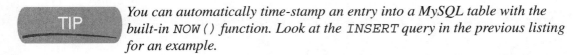

You can automatically time-stamp an entry into a MySQL table with the built-in NOW() function. Look at the INSERT query in the previous listing for an example.

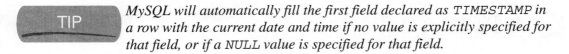

MySQL will automatically fill the first field declared as TIMESTAMP in a row with the current date and time if no value is explicitly specified for that field, or if a NULL value is specified for that field.

Deleting News Items

You'll remember, from the discussion of *list.php* a few pages back, that the script *delete.php* is passed a $id variable, which holds the unique record identifier for

16

the selected news item. This identifier is used by *delete.php* to delete the selected record from the database. The next listing illustrates this:

```
<html>
<head></head>
<body>

<!-- standard page header -->

<?php
// includes
include('../conf.php');
include('../functions.php');

// check for record ID
if ((!isset($_GET['id']) || trim($_GET['id']) == ''))
{
    die('Missing record ID!');
}

// open database connection
$connection = mysql_connect($host, $user, $pass) ↵
or die ('Unable to connect!');

// select database
mysql_select_db($db) or die ('Unable to select database!');

// generate and execute query
$id = $_GET['id'];
$query = "DELETE FROM news WHERE id = '$id'";
$result = mysql_query($query) ↵
or die ("Error in query: $query. " . mysql_error());

// close database connection
mysql_close($connection);

// print result
echo '<font size=-1>Deletion successful.';
echo '<a href=list.php>Go back to the main menu</a>.</font>';
?>
```

```
<!-- standard page footer -->

</body>
</html>
```

This is so simple, it hardly requires any explanation. The ID passed to the script via the `$id` variable is used to construct and execute a `DELETE` query, which removes the corresponding record from the database.

Figure 16-6 illustrates the output of a successful deletion.

Editing News Items

The last task on the to-do list involves updating, or editing, a news item. The script that does this is called *edit.php,* and it's a combination of both *add.php* and *delete.php.* Like *delete.php, edit.php* also receives the record's unique identifier via the `$id` variable. It now needs to display a form similar to that used by *add.php,* except this

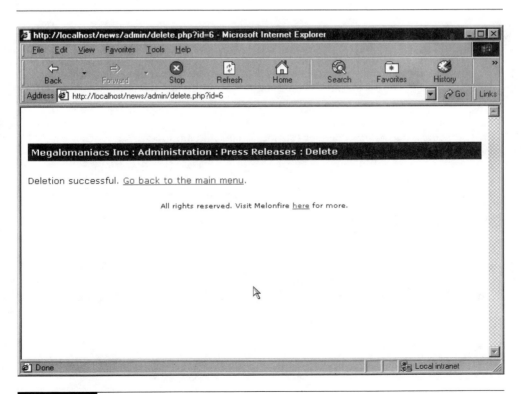

FIGURE 16-6   Successful deletion of a news item from the database

form needs to be prefilled with the data for that news item. Once the user changes the data and submits the form, the script has to execute an UPDATE query using the record identifier to save the changes to the database.

This sounds like a lot of work . . . and it is! Here's the first part of the listing:

```
<html>
<head></head>
<body>

<!-- standard page header -->

<?php
// includes
include('../conf.php');
include('../functions.php');

// form not yet submitted
// display initial form with values pre-filled
if (!$_POST['submit'])
{
    // check for record ID
    if ((!isset($_GET['id']) || trim($_GET['id']) == ''))
    {
        die('Missing record ID!');
    }

    // open database connection
    $connection = mysql_connect($host, $user, $pass) ↵
or die ('Unable to connect!');

    // select database
    mysql_select_db($db) or die ('Unable to select database!');

    // generate and execute query
    $id = $_GET['id'];
    $query = "SELECT title, content, contact FROM news ↵
WHERE id = '$id'";
    $result = mysql_query($query) ↵
or die ("Error in query: $query. " . mysql_error());

    // if a result is returned
    if (mysql_num_rows($result) > 0)
```

```php
        {
            // turn it into an object
            $row = mysql_fetch_object($result);

            // print form with values pre-filled
?>
<table cellspacing="5" cellpadding="5">
<form action="<?php echo $_SERVER['PHP_SELF']; ?>" method="POST">
<input type="hidden" name="id"  value="<?php echo $id; ?>">
<tr>
    <td valign="top"><b><font size="-1">Title</font></b></td>
    <td>
      <input size="50" maxlength="250" type="text" name="title"
value="<?php echo $row->title; ?>">
    </td>
</tr>
<tr>
    <td valign="top"><b><font size="-1">Content</font></b></td>
    <td>
      <textarea name="content" cols="40" rows="10">
      <?php echo $row->content; ?>
      </textarea>
    </td>
</tr>
<tr>
    <td valign="top"><font size="-1">Contact person</font></td>
    <td>
      <input size="50" maxlength="250" type="text" name="contact"
      value="<?php echo $row->contact; ?>">
    </td>
</tr>
<tr>
    <td colspan=2>
      <input type="Submit" name="submit" value="Update">
    </td>
</tr>
</form>
</table>
<?php
        }
    // no result returned
    // print graceful error message
    else
    {
        echo '<font size=-1>That press release could not be located ↵
in our database.</font>';
    }
}
```

```
else
{
// form submitted
// start processing it
}
?>

<!-- standard page footer -->

</body>
</html>
```

Using the identifier provided by *list.php*, *edit.php* queries the database for the fields relevant to that particular record and uses that information to prefill an HTML form. Figure 16-7 illustrates what this form might look like.

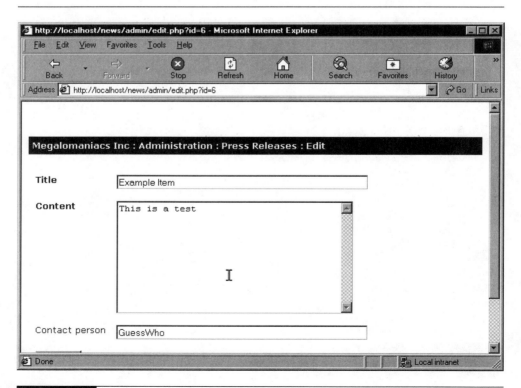

FIGURE 16-7   A form to edit news items

Locking the Doors

You might be wondering why the listing includes a check for the number of rows returned by the query. This is necessary because if the identifier provided to *edit.php* is invalid or nonexistent, the query will return zero rows, and the administrator will be faced with a form with no data in it. Always perform such "boundary condition" checks to ensure that your script doesn't behave in an unexpected manner.

Most of the time, this additional check is redundant because the identifier will be generated from *list.php* and will, therefore, usually be valid. However, if someone (say, a malicious hacker) decides to experiment with the URL string, changing the ID that gets appended to it to an invalid value, this could result in a series of ugly error messages or even cause the application to break. Therefore, by adding this check, not only does the overall security of the application improve, but also the possibility of errors reduces.

NOTE   *The $id variable is attached to the form as a hidden variable and is submitted together with the other values. This ID will be used by the form processor when constructing the UPDATE query in the second part of the script.*

Once the form is submitted, the data entered into it needs to be validated and integrated into an UPDATE query. This is handled by the second part of the listing, as shown in the following:

```
<html>
<head></head>
<body>

<!-- standard page header -->

<?php

if (!$_POST['submit'])
```

16

```php
{
// display initial form with values pre-filled
}
else
{
    // set up error list array
    $errorList = array();

    $title = $_POST['title'];
    $content = $_POST['content'];
    $contact = $_POST['contact'];
    $id = $_POST['id'];

    // check for record ID
    if ((!isset($_POST['id']) || trim($_POST['id']) == ''))
    {
      die ('Missing record ID!');
    }

    // validate text input fields
    if (trim($_POST['title']) == '')
    {
      $errorList[] = 'Invalid entry: Title';
    }

    if (trim($_POST['content']) == '')
    {
      $errorList[] = "Invalid entry: Content";
    }

    // set default value for contact person
    if (trim($_POST['contact']) == '')
    {
      $contact = $def_contact;
    }

    // check for errors
    // if none found...
    if (sizeof($errorList) == 0)
    {
        // open database connection
        $connection = mysql_connect($host, $user, $pass) ↵
or die ('Unable to connect!');
```

```
        // select database
        mysql_select_db($db) ↵
or die ('Unable to select database!');

        // generate and execute query
        $query = "UPDATE news SET title = '$title', ↵
content = '$content', contact = '$contact', timestamp = NOW() ↵
WHERE id = '$id'";
        $result = mysql_query($query) ↵
or die ("Error in query: $query. " . mysql_error());

        // print result
        echo '<font size=-1>Update successful.';
        echo '<a href=list.php>Go back to the main menu</a>.</font>';

        // close database connection
        mysql_close($connection);
    }
    else
    {
        // errors occurred
        // print as list
        echo '<font size=-1>The following errors were encountered:';
        echo '<br>';
        echo '<ul>';
        for ($x=0; $x<sizeof($errorList); $x++)
        {
            echo "<li>$errorList[$x]";
        }
        echo '</ul></font>';
    }
}
?>

<!-- standard page footer -->

</body>
</html>
```

16

This part of the script is almost identical to the code previously used in *add.php*, with the obvious difference that this query string uses an UPDATE command instead of an INSERT command.

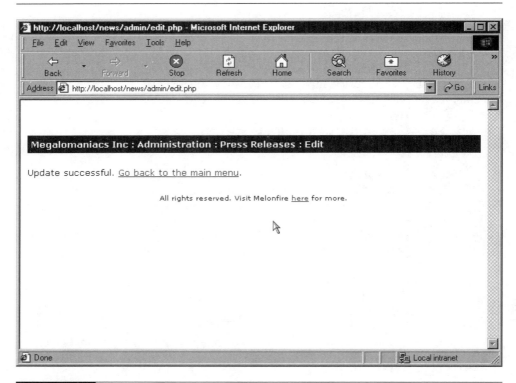

FIGURE 16-8   Successful update of a news item in the database

Figure 16-8 illustrates what the result of a successful update looks like.

At this point, you have an application that meets all the requirements outlined in the section "Understanding Requirements." You can now proceed to upload it to your web server and begin using it to manage the content of your web site. But first, a few words about security.

Protecting the Administration Module

The way the application has been built thus far, all the scripts are accessible to anyone with a web browser. This is fine for the "public" component of the application, but unacceptable for the "private" administration module. What you really need is a way to protect the administrative scripts so that only authorized users (that is, administrators) can get in to futz with the database content.

If you're using Apache, a simple way to accomplish this is with Apache's built-in user-authentication mechanism. This mechanism is based on the traditional username-password challenge. When the web server receives a request for a directory or file that it knows is a protected resource, it responds by sending the client browser an authentication challenge. Only after receiving a valid username and password back from the client browser is access granted to the directory or file.

The following instructions apply to Windows and UNIX versions of the Apache 1.3.x web server.

To see how this works, move the four administration scripts—*list.php, add.php, edit.php,* and *delete.php*—into a separate directory under the server root (let's call it *admin/*) and create a file named *.htaccess* in this directory. Open the file in a text editor and add the following lines to it:

```
AuthType Basic
AuthName "Administration Module"
AuthUserFile /usr/local/apache/users
require valid-user
```

The `AuthType` directive specifies the type of authentication, while the `AuthName` directive specifies a name or description for the resource (this description will appear in the client browser when the user attempts to access the protected directory, so you should choose something descriptive). The `AuthUserFile` directive specifies the location for the file containing the list of authorized users and passwords (in this example, */usr/local/apache/users*).

CAUTION

The file containing usernames and passwords should always be placed outside the web server root, in a directory not accessible through a browser . . . or else absolutely anyone will be able to download it! That said, note that the default Apache configuration blocks remote retrieval of any file beginning with `.ht`.

Next, open your main Apache configuration file, *httpd.conf,* and look for the `<Directory>` tags that reference your web server root. These tags should look something like this:

```
<Directory "/usr/local/apache/htdocs">
...
</Directory>
```

16

The Final Authority

The `AllowOverride` directive tells the server whether global configuration parameters can be overridden by local ones, like the parameters in the *.htaccess* file.

Ensure this `<Directory>` block contains the line

```
AllowOverride All
```

If this line isn't there, add it, and save the file. Restart the server for this change to take effect.

Next, create the password file itself, by running Apache's *htpasswd* program (usually in the *bin/* subdirectory of the Apache installation directory). Pass the program two parameters: the location to which the file should be written and a username (in this example, `newsadmins`).

```
$ ./htpasswd -c /usr/local/apache/users newsadmins
Adding password for newsadmins.
New password:
Re-type new password:
```

First Time Flag

You can add as many users as you like using the previous method. However, omit the `-c` parameter for all users after the first because the `-c` parameter is only used when creating the file for the first time.

FIGURE 16-9   Password-protecting a directory with Apache

   *The username passed to* htpasswd *need not be an actual user on the system; it exists only within the context of the Apache security mechanism.*

   *On Windows, the operating system will not let you create a file name beginning with a period. To work around this, open an MS-DOS command shell and issue the command* REN htaccess .htaccess *to rename the file.*

A password file named *users* should now be created in the named location, containing the username and the password (in encrypted form) you just entered.

With everything in place, start up your browser and point it to the directory you just protected. The web server should immediately pop up a dialog box asking for a username and password and will only let you view the contents of the directory if you enter the correct values. Figure 16-9 shows what this looks like.

This simple authentication system will prevent random visitors (or not-so-random hackers) from gaining access to the administration module and manipulating your MySQL database without your knowledge.

Summary

As you can see, building a simple publishing system with PHP and MySQL is extremely easy. The two technologies, combined together, are so powerful that putting together dynamic, robust web applications, like the one just described, is a snap. They're also great for rapid development, which can come in handy when working against aggressive deadlines.

To learn more about the techniques discussed in this chapter or to read more case studies, consider visiting the following links:

- Case study of an online polling system, at **http://www.melonfire.com/community/columns/trog/article.php?id=59**

- Case study of a web-based file management system, at **http://www.melonfire.com/community/columns/trog/article.php?id=64**

- Case study of a web-based e-mail client, at **http://www.melonfire.com/community/columns/trog/article.php?id=100**

- Case study of a time/resource tracking system, at **http://www.melonfire.com/community/columns/trog/article.php?id=92**

- Case study of a resume management system for recruitment personnel, at **http://www.melonfire.com/community/columns/trog/article.php?id=74**

- Case study of a web page monitoring system, at **http://www.melonfire.com/community/columns/trog/article.php?id=160**

- Apache tricks and tweaks, at **http://www.melonfire.com/community/columns/trog/article.php?id=115**

- More articles and tutorials on PHP, at **http://www.melonfire.com/community/columns/trog/archives.php?category=PHP**

You've now reached the end of this book. I hope you now have a clearer idea of what you can do with PHP and MySQL, both individually and together. I also hope you feel you have the grounding you need to go out there and begin creating dynamic web applications of your own.

Index

Symbols

-- (auto-decrement) operator
    effect of, 71
    example of, 75
$ (dollar) symbol, using before variables, 64
$_SESSION['cart'] associative array, example of, 136–144
% (division/modulus) operator, effect of, 71
& (ampersand), rendering correctly, 302–304
&& (logical AND) operator, effect of, 71
* (asterisk)
    appearance in queries, 187
    as multiplication operator, effect of, 71
    as wildcard used with privileges, 212
@ error-suppression operator, using with mysql_ connect, 245
[] (square braces), using with arrays, 103
_ (underscore), using with variables, 64
` (backticks)
    using with database names, 163
    using with external programs and scripts, 130
|| (logical OR) operator, effect of, 71
++ (auto-increment) operator, example of, 71, 75
< (left angle bracket), rendering correctly, 302–304
< (less than) operator, effect of, 71
<= (less than or equal to) operator, effect of, 71
<?=$variable?> syntax, displaying variable values with, 88
<> (not equal to/not of same type) operator, effect of, 71
= (assignment operator), using with variable values, 65

!= (not equal to) operator, effect of, 71
== (equal to) operator, effect of, 71
!== (not equal to/not of same type) operator, effect of, 71
=== (equal to/of same type) comparison operator, example of, 71, 73–74
-> (continuation character), using with MySQL, 158
> (right angle bracket), rendering correctly, 302–304
> (greater than) operator, effect of, 71
>= (greater than or equal to) operator, effect of, 71
\ (backslash), escaping quotation marks with, 184
" (quotes)
    escaping, 184
    escaping user input with, 131
    using with string and date values, 184
    using with string values, 69
; (semicolon)
    advisory about using with mysql_query(), 247
    omitting from PHP blocks, 63
' (single quote), using with field templates, 309
. (string concatenation operator), example of, 72, 289–290
? (ternary operators)
    using with if-else() blocks, 85
    validating data with, 266
' '/ " " (empty strings)
    comparing to white space, 266
    distinguishing from NULL values, 261
/ (division/quotient) operator, effect of, 71
! (logical NOT) operator, effect of, 71
. (string concatenation) operator, effect of, 71–72, 289–290

INTERNATIONAL CONTACT INFORMATION

AUSTRALIA
McGraw-Hill Book Company
Australia Pty. Ltd.
TEL +61-2-9900-1800
FAX +61-2-9878-8881
http://www.mcgraw-hill.com.au
books-it_sydney@mcgraw-hill.com

CANADA
McGraw-Hill Ryerson Ltd.
TEL +905-430-5000
FAX +905-430-5020
http://www.mcgraw-hill.ca

GREECE, MIDDLE EAST, & AFRICA
(Excluding South Africa)
McGraw-Hill Hellas
TEL +30-210-6560-990
TEL +30-210-6560-993
TEL +30-210-6560-994
FAX +30-210-6545-525

MEXICO (Also serving Latin America)
McGraw-Hill Interamericana Editores
S.A. de C.V.
TEL +525-1500-5108
FAX +525-117-1589
http://www.mcgraw-hill.com.mx
carlos_ruiz@mcgraw-hill.com

SINGAPORE (Serving Asia)
McGraw-Hill Book Company
TEL +65-6863-1580
FAX +65-6862-3354
http://www.mcgraw-hill.com.sg
mghasia@mcgraw-hill.com

SOUTH AFRICA
McGraw-Hill South Africa
TEL +27-11-622-7512
FAX +27-11-622-9045
robyn_swanepoel@mcgraw-hill.com

SPAIN
McGraw-Hill/
Interamericana de España, S.A.U.
TEL +34-91-180-3000
FAX +34-91-372-8513
http://www.mcgraw-hill.es
professional@mcgraw-hill.es

UNITED KINGDOM, NORTHERN,
EASTERN, & CENTRAL EUROPE
McGraw-Hill Education Europe
TEL +44-1-628-502500
FAX +44-1-628-770224
http://www.mcgraw-hill.co.uk
emea_queries@mcgraw-hill.com

ALL OTHER INQUIRIES Contact:
McGraw-Hill/Osborne
TEL +1-510-420-7700
FAX +1-510-420-7703
http://www.osborne.com
omg_international@mcgraw-hill.com